Alexander Pope (1688–1744) was the son of a linen merchant who moved his family to Binfield in Windsor Forest to escape discrimination against Catholics. After Pope contracted tubercular infection at the age of twelve, he grew only to four feet, six inches, developed curvature of the spine, and suffered from constant headaches. He came to public notice on the publication of "Pastorals" in Jacob Tonson's *Miscellany* (1709), and he gained much notoriety and acclaim for "The Rape of the Lock" (1712). By then, Pope had befriended Jonathan Swift, John Gay, Thomas Parnell, and Dr. John Arbuthnot, and together they formed the Scriblerus Club, which indirectly contributed to such works as Swift's *Gulliver's Travels* and Pope's own *Dunciad* (1728), as well as the *Memoirs of Martinus Scriblerus* (1741). Pope's translations of Homer's *Iliad* (1715–20) and *Odyssey* (1725–26) earned him financial success, as well as critical praise. *Imitations of Horace* (1733–38), a parody of the contemporary social and political scene, and his "pirated" letters, which he had devised to be published, would be his last works. At his death, Pope left the epic verse *Brutus* incomplete.

Christopher R. Miller teaches English at the College of Staten Island, City University of New York (CUNY). He is the author of *The Invention of Evening: Perception and Time in Romantic Poetry*, and he has completed a new study of surprise in the prose fiction and poetry of the eighteenth and early nineteenth centuries.

Elliott Visconsi is Associate Professor of English at the University of Notre Dame, where he writes about and teaches seventeenth-century and eighteenth-century English and American literature. The author of *Lines of Equity: Literature and the Origins of Law in Later Stuart England*, he works on writers such as Shakespeare, Milton, Pope, and Behn, particularly in relation to political theory, as well as First Amendment law, academic freedom, and the transformation of free expression in the digital age.

THE RAPE
OF THE LOCK
AND OTHER POEMS

Alexander Pope

Edited by
Martin Price

With an Introduction by
Christopher R. Miller
and a New Afterword by
Elliott Visconsi

SIGNET CLASSICS

SIGNET CLASSICS
Published by New American Library, a division of
Penguin Group (USA) Inc., 375 Hudson Street,
New York, New York 10014, USA
Penguin Group (Canada), 90 Eglinton Avenue East, Suite 700, Toronto,
Ontario M4P 2Y3, Canada (a division of Pearson Penguin Canada Inc.)
Penguin Books Ltd., 80 Strand, London WC2R 0RL, England
Penguin Ireland, 25 St. Stephen's Green, Dublin 2,
Ireland (a division of Penguin Books Ltd.)
Penguin Group (Australia), 250 Camberwell Road, Camberwell, Victoria 3124,
Australia (a division of Pearson Australia Group Pty. Ltd.)
Penguin Books India Pvt. Ltd., 11 Community Centre, Panchsheel Park,
New Delhi - 110 017, India
Penguin Group (NZ), 67 Apollo Drive, Rosedale, Auckland 0632,
New Zealand (a division of Pearson New Zealand Ltd.)
Penguin Books (South Africa) (Pty.) Ltd., 24 Sturdee Avenue,
Rosebank, Johannesburg 2196, South Africa

Penguin Books Ltd., Registered Offices:
80 Strand, London WC2R 0RL, England

Published by Signet Classics, an imprint of New American Library,
a division of Penguin Group (USA) Inc.

First Signet Classics Printing, May 1970
First Signet Classics Printing (Visconsi Afterword), April 2012
10 9 8 7 6 5 4 3 2 1

Contents

SATIRES AND EPISTLES OF HORACE IMITATED

Introduction

There is an old proverb that "to err is human, to forgive divine"—something we might recall when we give or accept an apology. It seems like an ageless and anonymous saying; but in fact, it entered the world in May of 1711, in a poem called "An Essay on Criticism," by a promising young writer named Alexander Pope. Its author would have been the first to admit that he was not making a terribly original claim about human fallibility; but he did intend to phrase the idea with what he called "wit":

> True wit is nature to advantage dressed,
>   What oft was thought, but ne'er so well expressed
> (297–98)

For Pope, as for us, wit meant having a talent for saying funny or clever things, but it also meant something closer to its origin in the Old English verb *witan,* "to know." In essence, wit was a kind of verbal knowledge—not just a truth, but a truth well phrased. It was best exercised in understanding "nature," which meant not just the outdoor world of trees, oceans, and giraffes, but also the entire universe and the divine laws that shape and animate it. Nature encompassed both the inner life of human beings (their perception, thought, and behavior) and everything in the outer world that they strove to depict or understand.

In Pope's conception, God had created order in nature rather than chaos, and it was our duty to approximate that order in art and science, ethics and laws. Later in the eighteenth century, Thomas Jefferson implied a similar idea in the opening of the Declaration of Independence: "We hold these truths to be self-evident, that all men are created equal, that they are endowed by their Creator with certain unalienable rights, that among these are life, liberty, and the pursuit of happiness." If the inherent equality of all people was a "self-evident" law given by the divine Creator, it still needed to be articulated in human language with the highest possible precision. In Pope's terms, the Declaration can be described as a statement about basic natural rights that had never been so well expressed.

Wit can take many forms, but Pope favored the heroic couplet: two lines of rhyming iambic pentameter. This was not an inevitable choice for a writer of essays and epistles on such subjects as the place of human beings in the universe, the corrupting power of wealth, and the philosophy of gardening; and Pope acknowledged as much in his preface to a later poem, "An Essay on Man." Why not write in prose sentences? Because, Pope insists, the discipline of poetry forces him to use fewer words. Why not write in blank verse, the unrhymed iambic pentameter of Shakespeare's plays and Milton's *Paradise Lost*? Because rhymed lines, in Pope's opinion, make a stronger impression on the reader and are more likely to be remembered afterward. In this way, Pope implicitly refutes Milton, who in the preface to his epic had dismissed rhyme as a childishly "jingling" sound effect. To Pope's mind and ear, rhyme was not a distraction from serious thought but a complement to it. "The sound," as Pope says in the "Essay on Criticism," "must seem an echo to the sense" (365).

It is not rhyme alone that makes Pope's couplets striking, but also their elegant syntactic balance. In them, the poet might pose one idea against another, make a statement and elaborate it, define opposite extremes, or ask a question and provide an answer. In the couplet on "true wit," for instance, he states a premise in the first line and then explains it in the next; and within the second line, he neatly distinguishes between silent thought and public expression, between the ordinary and the rare. According to his own autobiographical claims in the "Epistle to Dr. Arbuthnot," Pope was practically born speaking in couplets. "I lisped in numbers," he says, using the common term for metrical verse, "for the numbers came" (128). Nevertheless, Pope knew that his precocious talent would have been wasted if he had not cultivated it through wide reading and long practice. As he put it in the "Essay on Criticism," "True ease in writing comes from art, not chance,/As those move easiest who have learned to dance" (362–63). In fact, it was *only* in writing that Pope gracefully moved and danced, for in his youth he had been stricken with a tubercular infection that curved his spine, severely stunted his growth, and caused unending pain.

In Pope's worldview, everything is part of a divine plan that can only be imperfectly understood by mere mortals; and the gift of poetic "numbers" can be seen as a compensation for the curse of ill health that plagued the poet throughout what he called "this long disease my life." Pope's other handicap was to have been born and raised a Catholic in Protestant Britain, at a time when Catholics were forbidden from forming congregations, holding public office, receiving a university degree, or living within a ten-mile radius of London. Because of this last restriction, he spent his youth and early adulthood in Windsor Forest, north of London, and his later life at a villa in Twickenham (pronounced "Twit'nam") on the river Thames southwest of the great metropolis. At the latter residence, Pope sculpted and tended his gardens as meticulously as he wrote his couplets; and he built an artificial cave where he could sit in peaceful meditation or in conversation with friends. The place became an extension of Pope's personality, and a vantage point from which he could view the literary scene of London as a wry observer; and in the "Epistle to Dr. Arbuthnot," he describes himself as a literary celebrity desperately trying to hide from hordes of fans, enemies, and imitators who scale his walls and interrupt his dinner.

Everywhere Pope looked, he saw imperfection—in his own body, in his country's institutions, in the bad writing of his contemporaries, in the behavior of his fellow citizens—but he was convinced that his poetry, in contrast, could achieve a degree of formal precision and moral clarity. For instance, if he could not single-handedly reverse government policy, he could at least set the record straight on anti-Catholic slander. In 1666, a great fire had ravaged London, and a monumental pillar was later erected to commemorate the event, complete with an inscription that wrongly blamed it on Catholic arsonists. Pope refuted this piece of towering propaganda in one famous couplet, in which he refers to the site

> Where London's column, pointing at the skies,
> Like a tall bully, lifts the head, and lies.
>   ("Epistle to Bathurst," 330–31)

David thus takes aim at Goliath: in the slingshot of a single couplet, Pope avenges both his short stature and his social disadvantage with a well-turned metaphor of the monument as thuggish giant. The first line seems to represent the London landmark as a symbol of heavenward aspiration; but the next one pulls that lofty idea down to earth, in a slow progression, paced by commas, that culminates in a damning verb. Here, as elsewhere, Pope chooses his rhyming words for a reason: the monument sours into the "skies," but it is anchored in a foundation of "lies."

Religious persecution aside, Pope was free to write

and publish; and he began his literary career in earnest at the age of twenty-three with the "Essay on Criticism." The poem can be classified as an ars poetica, an instruction manual on the principles of good writing, founded on the Roman poet Horace's maxim that poetry ought to delight as well as instruct. Pope's poem is also a collection of epigrammatic sayings reminiscent of biblical proverbs. In the Bible, a typical proverb distinguishes between wise men and fools, the good and the wicked, and Pope applies these distinctions to the creation and judgment of art: there are both witty and dull poets, just as there are both astute and stupid critics. Several years later, Pope would condemn a whole pantheon of boring writers in "The Dunciad," in which he imagines the playwright and poet Colley Cibber as son of "Dulness" and king of all dunces. If the "Essay on Criticism" is a hopeful blueprint for new works of true wit, "The Dunciad" is a dark survey of the ruins: a vision of London overrun by untalented and overrated hacks who produce plays and poems whose greatest power is to put people to sleep.

In essence, Pope argued that the ethics of writing should correspond to the standards of polite conduct in a civil society. That is, good writing should not be tedious, and good criticism should treat its subject with intelligence, understanding, and tact. Today, we might watch television shows or read novels simply to be amused for a while, but Pope took his literary entertainment more seriously than that. Criticism was not merely the habit of finding fault with something, but rather the act of explaining what was worthwhile and what was not, the effort to say what interests us and why.

In the course of his career, Pope might seem to fall short of his ideal of polite criticism when making harshly satirical jabs at enemies and various people he judged as fools. In the "Epistle to Dr. Arbuthnot," Pope defends himself against the charge of cruelty by arguing that his targets are too stupid and self-satisfied to feel the pain of criticism. In any event, bad writers—mere "scribblers" in Pope's terminology—were simply too numerous and prolific to banish with a witty couplet:

> Who shames a scribbler? break one cobweb through,
> He spins the slight, self-pleasing thread anew:
> Destroy his fib or sophistry, in vain,
> The creature's at his dirty work again,
> Throned in the center of his thin designs,
> Proud of a vast extent of flimsy lines!
>
> (89–94)

If some spiders are makers of shoddy cobwebs, others are master architects; and in the "Essay on Man," Pope might well be describing his own poetic structures when he exclaims, "The spider's touch, how exquisitely fine!/Feels at each thread, and lives along the line" (217–18). In the measured rhythms of his couplets, Pope did live along the line, but the line itself might have a venomous sting at the end of it.

Pope's advice to aspiring poets and would-be critics in the "Essay on Criticism" can be briefly summarized as a warning against extremes and a counsel of humility. On the one hand, Pope insists that all criticism is deeply subjective: " 'Tis with our judgments as our watches; none/Go just alike, yet each believes his own" (9–10). On the other hand, he firmly believes that some opinions and some poems are better than others, just as some clock mechanisms are more finely crafted than others. Even so, Pope insists that no poem is perfect and that one of the worst mistakes that a critic can make is to hold it to an impossible standard: "Whoever thinks a faultless piece to see,/Thinks what ne'er was, nor is, nor e'er shall be" (253–54). One of the worst sins that a writer can commit is simply to be dull, and Pope spends many lines demonstrating the rules of good poetic writing: above all, to delight and surprise the reader with flowing lines, apt metaphors, and unexpected rhymes.

For literary models, Pope recommends the epic poems *The Iliad* and *The Odyssey:* "Be Homer's works your study and delight,/Read them by day, and meditate by night" (124–25). Beyond this edifying habit, Pope went so far as to translate the ancient Greek of *The Iliad* into English rhyming couplets. His translation became the eighteenth-century equivalent of a bestseller, and revenue from subscriptions to the edition made him independently wealthy. Today we take it for granted that professional writers earn advances and royalties from profit-making publishers; but in Pope's era, this mercantile model of authorship was relatively new, and writers often had to seek the support of affluent patrons.

Not content to translate another poet's words, Pope wrote his own version of a Homeric epic in "The Rape of the Lock." In *The Iliad,* the Trojan War is sparked by Paris' abduction of the Greek beauty Helen, daughter of Zeus and the mortal Leda. In Pope's poem, a quarrel erupts between two families over a stolen lock of hair, and the incident is playfully narrated as if it were a war. The poem is a *mock* epic in that it shrinks the immense scale of Homeric narrative down to domestic size: instead of a bloody battlefield, there is the "velvet plain" of a gaming table; instead of engaging in hand-to-hand combat, people slay each other with chilly glances and snide comments; instead of encompassing long, wearying years, the action takes place from noon (when spoiled aristocrats wake up) to nightfall (when the lock is magically transformed into stars); instead of a visit to Hades, there is a descent to the fanciful Cave of Spleen, the source of hypochondria and bad moods in the idle rich. Pope based the poem on a controversy reported to him by his friend John Caryll: the young Lord Petre had cut a lock of hair from the head of his intended, Arabella Fermor, and the latter retaliated by cutting off their wedding engagement. In a time before photography, keeping a snippet of a loved one's hair as a souvenir was an ordinary custom, but doing so without the person's permission was simply rude. But was it a serious enough offense to cause such fury?

On the one hand, the answer is no, and by humorously treating the squabble as an event of epic proportions, Pope means to make the warring families laugh at their dispute and put it behind them. On the other hand, the loss of the lock is not so "trivial" as the opening lines of the poem would suggest. More than just a strand of hair, Belinda's lock is a highly charged symbol: it is a small part that represents the whole body and its beauty; it is one half of a cascading pair of "shining ringlets," as balanced as a couplet; it is a "labyrinth" that traps the wandering eye and a baited "line" that tugs at the heart; and it is a product of both nature (spontaneous growth) and art (the daily work of combs and curlers). It is, in short, a fetish object: an ordinary thing endowed with extraordinary significance.

In this way, the lock represents the obsessions of the wealthy, rarefied society that Pope satirizes: a circle in which the smallest verbal and physical gestures are full of portentous meaning; a tribe in which solemn religious rituals take the form of playing cards, writing love letters, and getting dressed for a party; a culture of luxury in which all of the world's labors and riches culminate in the sparkling and fragrant goods of a dressing table and a coffee service. The cutting of the lock intimates the transience of such pleasures and the vanity of human wishes to prolong them:

> What time would spare, from steel receives its date,
> And monuments, like men, submit to fate!
>
> (171–72)

Pope well understands that the careful cultivation of beauty—whether in a lock of hair, a garden, or a poem—is no small thing, but he insists that this effort must be tempered by a mature sense of the fragile and ephemeral nature of all material things. The character of Clarissa, whose very name means clarity, serves as spokesperson for this view in the final canto of the poem. Without disparaging her society's values outright, she argues that all beauty and luxury ought to be balanced by "good sense" and "good humour": the intellectual judgment to recognize the difference between the loss of a lock and graver calamities; and the psychological disposition to weather misfortune and forgive error.

Clarissa's sermon is received with disdain by the people who hear it; but its spirit would live on in the "Essay on Man," a series of four moral epistles that Pope published in 1733 and 1734. In effect, Pope elaborates Clarissa's counsel of good sense and humour into a philosophical system. Where Clarissa urges that loss ought to be accepted with patience and wisdom, Pope argues in the "Essay" that all seemingly random events are part of a divine plan that we cannot comprehend. In many ways, the poem's panoramic vision of "man in the abstract" might seem like an attempt to see things from God's perspective, but Pope everywhere insists that we cannot transcend our limited points of view within the vast order of things. Pope's most forceful statement of God's inscrutable plan concludes the first epistle:

> And, spite of Pride, in erring Reason's spite
> One truth is clear, "WHATEVER IS, IS RIGHT."
> (293–94)

This single couplet has disturbed countless readers, including Pope's contemporary Voltaire, who wrote his famous novella *Candide* to attack the kind of naive optimism that such a statement might promote. (At the same time, Voltaire admired Pope's poetry and knew that the "Essay" was more complex and subtle than this one couplet might suggest.) Does Pope mean that all natural disasters and man-made calamities are, in the scheme of things, right? From any compassionate and ethical perspective, such a claim would seem outrageous—a permission for smug complacency and moral neutrality. Why attempt to change the world or alleviate suffering if everything is already part of God's plan? Why, if you are Alexander Pope, would you even bother to write satirical poems with the intent to mock and correct human foibles?

The problem of Pope's famous statement lies in the word "right." In some sense, there is no adjective in the dictionary for the divine perspective that Pope attempts to describe: the word that we use to define the factually correct or morally just is only an approximation of God's unknowable design. Here, "right" rhymes with "spite," and it flies in the face of "Reason"; as so often happens in Pope's couplets, the chiming of words gives us a mild shock. Calling the world's evils "right" does seem to spite our rational attempts to judge and understand. Pope's dual vision is writ small in this couplet: he is a crisply rational thinker who knows the limits of rationality, a stringent moralist who understands the failings of abstract moral principles.

Pope might seem to recommend stoic resignation, but he also acknowledges the insatiable nature of human desire and the impulse to change "whatever is." Heaven might be a place of perfect order and harmony, but the world is another matter:

> Better for us, perhaps, it might appear,
> Were there all harmony, all virtue here;
> That never air or ocean felt the wind;
> That never passion discomposed the mind:
> But ALL subsists by elemental strife;
> And passions are the elements of life.
>
> ("Essay on Man," I, 165–70)

A passion is, simply defined, a strong emotion; and as Pope well knew, the Latin root of the word was a verb meaning "to suffer." Pope did not think of the human being as an abstract Cartesian "I" or a disembodied brain. While passion might often be opposed to reason, he saw it as a necessary complement to it.

"The surest virtues," he says, "thus from passions shoot" ("Essay on Man," II, 183): through the filtering effect of reason, lust can be refined into love, envy can be disciplined into emulation, and grief over loss can be turned into joy in what remains. Struggle, conflict, and suffering were all a necessary part of Pope's vision of the world. It is in this spirit that we might read "The Rape of the Lock": to see it not merely as an amusing spoof of high society but also as a drama of passions. The effort that Belinda expends on her lock and the "mighty rage" she feels at its violation are aspects of passionate feeling to be taken seriously and not simply swept under the rug.

On the subject of passion, Pope outdid himself in "Eloïsa to Abelard," a poem based on the legendary medieval love affair between the French philosopher Peter Abelard and his pupil Héloïse. The affair ended with a fierce punishment that makes the family dispute in "The Rape of the Lock" seem truly trivial by comparison: Héloïse was banished to a convent; and Abelard was castrated in retribution and lived out the rest of his life in a monastery. By adopting the voice of Héloïse and writing the poem as if it were a letter from her to Abelard, Pope gives the abstract idea of passion a personal perspective. For Pope, language was the medium of wit, but in "Eloïsa to Abelard," it is also the expression of deep feeling:

> Heav'n first taught letters for some wretch's aid,
> Some banish'd lover, or some captive maid;
> They live, they speak, they breathe, what love inspires,
> Warm from the soul, and faithful to its fires.
>
> (51–55)

In Pope's metaphor for "true wit" in the "Essay on Criticism," a poetic turn of phrase clothes the body of nature; but in Eloïsa's conception, language is itself the body of the writer—her breath, her speech, her physical and spiritual warmth. For a lover who can content herself only with letters rather than the intimate physical presence of her beloved, this idea is particularly potent. Eloïsa's expressions of rage, erotic longing, and self-doubt represent an important foil to Pope's famous statements of resignation to the way things are. Passion, it turns out, is not far from wit: the orderly form of the couplet crystallizes and regulates Eloïsa's violent and often conflicting emotions, just as it gives shape to Pope's own spectrum of feelings, from deep outrage to wry amusement. As Pope says of the woes represented in "Eloïsa to Abelard," "He best can paint 'em who shall feel 'em most" (366).

—Christopher R. Miller

A Note on This Edition

The text of this edition is eclectic, largely based upon the Warburton octavo edition of 1751, but with some earlier readings restored. The punctuation is modernized wherever this seems helpful, and capitalization is almost entirely reduced to modern usage. I have preserved capital letters in cases of clearly allegorical nouns and in some terms of direct address that might be read as titles. In a few instances, I have preserved capitalization of such a term as "Nature" in order to make clear that it carries a fuller meaning than its modern counterpart.

Elliptical spellings have been expanded, in the belief that the visual pattern they present is distracting and that an adequate reading cannot help but enforce the elisions that the earlier spelling indicated. Archaic spellings have been modernized where this causes no change in pronunciation.

I have glossed as fully as seemed possible in this format, trying to give at least the import of the many proper names, and citing Pope's notes or those of Pope and Warburton (as P-W) where they were inescapably apt. Occasionally Pope is cited from a letter or other source without specific indication. The task, as I have pursued it, has been to provide a serviceable text for the general reader and student. I am deeply indebted to the Twickenham Edition, which all readers are urged to consult.

The selections are such as seemed to me essential. I regret several omissions, notably the epistles to Cobham and Bathurst and the imitation of Horace's epistle to Augustus.

Chronology

1688 21 May. Alexander Pope born in London of Roman Catholic parents, Alexander Pope, a linen merchant, and Editha Turner Pope.

c. 1700 Pope's family moved to Binfield, in Windsor Forest.

1705 Pope first entered the literary society of London, notably that of Will's coffeehouse, the resort of Dryden until his death in 1700.

1709 May. Pope's "Pastorals," begun in 1704, published in Tonson's *Poetical Miscellanies*.

1711 May. "An Essay on Criticism" published, praised by Addison in *Spectator* No. 253, attacked by the established critic, John Dennis.

1712 May. The "Messiah" (conflating Isaiah and Virgil) published in *Spectator* No. 378. The early two-canto version of "The Rape of the Lock" published in Lintot's *Miscellaneous Poems*. Pope became friendly with Addison, Steele, and other Whig wits who met at Button's coffeehouse.

1713 March. "Windsor Forest." April. A prologue to Addison's tragedy, *Cato*. Contributions to Steele's *Guardian*. October. Proposals for a translation of the *Iliad*.

1714   March. The enlarged version of "The Rape of
        The Lock." Pope was attending meetings of
        the Scriblerus Club with such Tory wits as
        Jonathan Swift, Dr. John Arbuthnot, John
        Gay, Thomas Parnell, and the two chief minis-
        ters of the government, Robert Harley, Earl
        of Oxford, and Henry St. John, Viscount Bol-
        ingbroke. The group was dispersed and the
        ministry fell with the death of Queen Anne
        on August 1.

1715   June. *Iliad,* Books I–IV (a translation which
        was to occupy him for the next five years and
        win him economic independence of patrons).

1716   March. *Iliad,* volume II. Pope's family moved
        to Chiswick on the Thames outside London.

1717   June. *Iliad,* volume III and the first collected
        volume of Pope's *Works,* containing "Eloïsa
        to Abelard" and "Elegy to the Memory of an
        Unfortunate Lady." October. Death of Pope's
        father.

1718   June. *Iliad,* volume IV.

1719   Pope and his mother moved to the villa at
        Twickenham on the Thames, where he was to
        become much involved in building and
        gardening.

1720   May. *Iliad,* volumes V and VI.

1725   March. Pope's edition of Shakespeare (begun
        in 1721) published in six volumes. April. The
        translation of the *Odyssey,* assisted by William
        Broome and Elijah Fenton, began to appear:
        volumes I–III. Bolingbroke, returned from
        exile, settled near Pope at Dawley Farm,
        Uxbridge.

1726   March. Lewis Theobald's *Shakespeare Re-
        stored,* with attacks upon errors and omissions
        of Pope's edition. June. *Odyssey,* volumes
        IV–V. Pope visited by Swift, whose *Gulliver's
        Travels* appeared in October.

1727   June. The first two volumes of the *Miscellanies*
        by Pope and Swift.

1728   March. The "last" volume of the *Miscellanies*.
        May. The first version of "The Dunciad" in
        three books, with Lewis Theobald as hero.

1729   April. "The Dunciad Variorum," amplified
        with burlesque critical apparatus, including
        the "prolegomena" of Martinus Scriblerus.

1731   December. "Epistle to the Earl of Burl-
        ington" (Moral Essay IV).

1733   January. "Epistle to Bathurst" (Moral Essay
        III). February. The first of the Imitations of
        Horace, "Satire" II, i. February–May. The
        first three epistles of the "Essay on Man"
        published anonymously and widely praised.

1734   January. "Epistle to Cobham" (Moral Essay
        I) and the fourth epistle of the "Essay on
        Man." June. Pope's mother died at the age of
        ninety-one.

1735   January. "Epistle to Dr. Arbuthnot." Febru-
        ary. "To a Lady" (Moral Essay II). May. Ed-
        mund Curll published an unauthorized edition
        of Pope's letters.

1737   May. Pope's own edition of his letters.

1738   May–July. "Epilogue to the Satires." Pope by
        now was close to the leaders of the opposition
        to Sir Robert Walpole.

1740   Pope's meeting with William Warburton, later
        his literary executor and editor of the posthu-
        mous edition of his *Works* in 1751.

1742   March. "The New Dunciad," the fourth book,
        published and attacked by Colley Cibber.

1743   October. "The Dunciad" in four books, with
        Cibber replacing Theobald as hero.

1744   Pope and Warburton worked on a collected
        edition of Pope's works. May 30. Death of
        Pope.

THE RAPE
OF THE LOCK
AND OTHER POEMS

AN ESSAY ON CRITICISM

(1711)

'Tis hard to say, if greater want of skill
Appear in writing or in judging ill;
But, of the two, less dangerous is the offense
To tire our patience, than mislead our sense.
Some few in that, but numbers err in this,   5
Ten censure wrong for one who writes amiss;
A fool might once himself alone expose,
Now one in verse makes many more in prose.
    'Tis with our judgments as our watches; none
Go just alike, yet each believes his own.   10
In poets as true genius is but rare,
True taste as seldom is the critic's share;
Both must alike from Heaven derive their light,
These born to judge, as well as those to write.
Let such teach others who themselves excel,   15
And censure freely who have written well.
Authors are partial to their wit, 'tis true,
But are not critics to their judgment too?
    Yet if we look more closely, we shall find
Most have the seeds of judgment in their mind;   20
Nature affords at least a glimmering light;
The lines, though touched but faintly, are drawn
    right.
But as the slightest sketch, if justly traced,
Is by ill coloring but the more disgraced,

reader can ruin (margin note)

25 So by false learning is good sense° defaced;
    Some are bewildered in the maze of schools,°
    And some made coxcombs° Nature meant but
        fools.
    In search of wit these lose their common sense,
    And then turn critics in their own defense.
30 Each burns alike, who can, or cannot write,
    Or with a rival's or an eunuch's spite.
    All fools have still an itching to deride,
    And fain would be upon the laughing side;
    If Maevius° scribble in Apollo's° spite,
35 There are who judge still worse than he can write.
        Some have at first for wits, then poets past,
    Turned critics next, and proved plain fools at last;
    Some neither can for wits nor critics pass,
    As heavy mules are neither horse nor ass.

haha (margin note)

40 Those half-learnèd witlings, numerous in our isle,
    As half-formed insects on the banks of Nile;
    Unfinished things, one knows not what to call,
    Their generation's so equivocal:°
    To tell° 'em, would a hundred tongues require,
45 Or one vain wit's, that might a hundred tire.
        But you who seek to give and merit fame,
    And justly bear a critic's noble name,
    Be sure yourself and your own reach to know,
    How far your genius, taste, and learning go;
50 Launch not beyond your depth, but be discreet,
    And mark that point where sense and dulness
        meet.
    Nature to all things fixed the limits fit,
    And wisely curbed proud man's pretending wit:

25 **good sense** This looks back to the "glimmering light" and
"seeds of judgment," which may be fulfilled through learning
(as the drawn sketch is by coloring) or may be destroyed
through its misuse.   26 **schools** schools of thought or criticism,
with a glance at the schoolmen or scholastics, whose learning
often seemed arid   27 **coxcombs** vain pretenders   34 **Maevius**
a bad poet of Virgil's age   34 **Apollo** as god and inspirer of
true poetry   43 **equivocal** Insects and vermin were supposed to
be bred spontaneously from the mud of the Nile.   44 **tell** count

As on the land while here the ocean gains,
In other parts it leaves wide sandy plains;   55
Thus in the soul while memory prevails,
The solid power of understanding fails;
Where beams of warm imagination play,
The memory's soft figures melt away.
One science° only will one genius fit,   60
So vast is art, so narrow human wit;
Not only bounded to peculiar arts,
But oft in those confined to single parts.
Like kings we lose the conquests gained before,
By vain ambition still to make them more;   65
Each might his several province well command,
Would all but stoop to what they understand.
   First follow Nature, and your judgment frame
By her just standard, which is still° the same:
Unerring NATURE, still divinely bright,   70
One clear, unchanged, and universal light,
Life, force, and beauty, must to all impart,
At once the source, and end, and test of art.
Art from that fund each just supply provides,
Works without show, and without pomp presides: 75
In some fair body thus the informing soul
With spirits feeds, with vigor fills the whole,
Each motion guides, and every nerve sustains;
Itself unseen, but in the effects, remains.
Some to whom Heaven in wit has been profuse,   80
Want as much more, to turn it to its use;
For wit and judgment often are at strife,
Though meant each other's aid, like man and wife.
'Tis more to guide than spur the Muse's steed;°
Restrain his fury, than provoke his speed;   85
The wingèd courser, like a generous° horse,
Shows most true mettle when you check his
    course.
   Those RULES of old discovered, not devised,
Are Nature still, but Nature methodized;

60 **science** art or type of knowledge 69 **still** always
84 **Muse's steed** Pegasus 86 **generous** high-bred

90 Nature, like liberty, is but restrained
    By the same laws which first herself ordained.
        Hear how learnèd Greece her useful rules
            indites,
    When to repress, and when indulge our flights:
    High on Parnassus' top her sons she showed,
95 And pointed out those arduous paths they trod,
    Held from afar, aloft, the immortal prize,
    And urged the rest by equal steps to rise;
    Just precepts thus from great examples given,
    She drew from them what they derived from
        Heaven.
100 The generous critic fanned the poet's fire,
    And taught the world with reason to admire.
    Then criticism the Muses' handmaid proved,
    To dress her charms, and make her more beloved;
    But following wits from that intention strayed,
105 Who could not win the mistress, wooed the maid;
    Against the poets their own arms they turned,
    Sure to hate most the men from whom they
        learned.
    So modern 'pothecaries, taught the art
    By doctor's bills° to play the doctor's part,
110 Bold in the practice of mistaken° rules,
    Prescribe, apply, and call their masters fools.
    Some on the leaves° of ancient authors prey,
    Nor time nor moths e'er spoiled so much as they:
    Some drily plain, without invention's° aid,
115 Write dull receipts° how poems may be made:
    These leave the sense, their learning to display,
    And those explain the meaning quite away.
        You then whose judgment the right course
            would steer,
    Know well each ancient's proper character;
120 His fable,° subject, scope° in every page;

109 **bills** prescriptions 110 **mistaken** misunderstood 112
leaves The scholiasts and textual editors are seen as insects
and vermin. 114 **invention's** imagination's 115 **receipts**
formulas 120 **fable** plot 120 **scope** aim, chosen form

Religion, country, genius of his age:
Without all these at once before your eyes,
Cavil you may, but never criticize.
Be Homer's works your study and delight,
Read them by day, and meditate by night;   *125*
Thence form your judgment, thence your
    maxims bring,
And trace the Muses upward to their spring;
Still with itself compared, his text peruse;
And let your comment be the Mantuan Muse.°
   When first young Maro° in his boundless mind   *130*
A work to outlast immortal Rome designed,
Perhaps he seemed° above the critic's law,
And but from Nature's fountains scorned to draw:
But when to examine every part he came,
Nature and Homer were, he found, the same: *135*
Convinced, amazed, he checks the bold design,
And rules as strict his labored work confine,
As if the Stagirite° o'erlooked each line.
Learn hence for ancient rules a just esteem;
To copy nature is to copy them.   *140*
   Some beauties yet no precepts can declare,
For there's a happiness° as well as care.
Music resembles poetry, in each
Are nameless graces which no methods teach,
And which a master hand alone can reach.   *145*
If, where the rules not far enough extend,
(Since rules were made but to promote their end)
Some lucky licence answer to the full
The intent proposed, that licence is a rule.
Thus Pegasus, a nearer way to take,   *150*
May boldly deviate from the common track;
From vulgar bounds with brave° disorder part,

---

129 **Mantuan Muse** Virgil's poetry, the best commentary on
Homer's   130 **Maro** Virgil   132 **seemed** i.e., to himself
138 **Stagirite** Aristotle, whose *Poetics* analyzed the forms of
tragedy and epic   142 **happiness** felicity, good fortune (as
opposed to "care"); cf. "lucky licence" (line 148)   152 **brave**
(1) daring (2) brilliant, vivid

And snatch a grace beyond the reach of art,
Which, without passing through the judgment,
    gains
155 The heart, and all its end at once attains.
In prospects, thus, some objects please our eyes,
Which out of nature's common order rise,
The shapeless rock, or hanging precipice.
Great wits sometimes may gloriously offend,
160 And rise to faults true critics dare not mend.
But though the ancients thus their rules invade,
(As kings dispense with laws themselves have made)
Moderns, beware! or if you must offend
Against the precept, ne'er transgress its end;
165 Let it be seldom, and compelled by need,
And have, at least, their precedent to plead.
The critic else proceeds without remorse,
Seizes your fame, and puts his laws in force.
    I know there are, to whose presumptuous
      thoughts
170 Those freer beauties, even in them, seem faults:
Some figures monstrous and misshaped appear,
Considered singly, or beheld too near,
Which, but proportioned to their light or place,
Due distance reconciles to form and grace.
175 A prudent chief not always must display
His powers in equal ranks, and fair array,
But with the occasion and the place comply,
Conceal his force, nay seem sometimes to fly.
Those oft are stratagems which error seem,
180 Nor is it Homer nods, but we that dream.
    Still green with bays° each ancient altar° stands,
Above the reach of sacrilegious hands,
Secure from flames, from envy's fiercer rage,
Destructive war, and all-involving age.
See, from each clime the learned their incense
185   bring!
Hear, in all tongues consenting° paeans ring!

181 **bays** the laurel that crowns the poet   181 **altar** the works
of the ancients   186 **consenting** in harmony, unanimous

In praise so just, let every voice be joined,
And fill the general chorus of mankind!
Hail Bards triumphant! born in happier days;
Immortal heirs of universal praise!   190
Whose honors with increase of ages grow,
As streams roll down, enlarging as they flow!
Nations unborn your mighty names shall sound,
And worlds applaud that must not yet be found!
Oh may some spark of your celestial fire,   195
The last, the meanest of your sons inspire,
(That on weak wings, from far, pursues your
    flights;
Glows while he reads, but trembles as he writes)
To teach vain wits a science little known,
To admire superior sense, and doubt their own!   200
  Of all the causes which conspire to blind
Man's erring judgment, and misguide the mind,
What the weak head with strongest bias rules,
Is _pride_, the never-failing vice of fools.
Whatever Nature has in worth denied,   205
She gives in large recruits° of needful° pride;
For as in bodies, thus in souls, we find
What wants° in blood and spirits, swelled with
    wind;
Pride, where wit fails, steps in to our defense,
And fills up all the mighty void of sense.   210
If once right reason drives that cloud away,
Truth breaks upon us with resistless day;
Trust not yourself; but your defects to know,
Make use of every friend—and every foe.
  A _little learning_ is a dangerous thing;   215
Drink deep, or taste not the Pierian spring:°
There shallow draughts intoxicate the brain,
And drinking largely° sobers us again.
Fired at first sight with what the Muse imparts,
In fearless youth we tempt the heights of arts,   220

206 **recruits** additional supplies 206 **needful** (1) needed (2)
demanding, arrogant 208 **wants** is lacking 216 **Pierian spring**
a spring sacred to the Muses (the Pierides) 218 **largely**
deeply, fully

While from the bounded level of our mind,
Short views we take, nor see the lengths behind,
But more advanced, behold with strange surprise
New, distant scenes of endless science° rise!
225   So pleased at first, the towering Alps we try,
Mount o'er the vales, and seem to tread the sky;
The eternal snows appear already past,
And the first clouds and mountains seem the last:
But those attained, we tremble to survey
230   The growing labors of the lengthened way,
The increasing prospect tires our wandering eyes,
Hills peep o'er hills, and Alps on Alps arise!
    A perfect judge will read each work of wit
With the same spirit that its author writ:
235   Survey the WHOLE, nor seek slight faults to find,
Where nature moves, and rapture warms the
        mind;
Nor lose, for that malignant dull delight,
The generous pleasure to be charmed with wit.
But in such lays as neither ebb, nor flow,
240   Correctly cold, and regularly° low,
That shunning faults, one quiet tenor keep;
We cannot blame indeed—but we may sleep.
In wit, as nature, what affects our hearts
Is not the exactness° of peculiar° parts;
245   'Tis not a lip, or eye, we beauty call,
But the joint force and full result of all.
Thus when we view some well-proportioned
        dome,°
(The world's just wonder, and even thine O
        Rome!)
No single parts unequally surprise;
250   All comes united to the admiring° eyes;

224 **science** knowledge   240 **Correctly . . . regularly** obedient
to the rules but without imagination   244 **exactness** correctness
244 **peculiar** particular   247 **dome** building, whether domed or
not, although the dome provides a fine instance of unifying
structure, as in Michelangelo's dome for St. Peter's   250
admiring wondering, awestruck, as well as approving

No monstrous height, or breadth, or length
   appear;
The whole at once is bold, and regular.
   Whoever thinks a faultless piece to see,
Thinks what ne'er was, nor is, nor e'er shall be.
In every work regard the writer's end,   255
Since none can compass more than they intend;
And if the means be just, the conduct° true,
Applause, in spite of trivial faults, is due.
As men of breeding, sometimes men of wit,°
To avoid great errors, must the less commit,   260
Neglect the rules each verbal critic° lays,
For not to know some trifles, is a praise.
Most critics, fond of some subservient art,
Still make the whole depend upon a part,
They talk of principles, but notions° prize,   265
And all to one loved folly sacrifice.
   Once on a time, La Mancha's knight,° they say,
A certain bard encountering on the way,
Discoursed in terms as just, with looks as sage,
As e'er could Dennis° of the Grecian stage;   270
Concluding all were desperate sots and fools,
Who durst depart from Aristotle's rules.
Our author, happy in a judge so nice,
Produced his play, and begged the knight's advice,
Made him observe the subject and the plot,   275
The manners, passions, unities,° what not?
All which, exact to rule, were brought about,
Were but a combat in the lists left out.

257 **conduct** execution   259 **breeding . . . wit** The analogy is
of manners and poetic composition.   261 **verbal critic** are
concerned with details of language, with form rather than
function   265 **notions** prejudices, unexamined ideas   267 **La
Mancha's knight** Don Quixote (in a sequel to Cervantes'
novel)   270 **Dennis** John Dennis, a gifted but self-important
critic of Pope's day   276 **manners . . . unities** critical terms
derived from Aristotle, sometimes legalistically applied, as in
the doctrine of the three unities (of time, place, and subject)
limiting a play to one revolution of the sun, one locale, and a
uniform tone

"What! leave the Combat out?" exclaims the
　　knight;
280 Yes, or we must renounce the Stagirite.
"Not so by Heaven" (he answers in a rage)
"Knights, squires, and steeds, must enter on the
　　stage."
So vast a throng the stage can ne'er contain.
"Then build a new, or act it in a plain."
285 　Thus critics, of less judgment than caprice,
Curious,° not knowing, not exact, but nice,°
Form short ideas; and offend in arts
(As most in manners) by a love to parts.°
　Some to *conceit*° alone their taste confine,
290 And glittering thoughts struck out at every line;
Pleased with a work where nothing's just or fit;
One glaring chaos and wild heap of wit:
Poets like painters, thus, unskilled to trace
The naked nature and the living grace,
295 With gold and jewels cover every part,
And hide with ornaments their want of art.
True wit is nature to advantage dressed,
What oft was thought, but ne'er so well expressed,
Something, whose truth convinced at sight we find,
300 That gives us back the image of our mind:
As shades° more sweetly recommend the light,
So modest plainness sets off sprightly wit:
For works may have more wit than does 'em good,
As bodies perish through excess of blood.°
305 　Others for *language* all their care express,
And value books, as women men, for dress:
Their praise is still—the style is excellent:
The sense, they humbly take upon content.°

286 **curious** laborious, fussy　286 **nice** squeamishly
fastidious　288 **parts** isolated gifts, as in "a man of parts"　289
conceit farfetched comparisons or metaphors, such as had been
favored by the Metaphysical poets　301 **As shades** Cf.
"Windsor Forest," lines 17–18, and "To Richard Boyle, Earl
of Burlington," lines 53–56.　304 **excess of blood** as it was
believed, in apoplexy　308 **upon content** on trust

Words are like leaves; and where they most
    abound,
Much fruit of sense beneath is rarely found.   310
False eloquence, like the prismatic glass,
Its gaudy colors spreads on every place;
The face of nature we no more survey,
All glares alike, without distinction gay:
But true expression, like the unchanging sun,   315
Clears and improves whate'er it shines upon,
It gilds all objects, but it alters none.
Expression is the dress of thought, and still
Appears more decent° as more suitable;
A vile° conceit in pompous words expressed,   320
Is like a clown° in regal purple dressed;
For different styles with different subjects sort,
As several garbs with country, town, and court.
Some by old words° to fame have made pretence;
Ancients in phrase, mere moderns in their sense!   325
Such labored nothings, in so strange a style,
Amaze the unlearned, and make the learnèd smile.
Unlucky, as Fungoso in the play,°
These sparks° with awkward vanity display
What the fine gentleman wore yesterday;   330
And but so mimic ancient wits at best,
As apes° our grandsires in their doublets drest.
In words, as fashions, the same rule will hold;
Alike fantastic, if too new, or old;
Be not the first by whom the new are tried,   335
Nor yet the last to lay the old aside.
    But most by *numbers*° judge a poet's song,
And smooth or rough, with them, is right or
    wrong;

319 **decent** appropriate, attractive   320 **vile** inept or low in
tone   321 **clown** rustic   324 **old words** archaic diction, such as
Spenser affects at times, but used more crudely by lesser poets
of Pope's day   328 **play** Ben Jonson's *Every Man Out of His
Humor*   329 **sparks** wits, fops   332 **apes** Monkeys were often
dressed in elaborate dress for entertainment.   337 **numbers**
versification, sound patterns

In the bright Muse though thousand charms
    conspire,
340 Her voice is all these tuneful fools admire,
Who haunt Parnassus but to please their ear,
Not mend their minds; as some to church repair,
Not for the doctrine but the music there.
These equal syllables alone require,
345 Though oft the ear the open vowels tire,°
While expletives their feeble aid do join,
And ten low words oft creep in one dull line,
While they ring round the same unvaried chimes,
With sure returns of still expected rhymes.
350 Where'er you find "the cooling western breeze,"
In the next line, it "whispers through the trees;"
If crystal streams "with pleasing murmurs creep,"
The reader's threatened (not in vain) with
    "sleep."
Then, at the last and only couplet fraught
355 With some unmeaning thing they call a thought,
A needless Alexandrine° ends the song,
That, like a wounded snake, drags its slow
    length along.
Leave such to tune their own dull rhymes, and
    know
What's roundly smooth, or languishingly slow;
360 And praise the easy vigor of a line
Where Denham's strength, and Waller's
    sweetness° join.
True ease in writing comes from art, not chance,
As those move easiest who have learned to dance.
'Tis not enough no harshness gives offense,
365 The sound must seem an echo to the sense.

345 The line illustrates the pattern of "equal syllables" (line
344). 356 **Alexandrine** a line of twelve syllables and six
stresses, illustrated in line 357 361 **Denham's strength . . .
Waller's sweetness** These two poets of the seventeenth century
were praised for complementary virtues, which the Augustans
sought to fuse. Sir John Denham (1615–69) wrote concisely,
sometimes harshly; Sir Edmund Waller (1606–87) was cele-
brated for the harmony and musicality of his verse.

Soft is the strain° when Zephyr° gently blows,
And the smooth stream in smoother numbers
        flows;
But when loud surges lash the sounding shore,
The hoarse, rough verse should like the torrent
        roar.
When Ajax° strives, some rock's vast weight to
        throw,   370
The line too labors, and the words move slow;
Not so, when swift Camilla° scours the plain,
Flies o'er the unbending corn, and skims along
        the main.
Hear how Timotheus'° varied lays surprise,
And bid alternate passions fall and rise!   375
While, at each change, the son of Libyan Jove°
Now burns with glory, and then melts with love;
Now his fierce eyes with sparkling fury glow,
Now sighs steal out, and tears begin to flow:
Persians and Greeks like turns of nature° found,   380
And the world's victor stood subdued by sound!
The power of music all our hearts allow,
And what Timotheus was, is DRYDEN now.
    Avoid extremes; and shun the fault of such
Who still are pleased too little or too much: 385
At every trifle scorn to take offense;
That always shows great pride, or little sense;
Those heads, as stomachs, are not sure the best,
Which nauseate all, and nothing can digest.
Yet let not each gay turn° thy rapture move,   390
For fools admire,° but men of sense approve;°
As things seem large which we through mists
        descry,
                                        ———

366 **Soft is the strain** Here and throughout the next eight lines,
Pope illustrates line 365.   366 **Zephyr** the west wind   370 **Ajax**
the rough hero in Homer's *Iliad*   372 **Camilla** the female
warrior in Virgil's *Aeneid*   374 **Timotheus** the bard is shown in
Dryden's ode, "Alexander's Feast, or the Power of Music."
376 **son . . . Jove** Alexander the Great   380 **turns of nature**
emotions   390 **turn** play on words or sound   391 **admire** are
filled with awe   391 **approve** (1) test (2) judge favorably

Dulness is ever apt to magnify.
   Some foreign writers, some our own despise;
395 The ancients only, or the moderns prize:
(Thus wit, like faith, by each man is applied
To one small sect, and all are damned beside.)
Meanly they seek the blessing to confine,
And force that sun but on a part to shine,
400 Which not alone the southern wit sublimes,°
But ripens spirits in cold northern climes;
Which from the first has shone on ages past,
Enlights the present, and shall warm the last:
(Though each may feel increases and decays,
405 And see now clearer and now darker days.)
Regard not then if wit be old or new,
But blame the false, and value still the true.
   Some ne'er advance a judgment of their own,
But catch the spreading notion of the town;
410 They reason and conclude by precedent,
And own stale nonsense which they ne'er invent.
Some judge of authors' names, not works, and
    then
Nor praise nor blame the writings, but the men.
Of all this servile herd the worst is he
415 That in proud dulness joins with quality,
A constant critic at the great man's board,
To fetch and carry nonsense for my lord.
What woeful stuff this madrigal would be,
In some starved hackney sonneteer, or me?
420 But let a lord once own the happy lines,
How the wit brightens! how the style refines!
Before his sacred name flies every fault,
And each exalted stanza teems with thought!
   The vulgar thus through imitation err;
425 As oft the learned by being singular;
So much they scorn the crowd, that if the throng
By chance go right, they purposely go wrong;
So schismatics the plain believers quit,
And are but damned for having too much wit.

400 **sublimes** raises, purifies

Some praise at morning what they blame at
    night; 430
But always think the last opinion right.
A Muse by these is like a mistress used,
This hour she's idolized, the next abused,
While their weak heads, like towns unfortified,
Twixt sense and nonsense daily change their side. 435
Ask them the cause; they're wiser still, they say;
And still tomorrow's wiser than today.
We think our fathers fools, so wise we grow;
Our wiser sons, no doubt, will think us so.
Once school-divines° this zealous isle o'erspread; 440
Who knew most sentences° was deepest read;
Faith, Gospel, all, seemed made to be disputed,
And none had sense enough to be confuted.
Scotists and Thomists,° now, in peace remain,
Amidst their kindred cobwebs in Duck Lane.° 445
If faith itself has diffcrent dresses worn,
What wonder modes in wit should take their turn?
Oft, leaving what is natural and fit,
The current folly proves the ready wit,
And authors think their reputation safe, 450
Which lives as long as fools arc pleased to laugh.
    Some valuing those of their own side or mind,
Still make themselves the measure of mankind;
Fondly° we think we honor merit then,
When we but praise ourselves in other men. 455
Parties in wit attend on those of state,°
And public faction doubles private hate.
Pride, malice, folly, against Dryden rose,
In various shapes of parsons, critics, beaus;

440 **school-divines** schoolmen, scholastic theologians 441
sentences maxims and precepts; religious *sententiae* used in
debate 444 **Scotists and Thomists** followers of Duns Scotus
and St. Thomas Aquinas, opposed on theological issues 445
Duck Lane a London street where old and secondhand books
were sold 454 **Fondly** foolishly, complacently 456 **state** This
rcfers both to the state's hiring of hack writers to further
political interests and to the political element that entered into
literary judgments.

460 But sense survived, when merry jests were past;
    For rising merit will buoy up at last.
    Might he return, and bless once more our eyes,
    New Blackmores and new Milbourns° must arise;
    Nay should great Homer lift his awful° head,
465 Zoilus° again would start up from the dead.
    Envy will merit, as its shade, pursue;
    But like a shadow, proves the substance true;
    For envied wit, like Sol eclipsed, makes known
    The opposing body's grossness, not its own.
470 When first that sun too powerful beams displays,
    It draws up vapors which obscure its rays;
    But even those clouds at last adorn its way,
    Reflect new glories, and augment the day.
      Be thou the first true merit to befriend;
475 His praise is lost, who stays till all commend.
    Short is the date, alas, of modern rhymes;
    And 'tis but just to let them live betimes.
    No longer now that golden age appears,
    When patriarch wits survived a thousand years;
480 Now length of fame (our second life) is lost,
    And bare threescore is all even that can boast:
    Our sons their fathers' failing language see,
    And such as Chaucer is,° shall Dryden be.
    So when the faithful pencil has designed
485 Some bright idea° of the master's mind,
    Where a new world leaps out at his command,
    And ready nature waits upon his hand;
    When the ripe colors soften and unite,
    And sweetly melt into just shade and light,
490 When mellowing years their full perfection give,
    And each bold figure just begins to live;

463 **Blackmores . . . Milbourns** Sir Richard Blackmore and
Luke Milbourn were among the lesser writers who attacked
Dryden. 464 **awful** awe-inspiring 465 **Zoilus** grammarian
and pedantic commentator on Homer 483 **as Chaucer is** Pope
foresees continuing change in the English language, such as
had made interpreting Chaucer difficult and reading his words
aloud most uncertain. 485 **bright idea** with suggestions of the
Platonic ideas by which the world is formed

The treacherous colors the fair art betray,
And all the bright creation fades away!
　　Unhappy wit, like most mistaken things,
Atones not for that envy which it brings.　　　495
In youth alone its empty praise we boast,
But soon the short-lived vanity is lost:
Like some fair flower the early spring supplies,
That gaily blooms, but even in blooming dies.
What is this wit which must our cares employ?　500
The owner's wife, that other men enjoy;
Then most our trouble still when most admired,
And still the more we give, the more required;
Whose fame with pains we guard, but lose with
　　ease,
Sure some to vex, but never all to please;　　505
'Tis what the vicious fear, the virtuous shun;
By fools 'tis hated, and by knaves undone!
　　If wit so much from ignorance undergo,
Ah let not learning too commence its foe!
Of old, those met rewards who could excel,　　510
And such were praised who but endeavored well:
Though triumphs were to generals only due,
Crowns were reserved to grace the soldiers too.
Now, they who reach Parnassus' lofty crown,
Employ their pains to spurn some others down;　515
And while self-love each jealous writer rules,
Contending wits become the sport of fools:
But still the worst with most regret commend,
For each ill author is as bad a friend.
To what base ends, and by what abject ways,　520
Are mortals urged through sacred° lust of praise!
Ah ne'er so dire a thirst of glory boast,
Nor in the critic let the man be lost!
Good nature and good sense must ever join;
To err is human, to forgive, divine.　　　525
　　But if in noble minds some dregs remain,
Not yet purged off, of spleen and sour disdain,
Discharge that rage on more provoking crimes,

---

521 **sacred** in its other meaning of "accursed"

Nor fear a dearth in these flagitious° times.
530 No pardon vile obscenity should find,
Though wit and art conspire to move your mind;
But dulness with obscenity must prove
As shameful sure as impotence in love.
In the fat age° of pleasure, wealth, and ease,
Sprung the rank weed, and thrived with large
535   increase;
When love was all an easy monarch's care;
Seldom at council, never in a war:
Jilts° ruled the state, and statesmen farces writ;
Nay wits had pensions, and young lords had wit:
540 The fair sat panting at a courtier's play,
And not a mask° went unimproved away:
The modest fan was lifted up no more,
And virgins smiled at what they blushed before.
The following licence of a foreign reign
545 Did all the dregs of bold Socinus° drain;
Then unbelieving priests reformed the nation,
And taught more pleasant methods of salvation;
Where Heaven's free subjects might their rights
        dispute,
Lest God himself should seem too absolute.
550 Pulpits their sacred satire learned to spare,
And vice admired to find a flatterer there!
Encouraged thus, wit's Titans° braved the skies,
And the press groaned with licensed blasphemies.
These monsters, critics! with your darts engage,
555 Here point your thunder,° and exhaust your rage!
Yet shun their fault, who, scandalously nice,

529 **flagitious** wicked   534 **fat age** the Restoration reign of
Charles II   538 **Jilts** harlots   541 **mask** Women wore masks at
the theatre in the Restoration period.   545 **Socinus** (1539–1604)
the religious teacher who denied the divinity of Christ. In
William's reign greater religious toleration was permitted, and
this early version of Unitarianism was among the doctrines
freed from censorship.   552 **Titans** the gods, pent up in the
earth, who fought Zeus in the heavens; here deistic
writers   555 **thunder** recalling Zeus' thunderbolts

Will needs mistake° an author into vice;
All seems infected that the infected spy,
As all looks yellow to the jaundiced eye.

LEARN then what MORALS critics ought to show, *560*
For 'tis but half a judge's task, to know.
'Tis not enough, taste, judgment, learning, join;
In all you speak, let truth and candor° shine:
That not alone what to your sense is due
All may allow; but seek your friendship too.   *565*
Be silent always when you doubt your sense;
And speak, though sure, with seeming diffidence:
Some positive persisting fops we know,
Who, if once wrong, will needs be always so;
But you, with pleasure own your errors past,   *570*
And make each day a critic on the last.
'Tis not enough your counsel still be true;
Blunt truths more mischief than nice° falsehoods
    do;
Men must be taught as if you taught them not,
And things unknown proposed as things forgot.   *575*
Without good breeding, truth is disapproved;
That only makes superior sense beloved.
Be niggards of advice on no pretense;
For the worst avarice is that of sense:
With mean complacence° ne'er betray your trust, *580*
Nor be so civil as to prove unjust;
Fear not the anger of the wise to raise;
Those best can bear reproof, who merit praise.
'Twere well might critics still this freedom take;
But Appius° reddens at each word you speak,   *585*
And stares, tremendous!° with a threatening eye,
Like some fierce tyrant in old tapestry.

557 **mistake** misread 563 **candor** generosity, openness of
mind 573 **nice** delicate 580 **mean complacence** timidly
uncritical approval 585 **Appius** John Dennis, author of the
unsuccessful tragedy *Appius and Virginia,* was sensitive to
criticism. 586 **tremendous** Dennis was fond of this word and
used it often.

Fear most to tax an honorable° fool,
Whose right it is, uncensured to be dull;
590 Such without wit are poets when they please,
As without learning they can take degrees.°
Leave dangerous truths to unsuccessful satires,
And flattery to fulsome dedicators,
Whom, when they praise, the world believes no
        more,
595 Than when they promise to give scribbling o'er.
'Tis best sometimes your censure to restrain,
And charitably let the dull be vain:
Your silence there is better than your spite,
For who can rail so long as they can write?
600 Still humming on, their drowsy course they keep,
And lashed so long, like tops, are lashed asleep.°
False steps but help them to renew the race,
As after stumbling, jades° will mend their pace.
What crowds of these, impenitently bold,
605 In sounds and jingling syllables grown old,
Still run on poets in a raging vein,
Even to the dregs and squeezings of the brain;
Strain out the last, dull droppings of their sense,
And rhyme with all the rage of impotence!
610   Such shameless bards we have; and yet 'tis true,
There are as mad, abandoned critics too.
The bookful blockhead, ignorantly read,
With loads of learnèd lumber in his head,
With his own tongue still edifies his ears,
615 And always listening to himself appears.
All books he reads, and all he reads assails,
From Dryden's Fables down to Durfey's Tales.°
With him, most authors steal their works, or buy;

588 **honorable** noble   591 **degrees** Unearned degrees could be
awarded to privy councilors and other noblemen.   601 **asleep**
A top is said to "sleep" when its motion is so rapid as to be
imperceptible.   603 **jades** worn-out horses   617 **Dryden's . . .
Tales** Dryden's *Fables* includes excellent verse translations of
Chaucer, Boccaccio, and Ovid. Thomas Durfey, best known as
a writer and collector of songs, was also a literary hack.

Garth° did not write his own Dispensary.
Name a new play, and he's the poet's friend,   620
Nay showed his faults—but when would poets
    mend?
No place so sacred from such fops is barred,
Nor is Paul's church° more safe than Paul's
    churchyard:
Nay, fly to altars; there they'll talk you dead;
For fools rush in where angels fear to tread.   625
Distrustful sense with modest caution speaks;
It still looks home, and short excursion makes;
But rattling nonsense in full volleys breaks,
And never shocked,° and never turned aside,
Bursts out, resistless, with a thundering tide!   630
    But where's the man who counsel can bestow,
Still pleased to teach, and yet not proud to know?
Unbiased, or by favor or by spite;
Not dully prepossessed, nor blindly right;
Though learned, well-bred; and though well-
    bred, sincere;   635
Modestly bold, and humanly° severe?
Who to a friend his faults can freely show,
And gladly praise the merit of a foe?
Blest with a taste exact, yet unconfined;
A knowledge both of books and human kind;   640
Generous converse; a soul exempt from pride;
And love to praise, with reason on his side?
    Such once were critics, such the happy few,
Athens and Rome in better ages knew.
The mighty Stagirite first left the shore,   645
Spread all his sails, and durst the deeps explore;
He steered securely, and discovered far,
Led by the light of the Maeonian star.°
Poets, a race long unconfined and free,

619 **Garth** Sir Samuel Garth, author of *The Dispensary.*
623 **Paul's church** St. Paul's Cathedral and its churchyard were
often places of meeting in the seventeenth century.
629 **shocked** checked   636 **humanly** humanely   648 **Maeonian
star** Homer

650 Still fond and proud of savage liberty,
    Received his laws, and stood convinced 'twas fit
    Who conquered nature,° should preside o'er wit.
      Horace still charms with graceful negligence,
    And without method° talks us into sense,
655 Will like a friend familiarly convey
    The truest notions in the easiest way.
    He, who supreme in judgment, as in wit,
    Might boldly censure, as he boldly writ,
    Yet judged with coolness though he sung with fire;°
660 His precepts teach but what his works inspire.
    Our critics take a contrary extreme,
    They judge with fury, but they write with fle'me:°
    Nor suffers Horace more in wrong translations
    By wits, than critics in as wrong quotations.
665   See Dionysius° Homer's thoughts refine,
    And call new beauties forth from every line!
      Fancy and art in gay Petronius please,
    The scholar's learning, with the courtier's ease.
      In grave Quintilian's copious work we find
670 The justest rules, and clearest method joined;
    Thus useful arms in magazines° we place,
    All ranged in order, and disposed with grace,
    But less to please the eye, than arm the hand,
    Still fit for use, and ready at command.
675   Thee, bold Longinus!° all the Nine inspire,
    And bless their critic with a poet's fire.
    An ardent judge, who zealous in his trust,
    With warmth gives sentence, yet is always just;
    Whose own example strengthens all his laws,
680 And is himself that great sublime he draws.

652 **nature** referring to Aristotle's scientific works 654
without method Horace's chief critical work, the *Ars Poetica,*
is written as an informal verse letter to friends, unlike the more
methodical *Poetics* of Aristotle. 659 **sung with fire** referring
to Horace's odes 662 **fle'me** phlegm, coldness 665 **Dionysius**
i.e., of Halicarnassus, Greek rhetorician, first century A.D. 671
magazines armories 675 **Longinus** Greek author of *On the
Sublime,* the most enthusiastic and least rule-bound of ancient
critics, first century A.D.

Thus long succeeding critics justly reigned,
Licence repressed, and useful laws ordained.
Learning and Rome alike in empire grew,
And arts still followed where her eagles° flew;
From the same foes, at last, both felt their doom, 685
And the same age saw learning fall, and Rome.
With tyranny, then superstition joined,
As that the body, this enslaved the mind;
Much was believed, but little understood,
And to be dull was construed to be good; 690
A second deluge learning thus o'errun,
And the monks finished what the Goths begun.
At length Erasmus,° that great injured name,
(The glory of the priesthood, and the shame!)
Stemmed the wild torrent of a barbarous age, 695
And drove those holy Vandals off the stage.
But see! each Muse, in Leo's golden days,°
Starts from her trance, and trims her withered bays!
Rome's ancient genius, o'er its ruins spread,
Shakes off the dust, and rears his reverend head! 700
Then sculpture and her sister arts revive;
Stones leaped to form, and rocks began to live;
With sweeter notes° each rising temple rung;
A Raphael° painted, and a Vida° sung!

684 **eagles** the insignia of her armies 693 **Erasmus** (1466–1536), humanist and moderate churchman (cf. "Satire" II, i, 66–67). Pope felt that Erasmus had been "oppressed and persecuted" by narrower fellow-Catholics and was at last "vindicated after a whole age of obloquy" (cf. "shame," line 694). 697 **Leo's . . . days** Leo X, the son of Lorenzo de' Medici, the Magnificent, was pope from 1513 to 1521. A patron of learning and the arts, he established the first Greek printing press in Rome and made Raphael (line 704) custodian of classical antiquities. 703 **sweeter notes** recalling the myth of Amphion, who built the walls of Thebes by drawing stones into place with the music of his lyre; referring as well to Leo's love and sponsorship of music · 704 **Raphael** (1483–1520) named chief architect of St. Peter's in 1514, painted many of his greatest frescoes and prepared the great tapestry cartoons (now in London) under Leo X 704 **Vida** (1490?–1566) a celebrated neo-Latin poet who was treated with favor by Leo X

705 Immortal Vida! on whose honored brow
    The poet's bays and critic's ivy° grow:
    Cremona° now shall ever boast thy name,
    As next in place to Mantua, next in fame!
       But soon by impious arms° from Latium chased,
710 Their ancient bounds the banished muses passed;
    Thence arts o'er all the northern world advance;
    But critic learning flourished most in France.
    The rules, a nation born to serve,° obeys,
    And Boileau° still in right of Horace sways.
715 But we, brave Britons, foreign laws despised,
    And kept unconquered, and uncivilized,
    Fierce for the liberties of wit, and bold,
    We still defied the Romans, as of old.°
    Yet some there were, among the sounder few
720 Of those who less presumed, and better knew,
    Who durst assert the juster ancient cause,
    And here restored wit's fundamental laws.
    Such was the muse,° whose rules and practice tell,
    "Nature's chief masterpiece is writing well."
    Such was Roscommon°—not more learned than
725   good,
    With manners generous as his noble blood;
    To him the wit of Greece and Rome was known,

706 As the bays, or laurel, were originally associated with the
conqueror or emperor, so was ivy with the poet; but as the bays
became identified with the poet, so was the ivy with the man
of learning, here the critic (Vida was the author of an "art of
poetry" in verse).   707 **Cremona** the birthplace of Vida, as
Mantua (708) was of Virgil   709 **impious arms** the Sack of
Rome in 1527 by the troops of the Emperor Charles V   713
nation . . . serve Cf. "Dunciad," IV, 297–98   714 **Boileau**
(1636–1711) published a verse *Art of Poetry* and satires in
imitation of Horace.   718 As the Britons resisted Roman rule,
so these writers resisted classical form and precept.   723 **muse**
John Sheffield, Duke of Buckingham and Normandy (1648–1721),
whose *Essay upon Poetry* is quoted in the next line. He had
been a patron of Dryden and was a friend of the young
Pope.   725 **Roscommon** translated Horace's *Art of Poetry* and
wrote *An Essay on Translated Verse*.

And every author's merit,° but his own.
Such late was Walsh,°—the Muse's judge and
    friend,
Who justly knew to blame or to commend;   *730*
To failings mild, but zealous for desert;
The clearest head, and the sincerest heart.
This humble praise, lamented shade! receive,
This praise at least a grateful Muse may give!
The Muse, whose early voice you taught to sing,   *735*
Prescribed her heights, and pruned her tender
    wing,
(Her guide now lost) no more attempts to rise,
But in low numbers short excursions tries;
Content, if hence the unlearned their wants may
    view,
The learned reflect on what before they knew: *740*
Careless of censure, nor too fond of fame,
Still pleased to praise, yet not afraid to blame,
Averse alike to flatter, or offend,
Not free from faults, nor yet too vain to mend.

---

728 **merit** Roscommon was one of the first to praise Milton's
Paradise Lost. 729 **Walsh** William Walsh (1662–1708), poet
and critic, whose advice was valued by both Dryden and Pope

WINDSOR FOREST

(1713)

THY forests, Windsor! and thy green retreats,
At once the Monarch's and the Muse's seats,°
Invite my lays. Be present, sylvan maids!
Unlock your springs, and open all your shades.
5 Granville° commands; your aid, O Muses, bring!
What Muse for Granville can refuse to sing?
   The groves of Eden,° vanished now so long,
Live in description, and look green in song:
These, were my breast inspired with equal flame,
10 Like them in beauty, should be like in fame.
Here hills and vales, the woodland and the plain,
Here earth and water seem to strive again;
Not chaos-like together crushed and bruised,
But, as the world, harmoniously confused:°
15 Where order in variety we see,
And where, though all things differ, all agree.
Here waving groves a chequered scene display,
And part admit and part exclude the day;

2 **At once . . . seats** the royal forest preserve of Queen Anne
seen as the center of both England's natural beauty and its
culture, later of its history and its empire   5 **Granville** a poet
and friend of Pope, made Secretary of War in 1710 and created
a peer in 1712   7 **Eden** an allusion to Milton, *Paradise Lost,*
IV   14 **harmoniously confused** an echo of Ovid's *discors
concordia* (*Metamorphoses,* I, 433)

28

As some coy nymph her lover's warm address
Nor quite indulges, nor can quite repress.   *20*
There, interspersed in lawns and opening glades,
Thin trees arise that shun each other's shades.
Here in full light the russet plains extend:
There wrapped in clouds the bluish hills ascend.
Even the wild heath displays her purple dyes,   *25*
And midst the desert° fruitful fields arise,
That crowned with tufted trees and springing corn,
Like verdant isles the sable waste adorn.
Let India boast her plants, nor envy we
The weeping amber or the balmy tree,°   *30*
While by our oaks° the precious loads are borne,
And realms commanded which those trees adorn.
Not proud Olympus° yields a nobler sight,
Though gods assembled grace his towering height,
Than what more humble mountains offer here,   *35*
Where, in their blessings,° all those gods appear.
See Pan° with flocks, with fruits Pomona° crowned,
Here blushing Flora paints the enamelled ground,°
Here Ceres' gifts° in waving prospect stand,
And nodding tempt the joyful reaper's hand;   *40*
Rich Industry° sits smiling on the plains,
And peace and plenty tell, a Stuart reigns.
   Not thus the land appeared in ages past,
A dreary desert and a gloomy waste,

26 **desert** barrenness; cf. "waste" (line 28)   30 **weeping . . .
tree** Cf. Milton, *Paradise Lost,* IV, 248: "Groves whose rich
Trees wept odorous Gums and Balm."   31 **oaks** in the form
of the British ships of the spice trade or (line 32) the Royal
Navy   33 **Olympus** the high Greek mountain where the gods
dwelled   36 **blessings** in the form of their gifts   37 **Pan** as
shepherd   37 **Pomona** as goddess of fruit   38 **blushing
Flora . . . ground** The goddess of flowers, herself suffused with
their color, paints the earth as if it were a painter's surface,
prepared with a background coating.   39 **Ceres' gifts** wheat
41 **Industry** Pope domesticates Virgil's account of the Golden
Age, "Eclogue" IV, as a picture of English prosperity in a
time of peace. This is a tribute to the Peace of Utrecht (1713),
which ended the War of the Spanish Succession, begun under
William of Orange in 1701.

45   To savage beasts and savage laws a prey,
      And kings more furious and severe than they:
      Who claimed the skies, dispeopled air and floods,°
      The lonely lords of empty wilds and woods:
      Cities laid waste, they stormed the dens and caves,
50   (For wiser brutes were backward to be slaves.)
      What could be free when lawless beasts obeyed,
      And even the elements a Tyrant swayed?°
      In vain kind seasons swelled the teeming grain,
      Soft showers distilled, and suns grew warm in vain;
55   The swain with tears his frustrate labor yields,
      And famished dies amidst his ripened fields.
      What wonder then, a beast or subject slain
      Were equal crimes in a despotic reign;
      Both doomed alike, for sportive tyrants bled,
60   But while the subject starved, the beast was fed.
      Proud Nimrod° first the bloody chase began,
      A mighty hunter, and his prey was man.
      Our haughty Norman° boasts that barbarous
           name,
      And makes his trembling slaves the royal game.
      The fields are ravished from the industrious
65   swains,
      From men their cities, and from Gods their fanes:
      The levelled towns with weeds lie covered o'er;
      The hollow winds through naked temples roar;
      Round broken columns clasping ivy twined;
70   O'er heaps of ruin stalked the stately hind;

47 **claimed . . . floods** a reference to the wide hunting preserves
claimed by earlier kings 49–52 **Cities . . . swayed** The
metaphor of hunting expands to all predatory use of power,
and possibly (in line 52) to the doctrine of a God in the image
of the tyrant· (cf. "Essay on Man," III, 241–68). Tyranny is
associated throughout with social disorder, in contrast to the
"peace and plenty" of a just reign.   61 **Nimrod** described in
Genesis 10:8–9 as "a mighty one in the earth" and a "mighty
hunter before the lord"; by Milton, *Paradise Lost*, XII, 24–47,
as the first tyrant and hunter of men.   63 **Norman** William
the Conqueror, who created the New Forest by destroying the
existing towns, farms, and churches (cf. "fanes," line 66;
"temples," 68; "choirs," 72).

The fox obscene to gaping tombs retires,
And savage howlings fill the sacred choirs.
Awed by his Nobles, by his Commons curst,
The oppressor ruled tyrannic where he durst,
Stretched o'er the poor and church his iron rod,   75
And served alike his vassals and his God.
Whom even the Saxon spared and bloody Dane,
The wanton victims of his sport° remain.
But see, the man who spacious regions gave
A waste for beasts, himself denied a grave!°   80
Stretched on the lawn his second hope° survey,
At once the chaser, and at once the prey:
Lo Rufus, tugging at the deadly dart,
Bleeds in the forest like a wounded hart.
Succeeding monarchs heard the subjects' cries,   85
Nor saw displeased the peaceful cottage rise.
Then gathering flocks on unknown mountains fed,
O'er sandy wilds were yellow harvests spread,
The forests wondered at the unusual grain,
And secret transport touched the conscious°
    swain.   90
Fair Liberty, Britannia's goddess, rears
Her cheerful head, and leads the golden years.
  Ye vigorous swains! while youth ferments your
    blood,
And purer spirits swell the sprightly flood,°
Now range the hills, the gameful woods beset,   95
Wind the shrill horn, or spread the waving net.
When milder autumn summer's heat succeeds,
And in the new-shorn field the partridge feeds,
Before his lord the ready spaniel bounds,
Panting with hope, he tries the furrowed grounds;   100

78 **sport** (1) hunting (2) scornful whim   80 **grave** William's
burial place at Caen was claimed by another and had to be
bought anew by his son.   81 **second hope** William's second
son, Richard, who died in the New Forest, like his brother,
William Rufus (line 83)   90 **conscious** responsive   94 **spirits . . .
sprightly flood** a reference to the animal spirits, believed to
be a subtle vapor-like substance that moved in the blood and
animated the body

But when the tainted gales° the game betray,
Couched close he lies, and meditates the prey:
Secure they° trust the unfaithful field beset,
Till hovering o'er 'em sweeps the swelling net.
105 Thus (if small things we may with great compare)
When Albion sends her eager sons to war,
Some thoughtless town, with ease and plenty blest,
Near, and more near, the closing lines° invest;
Sudden they seize the amazed, defenseless prize,
110 And high in air Britannia's standard flies.
   See! from the brake° the whirring pheasant
      springs,
And mounts exulting on triumphant wings;
Short is his joy! he feels the fiery wound,
Flutters in blood, and panting beats the ground.
115 Ah! what avail his glossy, varying dyes,°
His purple crest, and scarlet-circled eyes,
The vivid green his shining plumes unfold,
His painted wings, and breast that flames with
     gold?
   Nor yet, when moist Arcturus° clouds the sky,
120 The woods and fields their pleasing toils deny.
To plains with well-breathed beagles we repair,
And trace the mazes of the circling hare:
(Beasts, urged by us, their fellow-beasts pursue,
And learn of man each other to undo.)
With slaughtering guns the unwearied fowler
125   roves,
When frosts have whitened all the naked groves;
Where doves in flocks the leafless trees o'ershade,
And lonely woodcocks haunt the watery glade.
He lifts the tube, and levels with his eye;
130 Straight a short thunder breaks the frozen sky.
Oft, as in airy rings they skim the heath,

101 **tainted gales** breezes that carry the scent of game
103 **they** the partridges 108 **lines** of siege 111 **brake**
thicket 115 **glossy . . . dyes** the pheasant's plumage seen as
regal splendor 119 **moist Arcturus** associated with storms as
it rose in September

The clamorous lapwings feel the leaden death:
Oft, as the mounting larks their notes prepare,
They fall, and leave their little lives in air.
  In genial spring, beneath the quivering shade,   *135*
Where cooling vapors breathe along the mead,
The patient fisher takes his silent stand,
Intent, his angle trembling in his hand;
With looks unmoved, he hopes the scaly breed,
And eyes the dancing cork and bending reed.   *140*
Our plenteous streams a various race supply,
The bright-eyed perch with fins of Tyrian dye,°
The silver eel, in shining volumes° rolled,
The yellow carp, in scales bedropped with gold,
Swift trouts, diversified with crimson stains,   *145*
And pikes, the tyrants° of the watery plains.
  Now Cancer° glows with Phoebus' fiery car;
The youth rush eager to the sylvan war,
Swarm o'er the lawns, the forest walks surround,
Rouse the fleet hart, and cheer the opening°
   hound.   *150*
The impatient courser pants in every vein,
And, pawing, seems to beat the distant plain:
Hills, vales, and floods appear already crossed,
And ere he starts, a thousand steps are lost.
See the bold youth strain up the threatening steep,   *155*
Rush through the thickets, down the valleys
   sweep,
Hang o'er their coursers' heads with eager speed,
And earth rolls back beneath the flying steed.
Let old Arcadia° boast her ample plain,
The immortal huntress,° and her virgin train;   *160*
Nor envy, Windsor! since thy shades have seen

142 **Tyrian dye** crimson or purple   143 **volumes** coils
146 **tyrants** so called for their voraciousness   147 **Cancer** the
zodiacal sign for the season that begins with the summer
solstice, when the sun is at its height ("Phoebus' fiery car")
150 **opening** giving tongue, baying   159 **Arcadia** the area of
Greece celebrated in pastoral poetry   160 **huntress** Diana,
celebrated for chastity and as goddess of the moon (cf. line 162)

As bright a goddess, and as chaste a Queen,°
Whose care, like hers, protects the sylvan reign,
The earth's fair light, and empress of the main.
165   Here too, 'tis sung, of old Diana strayed,
And Cynthus'° top forsook for Windsor shade;
Here was she seen o'er airy wastes to rove,
Seek the clear spring, or haunt the pathless grove;
Here armed with silver bows, in early dawn,
170 Her buskined virgins° traced° the dewy lawn.
   Above the rest a rural nymph was famed,
Thy offspring, Thames! the fair Lodona° named;
(Lodona's fate, in long oblivion cast,
The Muse shall sing, and what she sings shall last.)
Scarce could the goddess from her nymph be
175   known,
But by the crescent° and the golden zone.°
She scorned the praise of beauty and the care;
A belt her waist, a fillet binds her hair;
A painted quiver on her shoulder sounds,
180 And with her dart the flying deer she wounds.
It chanced, as eager of the chase, the maid
Beyond the forest's verdant limits strayed,
Pan° saw and loved, and, burning with desire,
Pursued her flight; her flight increased his fire.
185 Not half so swift the trembling doves can fly,
When the fierce eagle cleaves the liquid° sky;
Not half so swiftly the fierce eagle moves,
When through the clouds he drives the
   trembling doves;
As from the god she flew with furious pace,
190 Or as the god, more furious, urged the chase.
Now fainting, sinking, pale, the nymph appears;

162 **Queen** Anne, who often hunted   166 **Cynthus** the
mountain on the island of Delos where Diana was born
170 **buskined virgins** the nymphs who joined Diana in the hunt,
wearing high-laced sandals   170 **traced** traversed   172 **Lodona**
the mythical form of the river Loddon, here imagined as
Diana's nymph   176 **crescent** the moon emblem of
Diana   176 **zone** belt   183 **Pan** as the god of shepherds, often
imagined as a goatlike satyr   186 **liquid** clear

Now close behind, his sounding steps she hears;
And now his shadow reached her as she run
(His shadow lengthened by the setting sun),
And now his shorter breath, with sultry air,   195
Pants on her neck, and fans her parting hair.
In vain on father Thames she calls for aid,
Nor could Diana help her injured maid.
Faint, breathless, thus she prayed, nor prayed in
     vain;
"Ah, Cynthia!° ah—though banished from thy
     train,   200
Let me, O let me, to the shades repair,
My native shades—there weep and murmur
     there"
She said, and melting as in tears she lay,
In a soft, silver stream dissolved away.
The silver stream her virgin coldness keeps,   205
For ever murmurs, and for ever weeps;
Still bears the name the hapless virgin bore,
And bathes the forest where she ranged before.
In her chaste current oft the goddess laves,
And with celestial tears augments the waves.   210
Oft in her glass° the musing shepherd spies
The headlong mountains and the downward skies,
The watery landscape of the pendent woods,
And absent° trees that tremble in the floods;
In the clear azure gleam the flocks are seen,   215
And floating forests paint the waves with green,
Through the fair scene roll slow the lingering
     streams,
Then foaming pour along, and rush into the
     Thames.
   Thou, too, great father° of the British floods!°
With joyful pride surveyst our lofty woods;   220
Where towering oaks their growing honors° rear,
And future navies on thy shores appear.

200 **Cynthia** Diana, so named for Mt. Cynthus   211 **glass**
mirror   214 **absent** unseen except in reflection   219 **father**
Thames   219 **floods** rivers   221 **honors** foliage

Not Neptune's° self from all his streams receives
A wealthier tribute than to thine he gives.
225 No seas so rich, so gay no banks appear,
No lake so gentle, and no spring so clear.
Nor Po° so swells the fabling poet's lays,
While led along the skies his current strays,
As thine,° which visits Windsor's famed abodes,
230 To grace the mansion of our earthly gods:
Nor all his stars above a lustre show
Like the bright beauties on thy banks below;
Where Jove, subdued by mortal° passion still,
Might change Olympus for a nobler hill.
235   Happy the man whom this bright court approves,
His sovereign favors, and his country loves;
Happy next him, who to these shades retires,
Whom Nature charms, and whom the Muse
       inspires,
Whom humbler joys of home-felt quiet please,
240 Successive study, exercise, and ease.
He gathers health from herbs the forest yields,
And of their fragrant physic spoils the fields:
With chymic° art exalts the mineral powers,
And draws° the aromatic souls of flowers.
245 Now marks the course of rolling orbs on high;
O'er figured° worlds now travels with his eye.
Of ancient writ° unlocks the learnèd store,
Consults the dead, and lives past ages o'er.
Or wandering thoughtful in the silent wood,
250 Attends the duties of the wise and good,
To observe a mean,° be to himself a friend,
To follow Nature, and regard his end;°

223 **Neptune** as the sea receiving the tribute of the rivers; in
return a source of trade   227 **Po** the Italian river seen as the
constellation Eridanus, flowing through the heavens (cf. line
231)   229 **thine** the Thames as it flows by the royal castle
233 **mortal** for a mortal woman   243 **chymic** chemical or
alchemical (converting baser elements to gold)   244 **draws**
extracts in essences   246 **figured** charted, as on a globe of the
heavens   247 **writ** writings   251 **mean** the golden mean, or
temperate life   252 **end** proper function as well as fate

Or looks on heaven with more than mortal eyes,
Bids his free soul expatiate° in the skies,
Amid her kindred stars familiar roam,   255
Survey the region, and confess her home!
Such was the life great Scipio° once admired;
Thus Atticus,° and Trumbull° thus retired.
   Ye sacred Nine! that all my soul possess,
Whose raptures fire me, and whose visions bless,   260
Bear me, oh bear me to sequestered scenes,
The bowery mazes, and surrounding greens:
To Thames's banks, which fragrant breezes fill,
Or where ye Muses sport on Cooper's Hill.°
(On Cooper's Hill eternal wreaths shall grow,   265
While lasts the mountain, or while Thames shall
     flow.)
I seem through consecrated walks to rove,
I hear soft music die along the grove:
Led by the sound, I roam from shade to shade
By godlike poets venerable made: 270
Here his first lays majestic Denham° sung;
There the last numbers flowed from Cowley's°
     tongue.
O early lost! what tears the river shed,
When the sad pomp° along his banks was led!
His drooping swans on every note expire,   275
And on his willows hung each Muse's lyre.°
   Since fate relentless stopped their heavenly voice,
No more the forests ring or groves rejoice;

254 **expatiate** wander at will   257 **Scipio** the Roman general
who retired to his country estate   258 **Atticus** the friend of
Cicero who repudiated public life out of devotion to study
258 **Trumbull** Sir William, the retired statesman and friend of
the young Pope   264 **Cooper's Hill** the scene of Sir John
Denham's poem (1642), a model for this one   271 **Denham**
Sir John, the Royalist poet, "majestic" because of his epic vein
(1615–69)   272 **Cowley** the poet Abraham Cowley, who died
near Windsor Forest at the age of forty-nine   274 **pomp**
Cowley's body was borne down the Thames to London, where
it was buried in Westminster Abbey.   276 **each Muse's lyre** a
reference to the many forms of poetry in which Cowley
excelled

Who now shall charm the shades, where Cowley
    strung
280 His living harp, and lofty Denham sung?
But hark! the groves rejoice, the forest rings!
Are these revived? or is it Granville sings?
'Tis yours, my Lord, to bless our soft retreats,
And call the Muses to their ancient seats;
285 To paint anew the flowery sylvan scenes,
To crown the forests with immortal greens,
Make Windsor hills in lofty numbers° rise,
And lift her turrets nearer to the skies;
To sing those honors you deserve to wear,
290 And add new lustre to her silver star.°
    Here noble Surrey° felt the sacred rage,
Surrey, the Granville of a former age:
Matchless his pen, victorious was his lance,
Bold in the lists, and graceful in the dance:
295 In the same shades the cupids tuned his lyre,
To the same notes, of love, and soft desire:
Fair Geraldine,° bright object of his vow,
Then filled the groves, as heavenly Mira now.
    Oh wouldst thou sing what heroes Windsor
    bore,
300 What kings first breathed upon her winding shore,
Or raise old warriors, whose adored remains
In weeping vaults her hallowed earth contains!
With Edward's acts° adorn the shining page,
Stretch his long triumphs down through every age,
305 Draw monarchs chained, and Cressy's glorious field,°

287 **lofty numbers** exalted or heroic verse   290 **silver star** the
emblem of the Order of the Garter, founded at Windsor by
Edward III. It was these "honors" (line 289) that Granville
deserved.   291 **Surrey** "one of the refiners of the English
poetry, who flourished in the time of Henry VIII" (Pope)   297
Geraldine the object of Surrey's love poems, as "Mira" was of
Granville's (line 298)   303 **Edward's acts** the victories of
Edward III, whose forces captured kings of Scotland and of
France (line 305)   305 **Cressy's . . . field** Crécy was a great
victory of Edward's son, the Black Prince, which confirmed
Edward's claim to France and his quartering of her fleur-de-
lys on his shield.

The lilies blazing on the regal shield:
Then, from her roofs when Verrio's colors° fall,
And leave inanimate the naked wall,
Still in thy song should vanquished France appear,
And bleed for ever under Britain's spear.   *310*
   Let softer strains ill-fated Henry° mourn,
And palms eternal° flourish round his urn.
Here o'er the Martyr King the marble weeps,
And, fast beside him, once-feared Edward° sleeps:
Whom not the extended Albion° could contain,   *315*
From old Belerium° to the northern main,
The grave unites; where e'en the great find rest,
And blended lie the oppressor and the opprest!
   Make sacred Charles's° tomb for ever known
(Obscure the place, and uninscribed the stone),   *320*
Oh fact accurst! what tears has Albion shed,
Heavens, what new wounds! and how her old
     have bled!
She saw her sons with purple deaths° expire,
Her sacred domes involved in rolling fire,°
A dreadful series of intestine wars,   *325*
Inglorious triumphs and dishonest° scars.
At length great Anna said—"Let Discord cease!"
She said! the world obeyed, and all was Peace!

   In that blest moment from his oozy bed
Old father Thames advanced his reverend head.   *330*

307 **Verrio's colors** the ceiling paintings at Windsor which represented Charles II with France at his feet   311 **Henry** Henry VI (1421–71), probably murdered and regarded as a royal martyr   312 **palms eternal** as emblems of martyrdom   314 **Edward** Edward IV (1442–83), rival claimant to the throne, buried near Henry VI at Windsor   315 **extended Albion** all of Britain, since Henry VI fled from Edward IV to the north   316 **Belerium** Land's End, Cornwall   319 **Charles** Charles I, another royal martyr, buried in some tomb as Henry VIII without any service   323 **purple deaths** the Great Plague (1665)   324 **rolling fire** the Great Fire of London (1666)   326 **dishonest** shameful, especially if the plague and fire are seen as divine retribution for the execution of Charles I

His tresses dropped with dews, and o'er the
    stream
His shining horns° diffused a golden gleam:
Graved on his urn appeared the moon, that guides
His swelling waters, and alternate tides;
335 The figured° streams in waves of silver rolled,
And on their banks Augusta° rose in gold.
Around his throne the sea-born° brothers stood,
Who swell with tributary urns his flood.
First the famed authors of his ancient name,°
340 The winding Isis and the fruitful Thame:
The Kennet swift, for silver eels renowned;
The Loddon slow, with verdant alders crowned;
Cole, whose dark streams his flowery islands lave;
And chalky Wey, that rolls a milky wave:
345 The blue, transparent Vandalis appears;
The gulfy Lee his sedgy tresses rears;
And sullen Mole, that hides his diving flood;°
And silent Darent, stained with Danish blood.°
    High in the midst, upon his urn reclined
350 (His sea-green mantle waving with the wind),
The God appeared: he turned his azure eyes
Where Windsor domes and pompous turrets rise;
Then bowed and spoke; the winds forget to roar,
And the hushed waves glide softly to the shore.
355   "Hail, sacred Peace! hail, long-expected days,
That Thames's glory to the stars shall raise!
Though Tiber's streams immortal Rome behold,
Though foaming Hermus° swells with tides of
    gold,

332 **shining horns** The horns of a bull were the usual mythical
attributes of river gods, perhaps suggesting natural energy. The
"urn" (line 333), from which the river flows, is commonly
shown with the river god. 335 **figured** represented on the
urn 336 **Augusta** London 337 **sea-born** born, like all rivers,
of Oceanus 339 **authors . . . name** The Latin name Tamesis
is taken as a fusion of Thame and Isis. 347 **diving flood**
underground stream 348 **Danish blood** at Otford in 1016
358 **Hermus** a river of Asia Minor whose sands were covered
with gold

From heaven itself though sevenfold Nilus° flows,
And harvests on a hundred realms bestows;   *360*
These now no more shall be the Muse's themes,
Lost in my fame, as in the sea their streams.
Let Volga's bank with iron squadrons° shine,
And groves of lances glitter on the Rhine,°
Let barbarous Ganges° arm a servile train;   *365*
Be mine the blessings of a peaceful reign.
No more my sons shall dye with British blood
Red Iber's sands,° or Ister's foaming flood;°
Safe on my shore each unmolested swain
Shall tend the flocks, or reap the bearded grain;   *370*
The shady empire shall retain no trace
Of war or blood, but in the sylvan chase;
The trumpet sleep, while cheerful horns are
    blown,
And arms employed on birds and beasts alone.
Behold! the ascending villas on my side,   *375*
Project long shadows o'er the crystal tide.
Behold! Augusta's glittering spires increase,
And temples° rise, the beauteous works of Peace.
I see, I see, where two fair cities° bend
Their ample bow, a new Whitehall° ascend!   *380*
There mighty nations shall inquire their doom,
The world's great oracle in times to come;
There kings shall sue, and suppliant states be seen
Once more to bend before a British Queen.

359 **Nilus** The source of the Nile was still undiscovered in
Pope's day.   363 **iron squadrons** presumably of Charles XII of
Sweden, finally defeated by Peter the Great in 1709   364
Rhine a reference to Marlborough's campaigns in the recent
war   365 **Ganges** reference to wars of the Mogul Emperor
Aurangzeb against the rebellious Marathar (1689–1705)   368
Iber's sands the Ebro river in Spain, where the English fought
victoriously in 1710   368 **Ister's . . . flood** the Danube, where
Marlborough achieved the victory of Blenheim in 1704   378
temples the fifty new churches commissioned by Queen
Anne   379 **two fair cities** London and Westminster meet at a
circular sweep of the Thames.   380 **Whitehall** the royal palace
mostly destroyed by fire in 1698, for which many new plans
were considered, notably Sir Christopher Wren's

"Thy trees, fair Windsor! now shall leave their
385   woods,
    And half thy forests rush into thy floods,
    Bear Britain's thunder,° and her cross° display,
    To the bright regions of the rising day;°
    Tempt icy seas, where scarce the waters roll,
390 Where clearer flames glow round the frozen Pole;
    Or under southern skies exalt their sails,
    Led by new stars,° and borne by spicy gales!
    For me the balm° shall bleed, and amber flow,
    The coral redden, and the ruby glow,
395 The pearly shell its lucid globe infold,
    And Phoebus° warm the ripening ore to gold.
    The time shall come, when free as seas or wind
    Unbounded Thames° shall flow for all mankind,
    Whole nations enter with each swelling tide,
400 And seas but join the regions they divide;
    Earth's distant ends our glory shall behold,
    And the new world launch forth to seek the old.
    Then ships of uncouth form shall stem the tide,
    And feathered people° crowd my wealthy side,
405 And naked youths and painted chiefs admire
    Our speech, our color, and our strange attire!
    O stretch thy reign, fair Peace! from shore to
      shore,
    Till conquest cease, and slavery be no more;
    Till the freed Indians in their native groves
410 Reap their own fruits, and woo their sable loves,
    Peru once more a race of kings behold,
    And other Mexicos be roofed with gold.

387 **thunder** naval cannons   387 **cross** of Saint George on the
Union Jack   388 **rising day** Orient   392 **new stars** the southern
constellations   393 **balm** from openings cut in the bark to
secure precious gums   396 **Phoebus** The sun was believed to
ripen precious minerals in the earth.   398 **Unbounded Thames**
"A wish that London may be made a free port" (Pope). Cf.
Isaiah 60:3, "And the Gentiles shall come to thy light, and
kings to the brightness of thy rising," or 60:11, "Therefore thy
gates shall be open continually; they shall not be shut day nor
night."   404 **feathered people** like the four Iroquois chiefs who
were received by Queen Anne in 1710

Exiled by thee from earth to deepest hell,
In brazen bonds, shall barbarous Discord° dwell;
Gigantic Pride, pale Terror, gloomy Care,   *415*
And mad Ambition shall attend her there:
There purple Vengeance bathed in gore retires,
Her weapons blunted, and extinct her fires:°
There hateful Envy her own snakes shall feel,
And Persecution mourn her broken wheel:°   *420*
There Faction roar, Rebellion bite her chain,
And gasping Furies thirst for blood in vain."
   Here cease thy flight, nor with unhallowed lays
Touch the fair fame of Albion's golden days:
The thoughts of gods let Granville's verse recite,   *425*
And bring the scenes of opening fate to light.
My humble Muse, in unambitious strains,
Paints the green forests and the flowery plains,
Where Peace descending bids her olives spring,
And scatters blessings from her dovelike wing.   *430*
Even I more sweetly pass my careless days,
Pleased in the silent shade with empty praise;
Enough for me, that to the listening swains
First in these fields I sung the sylvan strains.

414 **Discord** banished from Heaven by Jupiter, but here by
Anne (line 327)   420 **wheel** the torturing rack

THE RAPE OF THE LOCK

AN HEROI-COMICAL POEM

TO MRS. ARABELLA FERMOR°

(1712–1714)

CANTO I

WHAT dire offense from amorous causes springs,
What mighty contests rise from trivial things,
I sing—This verse to CARYLL, Muse! is due;
This, even Belinda may vouchsafe to view:
5 Slight is the subject, but not so the praise,
If she inspire, and he approve my lays.
    Say what strange motive, Goddess! could
       compel
A well-bred Lord to assault a gentle Belle?
O say what stranger cause, yet unexplored,
10 Could make a gentle Belle reject a Lord?
In tasks so bold, can little men engage,
And in soft bosoms dwells such mighty rage?
    Sol through white curtains shot a timorous ray,

To Mrs. Arabella Fermor John Caryll, Pope's friend, was
concerned about the estrangement between two families
caused when Robert, Lord Petre, cut off a lock of Arabella
(known as "Belle") Fermor's hair. As Pope explained it,
Caryll, a "common acquaintance and well-wisher to both,
desired me to write a poem and make a jest of it, and laugh
them together again." Pope published an earlier version in two
cantos and, a year later, amplified it with full mock-heroic
devices.

And oped those eyes that must eclipse the day:
Now lapdogs give themselves the rousing shake,   15
And sleepless lovers, just at twelve, awake:
Thrice rung the bell, the slipper knocked the
     ground,
And the pressed watch° returned a silver sound.
Belinda still her downy pillow prest,
Her guardian Sylph° prolonged the balmy rest.   20
'Twas he had summoned to her silent bed
The morning dream that hovered o'er her head.
A youth more glittering than a birth-night Beau,°
(That even in slumber caused her cheek to glow)
Seemed to her ear his winning lips to lay,   25
And thus in whispers said, or seemed to say:
    Fairest of mortals, thou distinguished care
Of thousand bright inhabitants of air!
If e'er one vision touched thy infant thought,
Of all the nurse and all the priest° have taught,   30
Of airy elves by moonlight shadows seen,
The silver token, and the circled green,°
Or virgins visited by angel powers,
With golden crowns and wreaths of heavenly
     flowers,
Hear and believe! thy own importance know,   35
Nor bound thy narrow views to things below.
Some secret truths, from learnèd pride concealed,
To maids alone and children are revealed:
What though no credit doubting wits may give?
The fair and innocent shall still believe.   40
Know, then, unnumbered spirits round thee fly,

18 **pressed watch** It responds with chimes for the hour and the
nearest quarter hour. 20 **Sylph** one of the aerial creatures
serving as a counterpart to a guardian angel, although his
whisper (lines 25–26) may recall Satan's first temptation of Eve
in *Paradise Lost,* Book IV, and his appeal to her pride in the
later, successful temptation of Book IX. 23 **birth-night Beau**
courtier splendidly dressed for the royal birthday 30 **nurse ...
priest** considered as teachers of superstition 32 referring to
the phosphoric light ("fairy sparks") and the withered circles
in the grass ("fairy rings") that were taken as signs of
fairies' presence

The light militia of the lower sky;
These, though unseen, are ever on the wing,
Hang o'er the box, and hover round the Ring.°
45 Think what an equipage thou hast in air,
And view with scorn two pages and a chair.
As now your own, our beings were of old,
And once enclosed in woman's beauteous mold;
Thence, by a soft transition, we repair
50 From earthly vehicles° to these of air.
Think not, when woman's transient breath is fled,
That all her vanities at once are dead:
Succeeding vanities she still regards,
And though she plays no more, o'erlooks the cards.
55 Her joy in gilded chariots, when alive,
And love of ombre,° after death survive.
For when the fair in all their pride expire,
To their first elements° their souls retire:
The sprites of fiery termagants in flame
60 Mount up, and take a Salamander's name.°
Soft yielding minds to water glide away,
And sip, with nymphs, their elemental tea.°
The graver prude sinks downward to a Gnome,
In search of mischief still on earth to roam.
65 The light coquettes in Sylphs aloft repair,
And sport and flutter in the fields of air.
    Know farther yet; whoever fair and chaste
Rejects mankind, is by some Sylph embraced:
For spirits, freed from mortal laws, with ease
70 Assume what sexes and what shapes they please.°
What guards the purity of melting maids,

44 The theater **box** and the circular drive ("Ring") in Hyde Park were common scenes of flirtation. 50 **vehicles** both (1) the equipage (45) and (2) the form, ethereal or terrestrial, in which the soul is embodied 56 **ombre** See note to Canto III, line 27. 58 **first elements** the preponderant elements of the four (air, earth, fire, water) of which all material things are composed 60 **Salamander's name** for the animal which, traditionally, could live unharmed in the midst of fire 62 **tea** a perfect rhyme in Pope's time for "away" 70 As can the angels in *Paradise Lost*.

In courtly balls and midnight masquerades,
Safe from the treacherous friend, the daring spark,
The glance by day, the whisper in the dark;
When kind occasion prompts their warm desires,   75
When music softens, and when dancing fires?
'Tis but their Sylph, the wise celestials know,
Though *honor* is the word with men below.
   Some nymphs there are, too conscious of their
     face,
For life predestined to the Gnomes' embrace.   80
These swell their prospects and exalt their pride,
When offers are disdained, and love denied.
Then gay ideas crowd the vacant brain,
While peers and dukes, and all their sweeping
     train,
And garters, stars, and coronets° appear,   85
And in soft sounds, *Your Grace*° salutes their ear.
'Tis these that early taint the female soul,
Instruct the eyes of young coquettes to roll,
Teach infant cheeks a bidden blush to know,
And little hearts to flutter at a beau.   90
   Oft when the world imagine women stray,
The Sylphs through mystic mazes guide their way
Through all the giddy circle they pursue,
And old impertinence° expel by new.
What tender maid but must a victim fall   95
To one man's treat, but for another's ball?
When Florio speaks what virgin could withstand,
If gentle Damon did not squeeze her hand?
With varying vanities, from every part,
They shift the moving toyshop of their heart;   100
Where wigs with wigs, with sword-knots sword-
     knots strive,
Beaux banish beaux, and coaches coaches drive.°

---

85 **garters . . . coronets** emblems of high court honors 86
Your Grace the salutation to a peeress 94 **impertinence** (1)
triviality or frivolity (2) excessive freedoms 101–102 Cf. *Iliad*
IV, 508–509: "Now shield with shield, with helmet helmet
closed, / To armor armor, lance to lance opposed." ("sword-
knots," ornaments tied to the hilts of swords)

This erring mortals levity may call,
Oh blind to truth! the Sylphs contrive it all.
105   Of these am I, who thy protection claim,
A watchful sprite, and Ariel is my name.
Late, as I ranged the crystal wilds of air,
In the clear mirror of thy ruling star
I saw, alas! some dread event impend,
110 Ere to the main this morning sun descend.
But heaven reveals not what, or how, or where:
Warned by the Sylph, oh pious maid, beware!
This to disclose is all thy guardian can:
Beware of all, but most beware of man!
      He said; when Shock, who thought she slept
115   too long,
      Leaped up, and waked his mistress with his
             tongue.
'Twas then, Belinda, if report say true,
Thy eyes first opened on a billet-doux;
Wounds, charms and ardors were no sooner read,
120 But all the vision vanished from thy head.
      And now, unveiled, the toilet° stands displayed,
Each silver vase in mystic order laid.
First, robed in white, the nymph intent adores,
With head uncovered, the cosmetic powers.
125 A heavenly image in the glass appears,
To that she bends, to that her eyes she rears;
The inferior priestess,° at her altar's side,
Trembling, begins the sacred rites of pride.
Unnumbered treasures ope at once, and here
130 The various offerings of the world appear;
From each she nicely culls with curious° toil,
And decks the goddess with the glittering spoil.
This casket India's glowing gems unlocks,

121 **toilet** The dressing table is ironically presented as an altar,
where "cosmetic powers" (line 124) replace cosmic powers.
127 **The inferior priestess** the maid Betty (see line 148).
Belinda is superior priestess as well as the source of the
"heavenly image" (line 125) that is adored. 131 **curious**
elaborately careful

Empire / exotic / animals sacrificed to pride

And all Arabia° breathes from yonder box.
The tortoise here and elephant unite,   135
Transformed to combs, the speckled and the
        white.°
Here files° of pins extend their shining rows,
Puffs, powders, patches,° bibles, billet-doux.
Now awful° beauty puts on all its arms;
The fair each moment rises in her charms,   140
Repairs her smiles, awakens every grace,
And calls forth all the wonders of her face;
Sees by degrees a purer blush° arise,
And keener lightnings° quicken in her eyes.
The busy Sylphs surround their darling care;   145
These set the head, and those divide the hair,
Some fold the sleeve, whilst others plait the gown;
And Betty's praised for labors not her own.

CANTO II

NOT with more glories, in the ethereal plain,°
The sun first rises o'er the purpled main,°
Than issuing forth, the rival of his beams
Launched on the bosom of the silver Thames.°
Fair nymphs, and well-dressed youths around
        her shone,   5
But every eye was fixed on her alone.
On her white breast a sparkling cross she wore,

134 **Arabia** the source of perfumes   136 **speckled . . . white**
tortoiseshell and ivory   137 **files** as of soldiers in ranks ' 138
patches tiny pieces of black silk or court plaster worn on the
face to heighten the whiteness of the skin   139 **awful** majestic
or awe-inspiring, like the epic hero arming himself   143 **purer
blush** a more even redness, the result of rouge   144 **keener
lightnings** achieved by drops of belladonna   1 **ethereal plain**
the heavens   2 **purpled main** the sea reddened by dawn to the
color of "royal purple"   4 Belinda is about to sail from
London to Hampton Court.

Which Jews might kiss, and infidels adore.°
Her lively looks a sprightly mind disclose,
10   Quick as her eyes, and as unfixed as those:
Favors to none, to all she smiles extends,
Oft she rejects, but never once offends.
Bright as the sun, her eyes the gazers strike,
And, like the sun, they shine on all alike.
15   Yet graceful ease, and sweetness void of pride,
Might hide her faults, if belles had faults to hide:
If to her share some female errors fall,
Look on her face, and you'll forget 'em all.
       This nymph, to the destruction of mankind,
20   Nourished two locks, which graceful hung behind
In equal curls, and well conspired to deck
With shining ringlets the smooth ivory neck.
Love in these labyrinths his slaves detains,
And mighty hearts are held in slender chains.
25   With hairy springes° we the birds betray,
Slight lines of hair surprise the finny prey,
Fair tresses man's imperial race ensnare,
And beauty draws us with a single hair.
     The adventurous Baron the bright locks
            admired,
30   He saw, he wished, and to the prize aspired:
Resolved to win, he meditates the way,
By force to ravish, or by fraud betray;
For when success a lover's toil attends,
Few ask, if fraud or force attained his ends.
35   For this, ere Phoebus rose,° he had implored
Propitious heaven, and every power adored,
But chiefly Love—to Love an altar built,
Of twelve vast French romances,° neatly gilt.
There lay three garters, half a pair of gloves;
40   And all the trophies of his former loves.

8 The kissing or adoration of the cross would mark conversion
to a new faith.   25 **hairy springes** traps, often nooses, delicately
woven   35 **ere Phoebus rose** before sunrise   38 **French
romances** notoriously long and highly formalized love stories,
here handsomely bound as well ("neatly gilt")

With tender billets-doux he lights the pyre,
And breathes three amorous sighs to raise the fire;
Then prostrate falls, and begs with ardent eyes
Soon to obtain, and long possess, the prize:
The powers gave ear, and granted half his prayer;   45
The rest, the winds dispersed in empty air.°
  But now secure the painted vessel glides,
The sunbeams trembling on the floating tides,
While melting music steals upon the sky,
And softened sounds along the waters die.   50
Smooth flow the waves, the zephyrs gently play,
Belinda smiled, and all the world was gay.
All but the Sylph—with careful thoughts opprest,
The impending woe sat heavy on his breast.
He summons straight his denizens° of air;   55
The lucid squadrons round the sails repair:
Soft o'er the shrouds° aërial whispers breathe,
That seemed but zephyrs to the train beneath.
Some to the sun their insect wings unfold,
Waft on the breeze, or sink in clouds of gold;   60
Transparent forms, too fine for mortal sight,
Their fluid bodies half dissolved in light.
Loose to the wind their airy garments flew,
Thin glittering textures of the filmy dew;
Dipped in the richest tincture of the skies,   65
Where light disports in ever-mingling dyes,
While every beam new transient colors flings,
Colors that change whene'er they wave their
    wings.
Amid the circle, on the gilded mast,
Superior° by the head, was Ariel placed;   70
His purple pinions opening to the sun,
He raised his azure wand, and thus begun.
  Ye Sylphs and Sylphids, to your chief give ear,

45–46 Cf. *Aeneid*, II, 794–95: "Apollo heard, and granting half his prayer,/Shuffled in winds the rest, and tossed in empty air" (Dryden).   55 **denizens** inhabitants; more strictly, naturalized aliens   57 **shrouds** ropes (appropriate to a grander vessel than this rivercraft)   70 **Superior** taller, as is the typical epic hero

Fays, Fairies, Genii, Elves, and Daemons, hear!°
75 Ye know the spheres and various tasks assigned
By laws eternal to the aërial kind.
Some in the fields of purest aether play,
And bask and whiten in the blaze of day.
Some guide the course of wandering orbs° on
      high,
80· Or roll the planets through the boundless sky.
Some less refined, beneath the moon's pale light
Pursue the stars that shoot athwart the night,
Or suck the mists in grosser air below,
Or dip their pinions in the painted bow,°
85 Or brew fierce tempests on the wintry main,
Or o'er the glebe° distil the kindly rain.
Others on earth o'er human race preside,
Watch all their ways, and all their actions guide:
Of these the chief the care of nations own,
90 And guard with arms divine the British throne.
   Our humbler province is to tend the fair,
Not a less pleasing, though less glorious care.
To save the powder from too rude a gale,°
Nor let the imprisoned essences° exhale,
95 To draw fresh colors from the vernal flowers,
To steal from rainbows e'er they drop in showers
A brighter wash;° to curl their waving hairs,
Assist their blushes, and inspire their airs;
Nay oft, in dreams, invention we bestow,
100 To change a flounce, or add a furbelow.°
   This day, black omens threat the brightest fair
That e'er deserved a watchful spirit's care;
Some dire disaster, or by force, or slight,
But what, or where, the fates have wrapped in
      night.
105 Whether the nymph shall break Diana's law,°

73–74 Cf. *Paradise Lost,* V, 600–602: "Hear all ye Angels,
Progeny of Light,/Thrones, Dominations, Princedoms, Virtues,
Powers,/Hear my Decree. . . ." 79 **wandering orbs** comets?
84 **bow** rainbow 86 **glebe** farmland 93 **too rude a gale** too
rough a breeze 94 **essences** perfumes 97 **wash** tinting
rinse 100 **furbelow** ruffle 105 **Diana's law** virginity

Or some frail China jar receive a flaw,
Or stain her honor, or her new brocade,
Forget her prayers, or miss a masquerade,
Or lose her heart, or necklace, at a ball;
Or whether Heaven has doomed that Shock
    must fall.   110
Haste then, ye spirits! to your charge repair:
The fluttering fan be Zephyretta's care;
The drops to thee, Brillante, we consign;
And, Momentilla, let the watch be thine;
Do thou, Crispissa,° tend her favorite lock;   115
Ariel himself shall be the guard of Shock.
  To fifty chosen Sylphs, of special note,
We trust the important charge, the petticoat:
Oft have we known that sevenfold fence to fail,
Though stiff with hoops, and armed with ribs of
    whale.°   120
Form a strong line° about the silver bound,
And guard the wide circumference around.°
  Whatever spirit, careless of his charge,
His post neglects, or leaves the fair at large,
Shall feel sharp vengeance soon o'ertake his sins, 125
Be stopped in vials, or transfixed with pins;
Or plunged in lakes of bitter washes lie,
Or wedged whole ages in a bodkin's° eye:
Gums and pomatums shall his flight restrain,
While clogged he beats his silken wings in vain;   130
Or alum styptics with contracting power
Shrink his thin essence like a rivelled flower.
Or as Ixion° fixed, the wretch shall feel
The giddy motion of the whirling mill,
In fumes of burning chocolate shall glow,   135
And tremble at the sea that froths below!
  He spoke; the spirits from the sails descend;
Some, orb in orb, around the nymph extend,

---

115 **Crispissa** derives from "crisp," in its old sense of
"curl."   120 **whale** whalebone   121 **line** that is, of defense
119–22 The petticoat is described in terms that recall the hero's
shield in epic.   128 **bodkin's** needle's   133 **Ixion** was tortured.

Some thrid the mazy ringlets of her hair,
140 Some hang upon the pendants of her ear;
With beating hearts the dire event they wait,
Anxious, and trembling for the birth of fate.

CANTO III

CLOSE by those meads, for ever crowned with
     flowers,
Where Thames with pride surveys his rising
     towers,
145 There stands a structure° of majestic frame,
Which from the neighboring Hampton takes its
     name.
5 Here Britain's statesmen oft the fall foredoom
Of foreign tyrants, and of nymphs at home;
Here thou, great Anna!° whom three realms obey,
Dost sometimes counsel take—and sometimes tea.
     Hither the heroes and the nymphs resort,
10 To taste awhile the pleasures of a court;
In various talk the instructive hours they past,
Who gave the ball, or paid the visit last;
One speaks the glory of the British queen,
And one describes a charming Indian screen;
15 A third interprets motions, looks, and eyes;
At every word a reputation dies.
Snuff, or the fan, supply each pause of chat,
With singing, laughing, ogling, *and all that*.
     Meanwhile, declining from the noon of day,
20 The sun obliquely shoots his burning ray;
The hungry judges soon the sentence sign,
And wretches hang that jurymen may dine;
The merchant from the Exchange returns in
     peace,

3 **structure** Hampton Court, a royal residence   7 **great Anna**
Queen Anne, ruler of Great Britain and Ireland and claimant
to France

And the long labors of the toilet cease—
Belinda now, whom thirst of fame invites,   25
Burns to encounter two adventurous knights,
At ombre° singly to decide their doom;
And swells her breast with conquests yet to come.
Straight the three bands prepare in arms to join,
Each band the number of the sacred nine.°   30
Soon as she spread her hand, the aërial guard
Descend, and sit on each important card:
First Ariel perched upon a Matadore,°
Then each, according to the rank they bore;
For Sylphs, yet mindful of their ancient race,   35
Are, as when women, wondrous fond of place.°
   Behold, four Kings in majesty revered,°
With hoary whiskers and a forky beard;
And four fair Queens whose hands sustain a
      flower,
The expressive emblem of their softer power;   40
Four Knaves in garbs succinct,° a trusty band,
Caps on their heads, and halberts° in their hand;
And particolored troops, a shining train,
Draw forth to combat on the velvet plain.°
   The skilful nymph reviews her force with care; 45
Let spades be trumps! she said, and trumps they
      were.°
   Now move to war her sable Matadores,°
In show like leaders of the swarthy Moors.

27 **ombre** a card game related to whist or modern bridge,
played with forty cards, the 10's, 9's, and 8's removed from
the deck. The taking of each trick is here presented as epic
combat.   29–30 There were three players, each holding nine
cards.   30 **sacred nine** the Muses   33 **Matadore** the highest
trump card   36 **place** rank   37 ff. The epic review of forces is
parodied.   41 **succinct** tucked up   42 **halberts** battle-axes and
pikes on long handles   44 **velvet plain** typical epic term for a
field" here the velvet-covered card table. Cf. "verdant field"
(line 52) and "level green" (line 80).   46 Cf. Genesis 1:3:
"And God said, 'Let there be light,' and there was light."   47
Matadores The highest trumps seen as epic heroes taking the
field. They are the ace of spades (Spadillio), the two of spades
(Manillio), the ace of clubs (Basto).

Spadillio first, unconquerable lord!
50 Led off two captive trumps, and swept the board.
As many more Manillio forced to yield,
And marched a victor from the verdant field.
Him Basto followed, but his fate more hard
Gained but one trump and one plebeian card.
55 With his broad sabre next, a chief in years,
The hoary Majesty of Spades appears,
Puts forth one manly leg, to sight revealed;
The rest, his many-colored robe concealed.
The rebel Knave, who dares his prince engage,
60 Proves the just victim of his royal rage.
Even mighty Pam,° that kings and queens
          o'erthrew,
And mowed down armies in the fights of Lu,
Sad chance of war! now, destitute of aid,
Falls undistinguished by the victor spade!
65   Thus far both armies to Belinda yield;
Now to the Baron fate inclines the field.
His warlike Amazon° her host invades,
The imperial consort of the crown of spades.
The club's black tyrant first her victim died,
70 Spite of his haughty mien, and barbarous pride:
What boots the regal circle on his head,
His giant limbs in state unwieldy spread?
That long behind he trails his pompous robe,
And of all monarchs only grasps the globe?°
75   The Baron now his diamonds pours apace;
The embroidered King who shows but half his
          face,
And his refulgent Queen, with powers combined,
Of broken troops an easy conquest find.
Clubs, diamonds, hearts, in wild disorder seen,
80 With throngs promiscuous strew the level green.

61 **Pam** knave of clubs, strongest card in the game of loo
67 **Amazon** The queen of spades seen as a female warrior.
This is the first of the four tricks the Baron takes in
turn. 71–74 typical epic lament for the decline of glory Cf.
"Windsor Forest," lines 115 ff.

Thus when dispersed a routed army runs,
Of Asia's troops, and Afric's sable sons,
With like confusion different nations fly,
Of various habit and of various dye,
The pierced battalions disunited fall,
In heaps on heaps; one fate o'erwhelms them all.°   85
The Knave of Diamonds tries his wily arts,
And wins (oh shameful chance!) the Queen of
     Hearts.
At this, the blood the virgin's cheek forsook,
A livid paleness spreads o'er all her look;
She sees, and trembles at the approaching ill,   90
Just in the jaws of ruin, and Codille.°
And now (as oft in some distempered state)
On one nice trick° depends the general fate.
An Ace of Hearts steps forth: the King unseen   95
Lurked in her hand, and mourned his captive
     Queen.
He springs to vengeance with an eager pace,
And falls like thunder on the prostrate Ace.°
The nymph exulting fills with shouts the sky,
The walls, the woods, and long canals reply.   100
   Oh thoughtless mortals! ever blind to fate,
Too soon dejected, and too soon elate!
Sudden these honors shall be snatched away,
And cursed for ever this victorious day.°
   For lo! the board with cups and spoons is
     crowned,   105
The berries° crackle, and the mill turns round.
On shining altars of Japan° they raise
The silver lamp; the fiery spirits° blaze.

81–86 a parody of the epic simile   92 **Codille** the "elbow,"
defeat if the Baron gains a fifth trick   94 **trick** used in a double
sense, referring to both the game and the politics of "some
distempered state" (line 93)   98 **prostrate Ace** outranked by
the king in the red suits   101–104 the epic warning in the
moment of pride   106 **berries** coffee beans. The coffee service
parodies the epic feast.   107 **Japan** japanned or lacquered
tables   108 **spirits** in the spirit lamps that heat the coffee

From silver spouts the grateful liquors glide,
110 While China's earth° receives the smoking tide.
At once they gratify their scent and taste,
And frequent cups prolong the rich repast.
Straight hover round the fair her airy band;
Some, as she sipped, the fuming liquor fanned,
115 Some o'er her lap their careful plumes displayed,
Trembling, and conscious of the rich brocade.
Coffee, (which makes the politician wise,
And see through all things with his half-shut eyes)
Sent up in vapors to the Baron's brain
120 New stratagems, the radiant lock to gain.
Ah cease, rash youth! desist ere 'tis too late,
Fear the just gods, and think of Scylla's fate!°
Changed to a bird, and sent to flit in air,
She dearly pays for Nisus' injured hair!
125   But when to mischief mortals bend their will,
How soon they find fit instruments of ill!
Just then, Clarissa drew with tempting grace
A two-edged weapon from her shining case;
So ladies in romance assist their knight,
130 Present the spear, and arm him for the fight.
He takes the gift with reverence, and extends
The little engine on his fingers' ends;
This just behind Belinda's neck he spread,
As o'er the fragrant steams she bends her head.
135 Swift to the lock a thousand sprites repair,
A thousand wings, by turns, blow back the hair,
And thrice they twitched the diamond in her ear;
Thrice she looked back, and thrice the foe drew
     near.
Just in that instant, anxious Ariel sought
140 The close recesses of the virgin's thought;
As, on the nosegay° in her breast reclined,

110 **China's earth** the cups of earthenware or china
122 **Scylla's fate** Scylla plucked a purple hair (upon which his
power depended) from the head of her father, Nisus, in order
to give it to her lover. She was repudiated by her lover, and
both were changed to birds. Cf. Ovid, *Metamorphoses*, VIII.
141 **nosegay** corsage of flowers

He watched the ideas rising in her mind,
Sudden he viewed, in spite of all her art,
An earthly lover lurking at her heart.
Amazed, confused, he found his power expired,   145
Resigned to fate, and with a sigh retired.
    The peer now spreads the glittering forfex°
        wide,
To enclose the lock; now joins it, to divide.
Even then, before the fatal engine closed,
A wretched Sylph too fondly interposed;   150
Fate urged the shears, and cut the Sylph in twain
(But airy substance soon unites° again),
The meeting points the sacred hair dissever
From the fair head, for ever and for ever!
    Then flashed the living lightning from her eyes,   155
And screams of horror rend the affrighted skies.
Not louder shrieks to pitying heaven are cast,
When husbands or when lapdogs breathe their
        last,
Or when rich China vessels, fallen from high,
In glittering dust and painted fragments lie!   160
    "Let wreaths of triumph now my temples twine,"
(The victor cried) "the glorious prize is mine!
While fish in streams, or birds delight in air,
Or in a coach and six the British fair,
As long as Atalantis° shall be read,   165
Or the small pillow grace a lady's bed,
While visits shall be paid on solemn days,
When numerous wax-lights in bright order blaze,
While nymphs take treats, or assignations give,
So long my honor, name, and praise shall live!"   170
    What time would spare, from steel° receives
        its date,
And monuments, like men, submit to fate!
Steel could the labor of the gods destroy,

---

147 **forfex** high diction for the pair of scissors   152 **soon unites**
Cf. Milton, *Paradise Lost,* VI, 330–31   165 **Atalantis** a popular
book of the day, full of court scandal   171 **steel** the fatal power
of arms and warfare

And strike to dust the imperial towers of Troy;°
175 Steel could the works of mortal pride confound,
And hew triumphal arches to the ground.
What wonder then, fair nymph! thy hairs should
        feel
The conquering force of unresisted steel?

CANTO IV

[handwritten: Pope's Portrait of the female mind]

BUT anxious cares the pensive nymph oppressed,
And secret passions labored in her breast.
Not youthful kings in battle seized alive,
Not scornful virgins who their charms survive,
5 Not ardent lovers robbed of all their bliss,
Not ancient ladies when refused a kiss,
Not tyrants fierce that unrepenting die,
Not Cynthia when her manteau's° pinned awry,
E'er felt such rage, resentment, and despair,
10 As thou, sad virgin! for thy ravished hair.
    For, that sad moment, when the Sylphs withdrew,
And Ariel weeping from Belinda flew,
Umbriel,° a dusky melancholy sprite
As ever sullied the fair face of light,
15 Down to the central earth, his proper scene,
Repaired to search the gloomy Cave of Spleen.°
    Swift on his sooty pinions flits the Gnome,
And in a vapor reached the dismal dome.°
No cheerful breeze this sullen region knows,

[handwritten left margin: Spirit of Prude]

174 **Troy** supposed to have been built by the gods Apollo and
Poseidon 8 **manteau** mantua, loose upper gown or hood
13 **Umbriel** a gnome and former prude, named from
"umbra," or shadow 16 **Cave of Spleen** epic visit to the
underworld; suggestive also of Spenser's caves of Mammon,
Despair, and Night. Spleen was the name for the fashionable
psychosomatic ailment of the day, whose symptoms were
melancholy, self-pity, and hypochondria, sometimes called a
"fit of vapors." 18 **dome** dwelling

The dreaded East° is all the wind that blows.   *20*
Here, in a grotto, sheltered close from air,
And screened in shades from day's detested glare,
She sighs for ever on her pensive bed,
Pain at her side, and Megrim° at her head.
   Two handmaids wait the throne: alike in place,   *25*
But differing far in figure and in face.
Here stood Ill Nature like an ancient maid,
Her wrinkled form in black and white arrayed;
With store of prayers, for mornings, nights, and
        noons,
Her hand is filled; her bosom with lampoons.   · *30*
   There Affectation, with a sickly mien
Shows in her cheek the roses of eighteen,
Practiced to lisp, and hang the head aside,
Faints into airs, and languishes with pride;
On the rich quilt sinks with becoming woe,   *35*
Wrapped in a gown, for sickness, and for show.
The fair ones feel such maladies as these,
When each new nightdress gives a new disease.
   A constant vapor o'er the palace flies;
Strange phantoms° rising as the mists arise;   *40*
Dreadful, as hermit's dreams in haunted shades,
Or bright as visions of expiring° maids.
Now glaring fiends, and snakes on rolling spires,
Pale spectres, gaping tombs, and purple fires:
Now lakes of liquid gold, Elysian scenes,°   *45*
And crystal domes, and angels in machines.
   Unnumbered throngs on every side are seen
Of bodies changed° to various forms by Spleen.
Here living teapots stand, one arm held out,
One bent; the handle this, and that the spout: *50*

20 **East** The east wind was taken as a cause of spleen.
24 **Megrim** migraine headache   40 **phantoms** fantasies
42 **expiring** literally, dying; in the punning sense, reaching
sexual climax   45 **Elysian scenes** not only fantasies of heaven
but scenes such as the contemporary stage featured in lavish
operas and pantomimes   48 **bodies changed** fantasies more
psychotic than neurotic, clearly sexual in some cases, as the
prudish world of gnomes would lead one to expect

nightmare *hysteria*

A pipkin° there like Homer's tripod walks;
Here sighs a jar, and there a goose-pie° talks;
Men prove with child, as powerful fancy works,
And maids turned bottles, call aloud for corks.
  Safe passed the Gnome through this fantastic
55   band,
A branch of healing spleenwort° in his hand.
Then thus addressed the power: "Hail, wayward
      Queen!
Who rule the sex to fifty from fifteen,
Parent of vapors and of female wit,
60 Who give the hysteric, or poetic fit,
On various tempers act by various ways,
Make some take physic,° others scribble plays;
Who cause the proud their visits to delay,
And send the godly in a pet to pray.
65 A nymph there is, that all thy power disdains,
And thousands more in equal mirth maintains.
But oh! if e'er thy Gnome could spoil a grace,°
Or raise a pimple on a beauteous face,
Like citron-waters° matrons' cheeks inflame,
70 Or change complexions at a losing game;
If e'er with airy horns° I planted heads,
Or rumpled petticoats, or tumbled beds,
Or caused suspicion when no soul was rude,
Or discomposed the headdress of a prude,
75 Or e'er to costive° lapdog gave disease,
Which not the tears of brightest eyes could ease:
Hear me, and touch Belinda with chagrin;
That single act gives half the world the spleen."
  The goddess with a discontented air
80 Seems to reject him, though she grants his prayer.

51 **pipkin** small earthenware boiler on a tripod. For Vulcan's
walking tripods, see *Iliad*, XVIII, 439 ff. 52 **goose-pie**
"Alludes to a real fact, a Lady of Distinction imagined herself
in this condition" (Pope). 56 **spleenwort** a protection against
the powers of spleen 62 **physic** medicine 67 **grace** both (1)
charm and (2) prayer (as in line 64) 69 **citron-waters** brandy
flavored with citron 71 **horns** as signs of the cuckold 75
costive constipated

A wondrous bag with both her hands she binds,
Like that where once Ulysses° held the winds;
There she collects the force of female lungs,
Sighs, sobs, and passions, and the war of tongues.
A vial next she fills with fainting fears,   85
Soft sorrows, melting griefs, and flowing tears.
The Gnome rejoicing bears her gifts away,
Spreads his black wings, and slowly mounts to day.
    Sunk in Thalestris'° arms the nymph he found,
Her eyes dejected and her hair unbound.   90
Full o'er their heads the swelling bag he rent,
And all the furies issued at the vent.
Belinda burns with more than mortal ire,
And fierce Thalestris fans the rising fire.
"O wretched maid!" she spread her hands, and
    cried,   95
(While Hampton's echoes, "Wretched maid!"
    replied)
"Was it for this you took such constant care
The bodkin,° comb, and essence to prepare;
For this your locks in paper durance° bound,
For this with torturing irons wreathed around?   100
For this with fillets° strained your tender head,
And bravely bore the double loads of lead?
Gods! shall the ravisher display your hair,
While the fops envy, and the ladies stare!
Honor forbid! at whose unrivalled shrine   105
Ease, pleasure, virtue, all, our sex resign.
Methinks already I your tears survey,
Already hear the horrid things they say,
Already see you a degraded toast,°
And all your honor in a whisper lost!   110
How shall I, then, your helpless fame defend?

82 **Ulysses** when he was given the winds by Aeolus, *Odyssey,*
X, 19 ff. 89 **Thalestris** named for the Queen of the
Amazons 98 **bodkin** hairpin 99 **paper durance** high diction
for curling papers 101 **fillets** headbands, worn by priestesses
in the *Aeneid,* here machinery of hairdressing 109 **toast** one
whose health is often drunk

'Twill then be infamy to seem your friend!
And shall this prize,° the inestimable prize,
Exposed through crystal to the gazing eyes,
115 And heightened by the diamond's circling rays,
On that rapacious hand for ever blaze?
Sooner shall grass in Hyde Park Circus° grow,
And wits take lodgings in the sound of Bow;°
Sooner let earth, air, sea, to chaos fall,
120 Men, monkeys, lapdogs, parrots, perish all!"
     She said; then raging to Sir Plume repairs,
And bids her beau demand the precious hairs:
(Sir Plume, of amber snuffbox justly vain,
And the nice conduct of a clouded° cane)
125 With earnest eyes, and round unthinking face,
He first the snuffbox opened, then the case,
And thus broke out—"My Lord, why, what the
     devil?
Z—ds! damn the lock! 'fore Gad, you must be
     civil!
Plague on't! 'tis past a jest—nay prithee, pox!
130 Give her the hair"—he spoke, and rapped his box.
     "It grieves me much" (replied the peer again)
"Who speaks so well should ever speak in vain.
But by this lock, this sacred lock I swear,
(Which never more shall join its parted hair,
135 Which never more its honors shall renew,
Clipped from the lovely head where late it grew)
That while my nostrils draw the vital air,
This hand, which won it, shall for ever wear."
He spoke, and speaking, in proud triumph spread
140 The long-contended honors° of her head.
     But Umbriel, hateful Gnome! forbears not so;
He breaks the vial whence the sorrows flow.
Then see! the nymph in beauteous grief appears,
Her eyes half languishing, half drowned in tears;

113 **this prize** the lock encased in a ring   117 **Hyde Park Circus**
the fashionable Ring (I, 44)   118 **Bow** near St. Mary-le-Bow,
in the unfashionable merchants' quarter, as opposed to
Westminster   124 **clouded** fashionably mottled or veined   140
honors beauties

On her heaved bosom hung her drooping head,   *145*
Which, with a sigh, she raised; and thus she said:
  "For ever cursed by this detested day,
Which snatched my best, my favorite curl away!
Happy! ah ten times happy had I been,
If Hampton Court these eyes had never seen!   *150*
Yet am not I the first mistaken maid,
By love of courts to numerous ills betrayed.
Oh had I rather unadmired remained
In some lone isle, or distant northern land;
Where the gilt chariot never marks the way,   *155*
Where none learn ombre; none e'er taste bohea!°
There kept my charms concealed from mortal eye,
Like roses that in deserts bloom and die.
What moved my mind with youthful lords to
    roam?
O had I stayed, and said my prayers at home!   *160*
'Twas this, the morning omens seemed to tell;
Thrice from my trembling hand the patch box fell;
The tottering china shook without a wind,
Nay, Poll sat mute, and Shock was most unkind!
A Sylph too warned me of the threats of fate,   *165*
In mystic visions, now believed too late!
See the poor remnants of these slighted hairs!
My hands shall rend what even thy rapine spares:
These, in two sable ringlets taught to break,
Once gave new beauties to the snowy neck;   *170*
The sister lock now sits uncouth, alone,
And in its fellow's fate foresees its own;
Uncurled it hangs, the fatal shears demands;
And tempts once more thy sacrilegious hands.
Oh hadst thou, cruel! been content to seize   *175*
Hairs less in sight, or any hairs but these!"

156 **bohea** a kind of tea

CANTO V

SHE said: the pitying audience melt in tears,
But fate and Jove had stopped the Baron's ears.
In vain Thalestris with reproach assails,
For who can move when fair Belinda fails?
5   Not half so fixed the Trojan could remain,
While Anna° begged and Dido raged in vain.
Then grave Clarissa° graceful waved her fan;
Silence ensued, and thus the nymph began.
    "Say why are beauties praised and honored
        most,
10   The wise man's passion, and the vain° man's
        toast?
Why decked with all that land and sea afford,
Why angels called, and angel-like adored?
Why round our coaches crowd the white-gloved
        beaux,
Why bows the side-box from its inmost rows?
15   How vain are all these glories, all our pains,
Unless good sense preserve what beauty gains:
That men may say, when we the front-box grace,
'Behold the first in virtue, as in face!'
Oh! if to dance all night, and dress all day,
20   Charmed the smallpox,° or chased old age away,
Who would not scorn what housewife's cares
        produce,
Or who would learn one earthly thing of use?
To patch, nay ogle, might become a saint,
Nor could it sure be such a sin to paint.
25   But since, alas! frail beauty must decay,
Curled or uncurled, since locks will turn to gray;

6 **Anna** Dido's sister, who failed to persuade Aeneas to remain
with Dido; *Aeneid,* IV   7 **Clarissa** "A new character intro-
duced in the subsequent editions, to open more clearly the
moral of the poem, in a parody of the speech of Sarpedon to
Glaucus in Homer [*Iliad,* XII]" (Pope).   10 **vain** both foolish
and boastful   20 **smallpox** This disfiguring disease was still
very common.

Since painted or not painted, all shall fade,
And she who scorns a man, must die a maid;
What then remains, but well our power to use,
And keep good humor still whate'er we lose?   *30*
And trust me, dear! good humor can prevail,
When airs, and flights, and screams, and scolding
    fail.
Beauties in vain their pretty eyes may roll;
Charms strike the sight, but merit wins the soul."
   So spoke the dame, but no applause ensued;   *35*
Belinda frowned, Thalestris called her prude.
"To arms, to arms!" the fierce virago cries,
And swift as lightning to the combat flies.
All side in parties, and begin the attack;
Fans clap, silks rustle, and tough whalebones
    crack;   *40*
Heroes' and heroines' shouts confusedly rise,
And bass and treble voices strike the skies.
No common weapons in their hands are found,
Like gods they fight, nor dread a mortal wound.
   So when bold Homer makes the gods engage,   *45*
And heavenly breasts with human passions rage;
'Gainst Pallas, Mars; Latona, Hermes arms;
And all Olympus rings with loud alarms.
Jove's thunder roars, heaven trembles all around;
Blue Neptune storms, the bellowing deeps
    resound;   *50*
Earth shakes her nodding towers, the ground
    gives way;
And the pale ghosts start at the flash of day!
   Triumphant Umbriel on a sconce's height
Clapped his glad wings, and sat to view the fight:
Propped on their bodkin spears, the sprites survey   *55*
The growing combat, or assist the fray.
   While through the press enraged Thalestris flies,
And scatters death around from both her eyes,
A beau and witling perished in the throng,
One died in metaphor, and one in song.   *60*
"O cruel nymph! a living death I bear,"
Cried Dapperwit, and sunk beside his chair.

A mournful glance Sir Fopling upwards cast,
"Those eyes are made so killing"—was his last.
65 Thus on Maeander's flowery margin lies
The expiring swan,° and as he sings he dies.
    When bold Sir Plume had drawn Clarissa down,
Chloe stepped in, and killed him with a frown;
She smiled to see the doughty hero slain,
70 But at her smile, the beau revived again.
    Now Jove suspends his golden scales° in air,
Weighs the men's wits against the lady's hair;
The doubtful beam long nods from side to side;
At length the wits mount up, the hairs subside.
75   See, fierce Belinda on the Baron flies,
With more than usual lightning in her eyes;
Nor feared the Chief the unequal fight to try,
Who sought no more than on his foe to die.°
But this bold lord, with manly strength endued,
80 She with one finger and a thumb subdued:
Just where the breath of life his nostrils drew,
A charge of snuff the wily virgin threw;
The Gnomes direct, to every atom just,
The pungent grains of titillating dust.
85 Sudden, with starting tears each eye o'erflows,
And the high dome re-echoes to his nose.
    "Now meet thy fate," incensed Belinda cried,
And drew a deadly bodkin from her side.
(The same,° his ancient personage to deck,
90 Her great great grandsire wore about his neck
In three seal rings; which after, melted down,
Formed a vast buckle for his widow's gown:
Her infant grandame's whistle next it grew,
The bells she jingled, and the whistle blew;
95 Then in a bodkin graced her mother's hairs,

---

66 **swan** The swan, dying on the banks of the river Maeander,
is supposed to sing most sweetly as he dies. 71 **golden scales**
a typical epic omen, here at the expense of the light-witted
men 78 **to die** in the double sense of "expiring" (IV, 42), as
elsewhere in this section 89 **The same** a parody of epic
accounts of the descent of armor or of Agamemnon's scepter

Which long she wore, and now Belinda wears.)
  "Boast not my fall" (he cried) "insulting foe!
Thou by some other shalt be laid as low.
Nor think, to die dejects my lofty mind;
All that I dread is leaving you behind!   100
Rather than so, ah let me still survive,
And burn in Cupid's flames—but burn alive."
  "Restore the lock!" she cries; and all around
"Restore the lock!" the vaulted roofs rebound.
Not fierce Othello in so loud a strain   105
Roared for the handkerchief that caused his pain.
But see how oft ambitious aims are crossed,
And chiefs contend till all the prize is lost!
The lock, obtained with guilt, and kept with pain,
In every place is sought, but sought in vain: 110
With such a prize no mortal must be blest,
So heaven decrees! with heaven who can contest?
  Some thought it mounted to the lunar sphere,°
Since all things lost on earth are treasured there.
There heroes' wits are kept in ponderous vases,   115
And beaus' in snuffboxes and tweezer cases.
There broken vows, and deathbed alms are found,
And lovers' hearts with ends of riband bound;
The courtier's promises, and sick man's prayers,
The smiles of harlots, and the tears of heirs,   120
Cages for gnats, and chains to yoke a flea,
Dried butterflies, and tomes of casuistry.
  But trust the Muse—she saw it upward rise,
Though marked by none but quick, poetic eyes:
(So Rome's great founder° to the heavens
      withdrew,   125
To Proculus alone confessed in view.)
A sudden star, it shot through liquid° air,
And drew behind a radiant trail of hair.

113 **lunar sphere** reminiscent of Milton's Limbo of Vanity in
Paradise Lost. Cf. Ariosto, *Orlando Furioso,* XXXIV, stanzas
68 ff. for a common source. 125 **Rome's . . . founder**
Romulus, whose translation to heaven was witnessed by the
senator Proculus 127 **liquid** clear

Not Berenice's locks° first rose so bright,
130 The heavens bespangling with dishevelled light.
The Sylphs behold it kindling as it flies,
And pleased pursue its progress through the skies.
   This the beau monde° shall from the Mall° survey,
And hail with music its propitious ray.
135 This, the blest lover shall for Venus take,
And send up vows from Rosamonda's lake.°
This Partridge° soon shall view in cloudless skies,
When next he looks through Galileo's eyes;°
And hence the egregious wizard shall foredoom
140 The fate of Louis, and the fall of Rome.
   Then cease, bright nymph! to mourn thy ravished hair
Which adds new glory to the shining sphere!
Not all the tresses that fair head can boast
Shall draw such envy as the lock you lost.
145 For, after all the murders of your eye,
When, after millions slain, yourself shall die;
When those fair suns shall set, as set they must,
And all those tresses shall be laid in dust;
This lock, the Muse shall consecrate to fame,
150 And midst the stars inscribe Belinda's name!

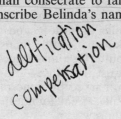

129 **Berenice's locks** The Queen's hair, offered by her to ensure her husband's safety in battle, was translated into a constellation. 133 **beau monde** fashionable world 133 **Mall** the promenade in St. James's Park 136 **Rosamonda's lake** a pond in St. James's Park, associated with unhappy love 137 **Partridge** an astrologer who predicted momentous public events 138 **Galileo's eyes** telescope

ELEGY TO THE MEMORY OF
AN UNFORTUNATE LADY

(1717)

WHAT beckoning ghost, along the moonlight
    shade
Invites my steps, and points to yonder glade?
'Tis she!—but why that bleeding bosom gored,
Why dimly gleams the visionary sword?
Oh ever beauteous, ever friendly! tell,   5
Is it, in heaven, a crime to love too well?
To bear too tender, or too firm a heart,
To act a lover's or a Roman's part?°
Is there no bright reversion° in the sky,
For those who greatly think, or bravely die?   10
   Why bade ye else, ye Powers! her soul aspire
Above the vulgar flight of low desire?
Ambition first sprung from your blest abodes;
The glorious fault of angels and of gods:°
Thence to their images on earth it flows,   15
And in the breasts of kings and heroes glows.
Most souls, 'tis true, but peep out once an age,
Dull sullen prisoners in the body's cage:

8 **act . . . a Roman's part** commit suicide 9 **reversion** return
to the former state; used legally of the return of an estate to
the owner after the expiration of a temporary grant 14
angels . . . gods referring to the rebellious angels of Milton's
Paradise Lost or to the wars of the Titans in classical
mythology

Dim lights of life, that burn a length of years
20 Useless, unseen, as lamps in sepulchres;
Like eastern kings a lazy state they keep,
And close confined to their own palace, sleep.
　　From these perhaps (ere nature bade her die)
Fate snatched her early to the pitying sky.
25 As into air the purer spirits flow,
And separate from their kindred dregs below;°
So flew the soul to its congenial place,
Nor left one virtue to redeem her race.
　　But thou, false guardian of a charge too good,
30 Thou, mean deserter of thy brother's blood!
See on these ruby lips the trembling breath,
These cheeks, now fading at the blast of death;
Cold is that breast which warmed the world
　　　before,
And those love-darting eyes must roll no more.
35 Thus, if eternal justice rules the ball,
Thus shall your wives, and thus your children fall:
On all the line a sudden vengeance waits,
And frequent hearses shall besiege your gates.
There passengers shall stand, and pointing say,
40 (While the long funerals blacken all the way)
Lo these were they, whose souls the Furies
　　　steeled,
And cursed with hearts unknowing how to yield.
Thus unlamented pass the proud away,
The gaze of fools, and pageant of a day!
45 So perish all, whose breast ne'er learned to glow
For others' good, or melt at others' woe.
　　What can atone (oh ever-injured shade!)
Thy fate unpitied, and thy rites unpaid?
No friend's complaint, no kind domestic tear
50 　　Pleased thy pale ghost, or graced thy mournful
　　　bier.
By foreign hands thy dying eyes were closed,
By foreign hands thy decent limbs composed,
By foreign hands thy humble grave adorned,

25–26 The image is of chemical distillation.

By strangers honored, and by strangers mourned!
What though no friends in sable weeds appear,　　55
Grieve for an hour, perhaps, then mourn a year,
And bear about the mockery of woe
To midnight dances, and the public show?
What though no weeping Loves° thy ashes grace,
Nor polished marble emulate° thy face?　　60
What though no sacred earth° allow thee room,
Nor hallowed dirge be muttered o'er thy tomb?
Yet shall thy grave with rising flowers be drest,
And the green turf lie lightly on thy breast:
There shall the morn her earliest tears bestow,　　65
There the first roses of the year shall blow;
While angels with their silver wings o'ershade
The ground, now sacred by thy reliques° made.
　　So peaceful rests, without a stone, a name,
What once had beauty, titles, wealth, and fame.　　70
How loved, how honored once, avails thee not,
To whom related, or by whom begot;
A heap of dust alone remains of thee,
'Tis all thou art, and all the proud shall be!
　　Poets themselves must fall, like those they sung,　　75
Deaf the praised ear, and mute the tuneful tongue.
Even he, whose soul now melts in mournful lays,
Shall shortly want the generous tear he pays;
Then from his closing eyes thy form shall part,
And the last pang shall tear thee from his heart,　　80
Life's idle business at one gasp be o'er,
The Muse forgot, and thou beloved no more!

---

59 **Loves** funeral monuments in the form of mourning cupids
60 **emulate** rival, reproduce　61 **sacred earth** Presumably
because of her suicide, the lady is not allowed Christian
burial.　68 **reliques** remains, often used of saint's remains; here
they sanctify the ground, just as nature pays the tribute man
has denied (lines 63–66).

ELOÏSA TO ABELARD

(1717)

ARGUMENT

Abelard and Eloïsa flourished in the twelfth century; they were two of the most distinguished persons of their age in learning and beauty, but for nothing more famous than for their unfortunate passion. After a long course of calamities, they retired each to a several convent, and consecrated the remainder of their days to religion. It was many years after this separation, that a letter of Abelard's to a friend, which contained the history of his misfortune, fell into the hands of Eloïsa. This awakening all her tenderness, occasioned those celebrated letters (out of which the following is partly extracted) which give so lively a picture of the struggles of grace and nature, virtue and passion.

In these deep solitudes and awful cells,
Where heavenly-pensive contemplation dwells,
And ever-musing melancholy reigns;
What means this tumult in a Vestal's° veins?
5   Why rove my thoughts beyond this last retreat?
Why feels my heart its long-forgotten heat?
Yet, yet I love!—From Abelard it° came,
And Eloïsa yet must kiss the name.
    Dear fatal name! rest ever unrevealed,
10   Nor pass these lips in holy silence sealed.
Hide it, my heart, within that close disguise,

4 **Vestal's** nun's   7 **it** the letter (see Argument)

74

Where mixed with God's, his loved idea° lies:
O write it not, my hand—the name appears
Already written—wash it out, my tears!
In vain lost Eloïsa weeps and prays,   15
Her heart still dictates, and her hand obeys.
   Relentless walls! whose darksome round
      contains
Repentant sighs, and voluntary pains:
Ye rugged rocks! which holy knees have worn;
Ye grots and caverns shagged with horrid thorn!°   20
Shrines! where their vigils pale-eyed virgins keep,
And pitying saints, whose statues learn to weep!
Though cold like you, unmoved and silent grown,
I have not yet forgot myself to stone.°
All is not Heaven's while Abelard has part,   25
Still rebel nature holds out half my heart;
Nor prayers nor fasts its stubborn pulse restrain,
Nor tears for ages taught to flow in vain.
   Soon as thy letters trembling I unclose,
That well-known name awakens all my woes.   30
Oh name for ever sad! for ever dear!
Still breathed in sighs, still ushered with a tear.
I tremble too, where'er my own I find,
Some dire misfortune follows close behind.
Line after line my gushing eyes o'erflow,   35
Led through a sad variety of woe:
Now warm in love, now withering in thy bloom,
Lost in a convent's° solitary gloom!
There stern religion quenched the unwilling flame,
There died the best of passions, love and fame.   40
   Yet write, oh write me all, that I may join
Griefs to thy griefs, and echo sighs to thine.
Nor foes nor fortune take this power away.
And is my Abelard less kind than they?
Tears still are mine, and those I need not spare,   45
Love but demands what else were shed in prayer;

12 **idea** image   20 Cf. Milton, "Comus," 429: "By grots, and
caverns shag'd with horrid shades."   24 Cf. Milton, "Il
Penseroso," 42: "Forget thy self to marble."   38 **convent**
monastery

No happier task these faded eyes pursue;
To read and weep is all they now can do.
    Then share thy pain, allow that sad relief;
50 Ah, more than share it, give me all thy grief.
Heaven first taught letters for some wretch's aid,
Some banished lover, or some captive maid;
They live, they speak, they breathe what love
    inspires,
Warm from the soul, and faithful to its fires,
55 The virgin's wish without her fears impart,
Excuse° the blush, and pour out all the heart,
Speed the soft intercourse from soul to soul,
And waft a sigh from Indus° to the Pole.
    Thou knowst how guiltless first I met thy flame,
When Love approached me under Friendship's
60   name;
My fancy formed thee of angelic kind,
Some emanation° of the all-beauteous Mind.
Those smiling eyes, attempering every ray,
Shone sweetly lambent° with celestial day.
65 Guiltless I gazed; heaven listened while you sung;
And truths divine came mended° from that
    tongue.
From lips like those what precept failed to move?
Too soon they taught me 'twas no sin to love:
Back through the paths of pleasing sense I ran,
70 Nor wished an angel whom I loved a man.
Dim and remote the joys of saints I see,
Nor envy them that heaven I lose for thee.
    How oft, when pressed to marriage, have I said,
Curse on all laws but those which love has made?
75 Love, free as air, at sight of human ties,
Spreads his light wings, and in a moment flies.
Let wealth, let honor, wait the wedded dame,
August her deed, and sacred be her fame;

---

56 **excuse** make unnecessary   58 **Indus** the large river flowing
from Tibet to the Indian Sea   62 **emanation** as in Neoplatonic
thought, a radiation or flowing forth from Godhead   64 **lambent**
radiant   66 **mended** improved

Before true passion all those views remove;°
Fame, wealth, and honor! what are you to Love?   *80*
The jealous god, when we profane his fires,
Those restless passions in revenge inspires,
And bids them make mistaken mortals groan,
Who seek in love for aught but love alone.
Should at my feet the world's great master fall,   *85*
Himself, his throne, his world, I'd scorn 'em all:
Not Caesar's empress would I deign to prove;
No, make me mistress to the man I love;
If there be yet another name more free,
More fond than mistress, make me that to thee!   *90*
Oh! happy state! when souls each other draw,
When love is liberty, and nature, law:
All then is full, possessing, and possessed,
No craving void left aching in the breast:
Even thought meets thought ere from the lips it
     part,   *95*
And each warm wish springs mutual from the
     heart.
This sure is bliss (if bliss on earth there be)
And once the lot of Abelard and me.
     Alas, how changed! what sudden horrors rise!
A naked lover bound and bleeding lies!   *100*
Where, where was Eloïse? her voice, her hand,
Her poniard, had opposed the dire command.
Barbarian, stay! that bloody stroke° restrain;
The crime was common, common be the pain.
I can no more; by shame, by rage suppressed,   *105*
Let tears and burning blushes speak the rest.
     Canst thou forget that sad, that solemn day,
When victims at yon altar's foot we lay?
Canst thou forget what tears that moment fell,
When, warm in youth, I bade the world farewell?   *110*
As with cold lips I kissed the sacred veil,
The shrines all trembled, and the lamps grew pale:
Heaven scarce believed the conquest it surveyed,

79 **remove** depart   103 **bloody stroke** referring to the emascula-
tion of Abelard upon the orders of Eloïsa's uncle

And saints with wonder heard the vows I made.
115 Yet then, to those dread altars as I drew,
Not on the cross my eyes were fixed, but you:
Not grace, or zeal, love only was my call,
And if I lose thy love, I lose my all.
Come! with thy looks, thy words, relieve my woe;
120 Those still at least are left thee to bestow.
Still on that breast enamored let me lie,
Still drink delicious poison from thy eye,
Pant on thy lip, and to thy heart be pressed;
Give all thou canst—and let me dream the rest.
125 Ah no! instruct me other joys to prize,
With other beauties charm my partial eyes,
Full in my view set all the bright abode,
And make my soul quit Abelard for God.
    Ah, think at least thy flock° deserves thy care,
130 Plants of thy hand, and children of thy prayer.
From the false world in early youth they fled,
By thee to mountains, wilds, and deserts led.
You raised these hallowed walls; the desert
        smiled,
And paradise was opened in the wild.
135 No weeping orphan saw his father's stores
Our shrines irradiate, or emblaze the floors;
No silver saints, by dying misers given,
Here bribed the rage of ill-requited heaven:
But such plain roofs as piety could raise,
140 And only vocal with the Maker's praise.
In these lone walls (their days eternal bound)
These moss-grown domes with spiry turrets
        crowned,
Where awful arches make a noonday night,
And the dim windows shed a solemn light;
145 Thy eyes diffused a reconciling ray,
And gleams of glory brightened all the day.
But now no face divine contentment wears,
'Tis all blank sadness or continual tears.

129 **flock** Eloïsa's convent, the Paraclete, was founded by Abelard and given to her nuns.

See how the force of others' prayers I try,
(O pious fraud of amorous charity!)   *150*
But why should I on others' prayers depend?
Come thou, my father, brother, husband, friend!
Ah let thy handmaid, sister, daughter move,
And all those tender names in one, thy love!
The darksome pines that o'er yon rocks reclined   *155*
Wave high, and murmur to the hollow wind,
The wandering streams that shine betwcen the
      hills,
The grots that echo to the tinkling rills,
The dying gales that pant upon the trees,
The lakes that quiver to the curling breeze;   *160*
No more these scenes my meditation aid
Or lull to rest the visionary maid.
But o'er the twilight groves and dusky caves,
Long-sounding aisles, and intermingled graves,
Black Melancholy sits, and round her throws   *165*
A deathlike silcnce, and a dread repose:
Her gloomy presence saddens all the scene,
Shades every flower, and darkens every grcen,
Deepens the murmur of the falling floods,
And breathes a browner horror on the woods.   *170*
   Yet here for ever, ever must I stay;
Sad proof how well a lover can obey!
Death, only death, can break the lasting chain;
And here, even then, shall my cold dust remain,
Here all its frailties, all its flames resign,   *175*
And wait till 'tis no sin to mix with thine.
   Ah wretch! believed the spouse of God in vain,
Confessed within the slave of love and man.
Assist me, heaven! but whence arose that prayer?
Sprung it from piety, or from despair?   *180*
Even here, where frozen chastity retires,
Love finds an altar for forbidden fires.
I ought to grieve, but cannot what I ought;
I mourn the lover, not lament the fault;
I view my crime, but kindle at the view,   *185*
Repent old pleasures, and solicit new;
Now turned to heaven, I weep my past offense,

Now think of thee, and curse my innocence.
Of all affliction taught a lover yet,
190 'Tis sure the hardest science to forget!
How shall I lose the sin, yet keep the sense,
And love the offender, yet detest the offense?
How the dear object from the crime remove,
Or how distinguish penitence from love?
195 Unequal task! a passion to resign,
For hearts so touched, so pierced, so lost as mine.
Ere such a soul regains its peaceful state,
How often must it love, how often hate!
How often hope, despair, resent, regret,
200 Conceal, disdain,—do all things but forget.
But let heaven seize it, all at once 'tis fired:
Not touched, but rapt; not wakened, but inspired!
Oh come! oh teach me nature to subdue,
Renounce my love, my life, myself—and you.
205 Fill my fond heart with God alone, for he
Alone can rival, can succeed to thee.
  How happy is the blameless Vestal's lot!
The world forgetting, by the world forgot:
Eternal sunshine of the spotless mind!
210 Each prayer accepted, and each wish resigned;
Labor and rest, that equal periods keep;
"Obedient slumbers that can wake and weep;"°
Desires composed, affections ever even;
Tears that delight, and sighs that waft to heaven.
215 Grace shines around her with serenest beams,
And whispering angels prompt her golden dreams.
For her the unfading rose of Eden blooms,
And wings of Seraphs shed divine perfumes,
For her the spouse prepares the bridal ring,
220 For her white virgins hymeneals° sing,
To sounds of heavenly harps she dies away,
And melts in visions of eternal day.
  Far other dreams my erring soul employ,

212 Taken from Richard Crashaw, *Description of a Religious
House,* line 16   220 **hymeneals** wedding songs for the *spouse
of God* (cf. line 177)

Far other raptures, of unholy joy:
When at the close of each sad, sorrowing day,   225
Fancy restores what vengeance snatched away,
Then conscience sleeps, and leaving nature free,
All my loose soul unbounded springs to thee.
Oh cursed, dear horrors of all-conscious night!
How glowing guilt exalts the keen delight!   230
Provoking demons all restraint remove,
And stir within me every source of love.
I hear thee, view thee, gaze o'er all thy charms,
And round thy phantom glue my clasping arms.
I wake:—no more I hear, no more I view,   235
The phantom flies me, as unkind as you.
I call aloud; it hears not what I say:
I stretch my empty arms; it glides away.
To dream once more I close my willing eyes;
Ye soft illusions, dear deceits, arise!   240
Alas, no more! methinks we wandering go
Through dreary wastes, and weep each other's
    woe,
Where round some moldering tower pale ivy
    creeps,
And low-browed rocks hang nodding o'er the
    deeps.
Sudden you mount, you beckon from the skies; . 245
Clouds interpose, waves roar, and winds arise.
I shriek, start up, the same sad prospect find,
And wake to all the griefs I left behind.
For thee the fates, severely kind, ordain
A cool suspense from pleasure and from pain;   250
Thy life a long dead calm of fixed repose;
No pulse that riots, and no blood that glows.
Still as the sea, ere winds were taught to blow,
Or moving spirit bade the waters flow;
Soft as the slumbers of a saint forgiven,   255
And mild as opening gleams of promised heaven.
    Come, Abelard! for what hast thou to dread?
The torch of Venus burns not for the dead.
Nature stands checked; religion disapproves;
Even thou art cold—yet Eloïsa loves.   260

Ah hopeless, lasting flames! like those that burn
To light the dead, and warm the unfruitful urn.
   What scenes appear where'er I turn my view?
The dear ideas, where I fly, pursue,
265 Rise in the grove, before the altar rise,
Stain all my soul, and wanton in my eyes.
I waste the matin lamp in sighs for thee,
Thy image steals between my god and me,
Thy voice I seem in every hymn to hear,
270 With every bead I drop too soft a tear.
When from the censer clouds of fragrance roll,
And swelling organs lift the rising soul,
One thought of thee puts all the pomp to flight,
Priests, tapers, temples, swim before my sight:
275 In seas of flame my plunging soul is drowned,
While altars blaze, and angels tremble round.
   While prostrate here in humble grief I lie,
Kind, virtuous drops just gathering in my eye,
While praying, trembling, in the dust I roll,
280 And dawning grace is opening on my soul:
Come, if thou darst, all charming as thou art!
Oppose thyself to heaven; dispute my heart;
Come, with one glance of those deluding eyes,
Blot out each bright idea of the skies;
Take back that grace, those sorrows, and those
285   tears;
Take back my fruitless penitence and prayers;
Snatch me, just mounting, from the blest abode;
Assist the fiends, and tear me from my God!
   No, fly me, fly me, far as Pole from Pole;
290 Rise Alps between us! and whole oceans roll!
Ah, come not, write not, think not once of me,
Nor share one pang of all I felt for thee.
Thy oaths I quit, thy memory resign;
Forget, renounce me, hate whate'er was mine.
295 Fair eyes, and tempting looks (which yet I view!)
Long loved, adored ideas, all adieu!
Oh Grace serene! oh virtue heavenly fair!
Divine oblivion of low-thoughted care!
Fresh blooming Hope, gay daughter of the sky!

And Faith, our early immortality!   300
Enter, each mild, each amicable guest;
Receive, and wrap me in eternal rest!
   See in her cell sad Eloïsa spread,
Propped on some tomb, a neighbor of the dead.
In each low wind methinks a Spirit calls,   305
And more than echoes talk along the walls.
Here, as I watched the dying lamps around,
From yonder shrine I heard a hollow sound.
"Come, sister, come!" (it said, or seemed to say)
"Thy place is here, sad sister, come away!   310
Once like thyself, I trembled, wept, and prayed,
Love's victim then, though now a sainted maid:
But all is calm in this eternal sleep;
Here grief forgets to groan, and love to weep,
Even superstition loses every fear: 315
For God, not man, absolves our frailties here."
   I come, I come! prepare your roseate bowers,
Celestial palms, and ever-blooming flowers.
Thither, where sinners may have rest, I go,
Where flames refined in breasts seraphic glow: 320
Thou, Abelard! the last sad office pay,
And smooth my passage to the realms of day;
See my lips tremble, and my eyeballs roll,
Suck my last breath, and catch my flying soul!
Ah no—in sacred vestments mayst thou stand,   325
The hallowed taper trembling in thy hand,
Present the cross before my lifted eye,
Teach me at once, and learn of me to die.
Ah then, thy once-loved Eloïsa see!
It will be then no crime to gaze on me.   330
See from my cheek the transient roses fly!
See the last sparkle languish in my eye!
Till every motion, pulse, and breath be o'er;
And even my Abelard be loved no more.
O Death all-eloquent! you only prove   335
What dust we dote on, when 'tis man we love.
   Then too, when fate shall thy fair frame destroy,
(That cause of all my guilt, and all my joy)
In trance ecstatic may thy pangs be drowned,

Bright clouds descend, and angels watch thee
340   round,
From opening skies may streaming glories shine,
And saints embrace thee with a love like mine.
   May one kind grave unite each hapless name,°
And graft my love immortal on thy fame!
345 Then, ages hence, when all my woes are o'er,
When this rebellious heart shall beat no more;
If ever chance two wandering lovers brings
To Paraclete's white walls and silver springs,
O'er the pale marble shall they join their heads,
350 And drink the falling tears each other sheds;
Then sadly say, with mutual pity moved,
"Oh may we never love as these have loved!"
From the full choir when loud hosannas rise,
And swell the pomp of dreadful sacrifice,
355 Amid that scene if some relenting eye
Glance on the stone where our cold relics° lie,
Devotion's self shall steal a thought from heaven,
One human tear shall drop, and be forgiven.
And sure, if fate some future bard shall join
360 In sad similitude of griefs to mine,
Condemned whole years in absence to deplore,
And image charms he must behold no more;
Such if there be, who loves so long, so well;
Let him our sad, our tender story tell;
365 The well-sung woes will soothe my pensive ghost;
He best can paint 'em who shall feel 'em most.

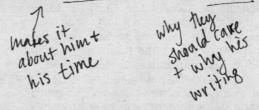

ends w/ Pope

makes it about him + his time

why they should care + why his writing

343 "Abelard and Eloïsa were interred in the same grave, or
in monuments adjoining in the monastery of the Paraclete: he
died in the year 1142, she in 1163" (Pope).   356 **relics** remains

AN ESSAY ON MAN

IN FOUR EPISTLES

TO HENRY ST. JOHN, LORD BOLINGBROKE°

(1733–1734)

EPISTLE I

AWAKE, my ST. JOHN! leave all meaner things
To low ambition, and the pride of kings.
Let us (since life can little more supply
Than just to look about us and to die)
Expatiate free o'er all this scene of Man;   *5*
A mighty maze! but not without a plan;
A wild, where weeds and flowers promiscuous
    shoot,
Or garden, tempting with forbidden fruit.°
Together let us beat this ample field,°
Try what the open, what the covert yield;   *10*
The latent tracts, the giddy heights, explore
Of all who blindly creep, or sightless soar;
Eye nature's walks, shoot folly as it flies,
And catch the manners living as they rise;
Laugh where we must, be candid where we can;   *15*

Bolingbroke See "Imitations of Horace," Epistle I, i. 7–8 **A
wild . . . fruit** with suggestions of Milton's Eden, which required
cultivation by Adam and Eve, fused goodness with latent evil
and disorder, and was the scene of their fall 9 **beat . . . field** as
might hunters of birds

But vindicate the ways of God to man.°
   I. Say first, of God above, or Man below,
What can we reason, but from what we know?
Of Man, what see we but his station here,
20 From which to reason, or to which refer?
Through worlds unnumbered though the God be
     known,
'Tis ours to trace him only in our own.
He, who through vast immensity can pierce,
See worlds on worlds compose one universe,
25 Observe how system into system runs,
What other planets circle other suns,
What varied being peoples every star,
May tell why Heaven has made us as we are.
But of this frame the bearings, and the ties,
30 The strong connections, nice° dependencies,
Gradations just, has thy pervading soul
Looked through? or can a part contain the whole?
   Is the great chain,° that draws all to agree,
And drawn supports, upheld by God, or thee?
   II. Presumptuous Man! the reason wouldst
35   thou find,
Why formed so weak, so little, and so blind!
First, if thou canst, the harder reason guess,
Why formed no weaker, blinder, and no less!
Ask of thy mother earth,° why oaks are made
40 Taller or stronger than the weeds they shade?
Or ask of yonder argent fields above,

15–16 **Laugh . . . God to man** echoing in a lighter vein (the tentative tone of an "essay") Milton's "justify the ways of God to man" (*Paradise Lost*, I, 26) 30 **nice** subtle, precise (here as throughout lines 29–31 the delicate equilibrium of the "plan" is stressed) 33 **great chain** the Great Chain of Being, the metaphor which sees all kinds of creatures as links in a continuous chain descending from God through the levels of being: from angelic to human, from intelligent to merely sentient, from animate to inanimate. Man's place is the most precarious, for he is the lowest of rational creatures and the highest of passionate, most complex and unstable in his structure, free to fall and easily deluded by pride. 39 **thy mother earth** a reminder of man's less than angelic nature

Why Jove's satellites° are less than Jove?
  Of systems possible, if 'tis confest
That wisdom infinite must form the best,
Where all must full or not coherent° be,   45
And all that rises, rise in due degree;
Then, in the scale of reasoning life, 'tis plain
There must be, somewhere, such a rank as Man;
And all the question (wrangle e'er so long)
Is only this, if God has placed him wrong?°   50
  Respecting Man, whatever wrong we call,
May, must be right, as relative to all.°
In human works, though labored on with pain,
A thousand movements scarce one purpose gain;
In God's, one single can its end produce;   55
Yet serves to second too some other use.
So Man, who here seems principal alone,
Perhaps acts second to some sphere unknown,
Touches some wheel, or verges to some goal;°
'Tis but a part we see, and not a whole.   60
  When the proud steed shall know why Man
    restrains
His fiery course, or drives him o'er the plains;
When the dull ox, why now he breaks the clod,

42 **Jove's satellites** i.e., of the planet Jupiter; but also the lesser
Olympian gods 45 **full or not coherent** According to the
principle of plenitude, the Great Chain must include every
possible kind of creature if it is to represent God's goodness
and omnipotence; any gaps would be denials of these qualities,
and any failure to preserve an exact hierarchy of kinds ("due
degree," line 46) in the chain would represent a disordering
or unmaking of God's creation (see I, lines 243–46, 249–50).
49–50 **all the question . . . wrong** alluding to the frequent
complaints (1) that man was insufficiently prepared to maintain
his place, (2) that he was denied powers granted other
creatures, or (3) that he should be able to move freely
throughout the chain, assuming whatever place he chose 52
as relative to all when considered not as an end in himself
("principal," line 57) but as part of a large plan, in which his
existence serves the needs of other creatures as well ("to
second too some other use," as in line 56) 59 **Touches . . .
goal** recalling the imagery of a delicate machine, so delicate as
to suggest an organism, as in lines 29–31

Is now a victim, and now Egypt's god:°
65 Then shall Man's pride and dulness comprehend
His actions', passions', being's, use and end;
Why doing, suffering, checked, impelled; and why
This hour a slave, the next a deity.
    Then say not Man's imperfect, Heaven in fault;
70 Say rather, Man's as perfect as he ought:
His knowledge measured to his state and place,
His time a moment, and a point his space.°
If to be perfect in a certain sphere,
What matter, soon or late, or here or there?
75 The blest today is as completely so,
As who began a thousand years ago.
    III. Heaven from all creatures hides the book
      of Fate,
All but the page prescribed, their present state;
From brutes what men, from men what spirits
      know:
80 Or who could suffer Being here below?
The lamb thy riot° dooms to bleed today,
Had he thy Reason, would he skip and play?
Pleased to the last, he crops the flowery food,
And licks the hand just raised to shed his blood.°
85 Oh blindness to the future! kindly given,
That each may fill the circle marked by Heaven;
Who sees with equal° eye, as God of all,
A hero perish, or a sparrow fall,°
Atoms or systems into ruin hurled,
90 And now a bubble burst, and now a world.

64 **Egypt's god** Apis, the sacred bull worshiped at Memphis
72 **His time . . . space** This contraction of man's mortal life
both stresses the limit of his knowledge and contrasts with the
eternity of beatitude of lines 75–76 (where timelessness makes
a difference of a "thousand years" meaningless).   81 **riot** self-
indulgence   84 **And licks . . . blood** stressing (1) blessed
ignorance of "the book of Fate" (line 77) and (2) the inevitable
cruelty of man's dispensations when he assumes a role like
God's, as in lines 117–18   87 **equal** impartial   88 **a sparrow
fall** Cf. Matthew 10:29: "Are not two sparrows sold for a
farthing? and one of them shall not fall to the ground without
your Father."

Hope humbly then; with trembling pinions soar;
Wait the great teacher Death, and God adore!
What future bliss, he gives not thee to know,
But gives that hope to be thy blessing now.
Hope springs eternal in the human breast: 95
Man never Is, but always To be blest:
The soul, uneasy and confined from home,°
Rests and expatiates in a life to come.
    Lo, the poor Indian, whose untutored mind
Sees God in clouds, or hears him in the wind;   100
His soul proud Science never taught to stray
Far as the solar walk, or milky way;
Yet simple Nature to his hope has given,
Behind the cloud-topped hill, an humbler heaven;
Some safer world in depth of woods embraced,   105
Some happier island in the watery waste,
Where slaves° once more their native land behold,
No fiends torment, no Christians thirst for gold!
To Be, contents his natural desire,
He asks no angel's wing, no seraph's fire;°   110
But thinks, admitted to that equal° sky,
His faithful dog shall bear him company.
    IV. Go, wiser thou! and in thy scale of sense
Weigh thy Opinion against Providence;
Call imperfection what thou fanciest such,   115
Say, here he° gives too little, there too much;
Destroy all creatures for thy sport or gust,°
Yet cry, If Man's unhappy, God's unjust;
If Man alone ingross° not Heaven's high care,
Alone made perfect here, immortal there: 120
Snatch from his hand the balance and the rod,°

97 **home** Heaven   107 **slaves** presumably, as an example, the
Indians who work the gold mines of Spanish America   110
seraph's fire a traditional attribute based on the supposed
derivation of "seraph" from the Hebrew root meaning "to
burn"; here associated with the consuming ambition of more
sophisticated men   111 **equal** available to all (see line
87)   116 **he** God   117 **gust** taste (food or pleasure)   119 **ingross** monopolize   121 **balance . . . rod** symbols of justice
and power

Re-judge his justice, be the GOD of GOD!
In Pride, in reasoning Pride, our error lies;
All quit their sphere, and rush into the skies.
125 Pride still is aiming at the blest abodes,
Men would be Angels, Angels would be Gods.
Aspiring to be Gods, if Angels fell,°
Aspiring to be Angels, Men rebel:
And who but wishes to invert the laws
130 Of ORDER, sins against the Eternal Cause.
      V. Ask for what end the heavenly bodies shine,
Earth for whose use? Pride answers, " 'Tis for
          mine:
For me kind Nature wakes her genial° power,
Suckles each herb, and spreads out every flower;
135 Annual for me, the grape, the rose renew
The juice nectareous, and the balmy dew;°
For me, the mine a thousand treasures brings;
For me, health gushes from a thousand springs;
Seas roll to waft me, suns to light me rise;
140 My footstool earth, my canopy the skies."°
      But errs not Nature from this gracious end,
From burning suns when livid deaths° descend,
When earthquakes swallow, or when tempests
          sweep
Towns to one grave, whole nations to the deep?
145 "No" ('tis replied)° "the first Almighty Cause
Acts not by partial, but by general laws;
The exceptions few; some change since all began,

127 **Aspiring . . . fell** recalling the rebellion of Satan and the
war in Heaven of *Paradise Lost* and (in line 128) Satan's
temptation of Eve   133 **genial** generative   136 **balmy dew**
fragrance   140 **My footstool . . . skies** Cf. Isaiah 66:1: "Thus
saith the Lord, the heaven is my throne, and the earth my
footstool." Here it is man who speaks as the "God of God"
(line 122).   142 **livid deaths** plagues, believed to be caused by
the sun's heat   145 **'tis replied** by Pride, qualifying the
anthropocentric view with a recognition of some limitations in
God's design, but never questioning whether the end of that
design may be misunderstood

And what created perfect?"—Why then Man?°
If the great end be human Happiness,
Then Nature deviates; and can Man do less?   150
As much that end a constant course requires
Of showers and sunshine, as of Man's desires;
As much eternal springs and cloudless skies,
As men for ever temperate, calm, and wise.
If plagues or earthquakes break not Heaven's
    design,   155
Why then a Borgia,° or a Catiline?°
Who knows but he, whose hand the lightning
    forms,
Who heaves old Ocean, and who wings the storms,
Pours fierce ambition in a Caesar's mind,
Or turns young Ammon° loose to scourge mankind? 160
From Pride, from Pride, our very reasoning springs;
Account for moral as for natural things:
Why charge° we Heaven in those, in these acquit?
In both, to reason right is to submit.

    Better for us, perhaps, it might appear,   165
Were there all harmony, all virtue here;
That never air or ocean felt the wind;
That never passion discomposed the mind:
But ALL subsists by elemental strife;°
And passions are the elements of life.   170
The general ORDER, since the whole began,
Is kept in Nature, and is kept in Man.

148 **Why then Man?** Why should Pride expect Man to be
created full of imperfections?   156 **Borgia** one of the Italian
Renaissance family that ruled with murder and deceit; Cesare
Borgia was the model of Machiavelli's "Prince."   156 **Catiline**
the conspirator against the Roman Republic, attacked by
Cicero for treachery and licentiousness 160 **young Ammon**
Alexander the Great, who claimed descent from Jupiter
Ammon 163 **charge** with error, in making Man less than
perfect 169 **But ALL . . . strife** The Whole is created by the
harmony of apparently discordant elements, as man's mind is
seen as a harmony of four humors, each corresponding in turn
to one of the elements, each capable of becoming a violent
force without the restraining power of the others.

    VI. What would this Man? Now upward will
       he soar,
And little less than Angel, would be more;
175 Now looking downwards,° just as grieved appears
To want the strength of bulls, the fur of bears.
Made for his use all creatures if he call,
Say what their use, had he the powers of all?
Nature to these, without profusion° kind,
180 The proper organs, proper powers assigned;
Each seeming want compénsated of course,°
Here with degrees of swiftness, there of force;
All in exact proportion to the state;
Nothing to add, and nothing to abate.
185 Each beast, each insect, happy in its own:
Is Heaven unkind to Man, and Man alone?
Shall he alone, whom rational we call,
Be pleased with nothing, if not blessed with all?
   The bliss of Man (could Pride that blessing find)
190 Is not to act or think beyond mankind;
No powers of body or of soul to share,
But what his nature and his state can bear.
Why has not Man a Microscopic eye?
For this plain reason, Man is not a Fly.
195 Say what the use, were finer optics° given,
To inspect a mite, not comprehend the heaven?
Or touch, if tremblingly alive all o'er,
To smart and agonize at every pore?
Or quick effluvia° darting through the brain,
200 Die of a rose in aromatic pain?
If nature thundered in his opening° ears,
And stunned him with the music of the spheres,°

175 **downwards** in the scale of creatures in the Great Chain of
Being   179 **profusion** excess   181 **of course** in due course
195 **finer optics** like the fly, which was believed to have
microscopic powers (contrasted in the next line with telescopic)
199 **quick effluvia** streams of invisible particles carrying odors
201 **opening** more perceptive   202 **music of the spheres** the
music, audible to angels but not to men, supposedly produced
by the motion of the heavenly spheres that held stars, planets,
etc.

How would he wish that Heaven had left him still
The whispering zephyr, and the purling rill?
Who finds not Providence all good and wise,   205
Alike in what it gives, and what denies?
    VII. Far as creation's ample range extends,
The scale of sensual,° mental powers ascends:
Mark how it mounts, to Man's imperial race,
From the green myriads in the peopled grass: 210
What modes of sight betwixt each wide extreme,
The mole's dim curtain, and the lynx's beam:°
Of smell, the headlong° lioness between,
And hound sagacious° on the tainted° green:
Of hearing, from the life that fills the flood,°   215
To that which warbles through the vernal wood:
The spider's touch, how exquisitely fine!
Feels at each thread, and lives along the line:
In the nice bee, what sense so subtly true
From poisonous herbs extracts the healing dew:°   220
How Instinct varies in the groveling swine,
Compared, half-reasoning elephant,° with thine:
Twixt that, and Reason, what a nice barrier;
For ever separate, yet for ever near!
Remembrance and Reflection how allied;   225
What thin partitions Sense from Thought divide:°
And middle natures,° how they long to join,
Yet never pass the insuperable line!
Without this just gradation, could they be
Subjected these to those, or all to thee?   230

208 **sensual** sensuous   212 **lynx's beam** traditionally the
keenest of all eyebeams   213 **headlong** lioness who hunted
by the sound rather than the scent of the prey   214 **sagacious**
quick of scent   214 **tainted** with an animal's scent   215 **life . . .
flood** fish, like the lioness an extreme of insensitivity   220
healing dew honey, once believed to be a dew and still used
medicinally   222 **elephant** famous for its memory and credited
with other mental powers   225–26 **Remembrance . . . divide**
making two parallel distinctions (1) between simple memory
and the ability to draw conclusions or make plans; (2) between
sensation and rationality   227 **middle natures** animals that fall
between classes, transitional species, that almost but not quite
join the powers distinguished in lines 225–26

The powers of all subdued by thee alone,
Is not thy Reason all these powers in one?
   VIII. See, through this air, this ocean, and this
      earth,
All matter quick,° and bursting into birth.
235 Above, how high progressive life may go!
Around, how wide! how deep extend below!
Vast chain of being, which from God began,
Natures ethereal, human, angel, man,
Beast, bird, fish, insect! what no eye can see,
240 No glass can reach! from Infinite to thee,°
From thee to Nothing!—On superior powers
Were we to press, inferior might on ours:
Or in the full creation leave a void,
Where, one step broken, the great scale's
      destroyed:
245 From Nature's chain whatever link you strike,
Tenth or ten thousandth, breaks the chain alike.
   And if each system in gradation roll,°
Alike essential to the amazing Whole,
The least confusion but in one, not all
250 That system only, but the Whole must fall.
Let Earth unbalanced from her orbit fly,
Planets and suns run lawless through the sky,
Let ruling Angels° from their spheres be hurled,
Being on being wrecked, and world on world,
255 Heaven's whole foundations to their center nod,
And Nature tremble to the throne of God:
All this dread ORDER break—for whom? for
      thee?
Vile worm!—Oh madness, pride, impiety!
   IX. What if the foot, ordained the dust to tread,
260 Or hand to toil, aspired to be the head?
What if the head, the eye, or ear repined
To serve mere engines° to the ruling mind?
Just as absurd for any part of claim

234 **quick** pregnant, living   240 **thee** Man   247 **roll** revolve
and rotate   253 **ruling Angels** believed to rule or govern the
movement of each sphere   262 **engines** instruments. For a
scriptural parallel to this passage see I Corinthians 12:12–27.

To be another, in this general frame:
Just as absurd, to mourn the tasks or pains   265
The great directing MIND of ALL ordains.
    All are but parts of one stupendous whole,
Whose body Nature is, and God the soul;
That, changed through all, and yet in all the same,
Great in the earth, as in the ethereal frame,   270
Warms in the sun, refreshes in the breeze,
Glows in the stars, and blossoms in the trees,
Lives through all life, extends through all extent,
Spreads undivided, operates unspent,
Breathes in our soul, informs our mortal part,   275
As full, as perfect, in a hair as heart;
As full, as perfect, in vile Man that mourns,
As the rapt Seraph that adores and burns;
To him no high, no low, no great, no small;
He fills, he bounds, connects, and equals all.°   280
    X. Cease then, nor ORDER imperfection name:
Our proper bliss depends on what we blame.
Know thy own point:° this kind, this due degree
Of blindness, weakness, Heaven bestows on thee.
Submit—in this, or any other sphere,   285
Secure to be as blest as thou canst bear:
Safe in the hand of one disposing Power,
Or in the natal, or° the mortal hour.
All Nature is but Art, unknown to thee:°
All Chance, Direction, which thou canst not see;   290
All Discord, Harmony, not understood;
All partial Evil,° universal Good:
And, spite of Pride, in erring Reason's spite,
One truth is clear, "WHATEVER IS, IS RIGHT."

280 **equals all** makes all equal   283 **point** as in line 72   288
Or . . . or whether . . . or   289 **All Nature . . . thee** alluding
to the traditional view that nature is the handiwork or art of
God   292 **partial Evil** evil to individuals

EPISTLE II

I. KNOW then thyself, presume not God to scan;°
The proper study of mankind is Man.
Placed on this isthmus of a middle state,
A being darkly wise, and rudely° great:
5   With too much knowledge for the Sceptic side,°
With too much weakness for the Stoic's pride,°
He hangs between; in doubt to act, or rest,
In doubt to deem himself a God, or Beast;°
In doubt his Mind or Body to prefer,
10   Born but to die, and reasoning but to err;
Alike in ignorance, his reason such,
Whether he thinks too little, or too much:
Chaos of Thought and Passion, all confused;
Still by himself abused, or disabused;
15   Created half to rise, and half to fall;
Great lord of all things, yet a prey to all;
Sole judge of Truth, in endless Error hurled:
The glory, jest, and riddle of the world!
   Go, wondrous creature! mount where Science
     guides,
20   Go, measure earth, weigh air, and state the tides;
Instruct the planets in what orbs to run,
Correct old Time, and regulate the Sun;
Go, soar with Plato to the empyreal sphere,°
To the first good, first perfect, and first fair;
25   Or tread the mazy round° his followers trod,

1 **scan** criticize, judge   4 **rudely** roughly, turbulently   5 **Sceptic side** the distrust of all possibility of certain knowledge   6 **Stoic's pride** the mastery of all passions   7–8 **in doubt . . . or Beast** choosing between the impassivity and serenity ("rest") of a God or the restless activity of satisfying animal appetite; so again in line 9, Mind and Body as opposed principles   23 **empyreal sphere** the outermost, where might dwell Plato's archetypal ("first," line 24) Ideas of the Good, True, and Beautiful (as in line 24) from which all earthly instances are imitated   25 **mazy round** Neoplatonists often fused metaphysics and mysticism, seeking to transcend the flesh in rapturous trances and to become godlike; likened here to the self-induced obliviousness of Eastern mystics who dizzy themselves (lines 27–28).

And quitting sense call imitating God;
As Eastern priests in giddy circles run,
And turn their heads to imitate the sun.
Go, teach Eternal Wisdom how to rule—
Then drop into thyself, and be a fool!   30

    Superior beings, when of late they saw
A mortal Man unfold all Nature's law,
Admired such wisdom in an earthly shape,
And showed a NEWTON as we show an Ape.°

    Could he, whose rules the rapid comet bind,   35
Describe or fix one movement of his mind?
Who saw its fires here rise, and there descend,
Explain his own beginning, or his end?
Alas what wonder! Man's superior part
Unchecked may rise, and climb from art to art: 40
But when his own great work is but begun,
What Reason weaves, by Passion is undone.°

    Trace Science° then, with modesty thy guide;
First strip off all her equipage of pride,
Deduct what is but vanity, or dress,   45
Or learning's luxury,° or idleness;
Or tricks to show the stretch of human brain,
Mere curious pleasure, or ingenious pain:
Expunge the whole, or lop the excrescent parts
Of all, our Vices have created Arts: 50
Then see how little the remaining sum,
Which served the past, and must the times to come!

    II. Two principles in human nature reign;
Self-love, to urge, and Reason, to restrain;
Nor this a good, nor that a bad we call,   55
Each works its end, to move or govern all:
And to their proper operation still,
Ascribe all good; to their improper, ill.

---

34 **And showed . . . Ape** with real esteem for his powers but
with powers of their own that far surpass his; at once a tribute
to Newton and a warning against pride   42 **What Reason . . .
undone** as in Penelope's undoing by night what she weaved by
day; here the distinctive problem of man's knowledge of Man
where his passions and interests are involved   43 **Science**
knowledge in general   46 **luxury** self-display

Self-love,° the spring of motion, acts° the soul;
60 Reason's comparing balance rules the whole.
Man, but for that, no action could attend,°
And, but for this, were active to no end;
Fixed like a plant on his peculiar spot,
To draw nutrition, propagate, and rot;
65 Or, meteor-like, flame lawless through the void,
Destroying others, by himself destroyed.
Most strength the moving principle requires;
Active its task, it prompts, impels, inspires.
Sedate and quiet the comparing lies,
70 Formed but to check, deliberate, and advise.
Self-love still stronger, as its objects nigh;
Reason's at distance, and in prospect lie:
That sees immediate good by present sense;
Reason, the future and the consequence.
75 Thicker than arguments, temptations throng,
At best more watchful this, but that more strong.
The action of the stronger to suspend
Reason still use, to Reason still attend:
Attention, habit and experience gains,
80 Each strengthens Reason, and Self-love restrains.°
Let subtle schoolmen° teach these friends to
fight,
More studious to divide than to unite,
And Grace and Virtue,° Sense° and Reason split,

59 **Self-love** in the sense of gratification of appetite, not merely
self-regard; see note to II, 7–8.   59 **acts** activates   61 **attend** give
himself to   75–80 **Thicker than . . . restrains** The linkages are
arguments–watchfulness–reason and temptations–strength–self-
love. In order to suspend the strength of self-love one must
invoke reason; attention to her dictates builds habits which
strengthen reason and enable her to restrain the initially stronger
power of self-love. 81 **subtle schoolmen** scholastic philo-
sophers, or any rigid theologians and moralists 83 **Grace and
Virtue** a much-discussed issue during the rise of radical
Protestantism, which dissociated the state of grace from mere
worldly morality or good works; the moderate position saw
virtue as a probable sign of grace and thus held them
together. 83 **Sense** probably used as "sensuality" or passion
rather than "sensation" or empiricism

With all the rash dexterity of wit:
Wits, just like fools, at war about a name,   85
Have full as oft no meaning, or the same.
Self-love and Reason to one end aspire,
Pain their aversion, pleasure their desire;
But greedy that its object would devour,
This taste the honey, and not wound the flower: 90
Pleasure, or wrong or rightly understood,
Our greatest evil, or our greatest good.
   III. Modes of Self-love the Passions we may call;
'Tis real good, or seeming, moves them all;
But since not every good we can divide,   95
And Reason bids us for our own provide;
Passions, though selfish, if their means be fair,
List° under Reason, and deserve her care;
Those, that imparted,° court a nobler aim,
Exalt their kind, and take some Virtue's name.   100
   In lazy apathy° let Stoics boast
Their virtue fixed; 'tis fixed as in a frost,
Contracted all, retiring to the breast;
But strength of mind is Exercise, not Rest:
The rising tempest puts in act the soul,   105
Parts it may ravage, but preserves the whole.°
On life's vast ocean diversely we sail,
Reason the card,° but Passion is the gale;
Nor God alone in the still calm we find,
He mounts the storm, and walks upon the wind.° 110
   Passions, like elements,° though born to fight,
Yet, mixed and softened, in his work unite:
These 'tis enough to temper and employ;
But what composes Man, can Man destroy?°

98 **List** enlist 99 **that imparted** under the guide of
reason 101 **apathy** impassivity, a conquest of passion or
feeling 106 **Parts . . . whole** suggesting the analogy of a ship,
torn by winds but lost without them 108 **card** mariner's
chart 110 **He mounts . . . wind** Cf. among other scriptural
passages, Psalms 104:3: "who maketh the clouds his chariot:
who walketh upon the wings of the wind." 111 **elements** as
in "elemental strife," I, 169, and note 114 **can Man destroy?**
i.e., can man hope to suppress his passions entirely?

115 Suffice that Reason keep to Nature's road,
     Subject, compound them, follow her and God.
     Love, Hope, and Joy, fair pleasure's smiling train,
     Hate, Fear, and Grief, the family of pain;
     These mixed with art, and to due bounds confined,
120 Make and maintain the balance of the mind:
     The lights and shades, whose well-accorded strife
     Gives all the strength and color of our life.
        Pleasures are ever in our hands or eyes,
     And when in act they cease, in prospect rise;
125 Present to grasp, and future still to find,
     The whole employ of body and of mind.
     All spread their charms, but charm not all alike;
     On different senses different objects strike;
     Hence different Passions more or less inflame,
130 As strong or weak, the organs of the frame;
     And hence one MASTER PASSION in the breast,
     Like Aaron's serpent,° swallows up the rest.
        As Man, perhaps, the moment of his breath,
     Receives the lurking principle of death;
135 The young disease, that must subdue at length,
     Grows with his growth, and strengthens with his
          strength:
     So, cast and mingled with his very frame,
     The mind's disease, its RULING PASSION came;
     Each vital humor° which should feed the whole,
140 Soon flows to this, in body and in soul.
     Whatever warms the heart, or fills the head,
     As the mind opens, and its functions spread,
     Imagination plies her dangerous art,
     And pours it all upon the peccant part.°

132 **Aaron's serpent** When Aaron cast down his rod before
the Pharaoh, it became a serpent; when the Egyptian magicians
did the same, Aaron's serpent devoured theirs (Exodus
7:10–12).   139 **vital humor** The "vital spirits" (found in the heart)
and "animal spirits" (found in the head) were believed to nourish
the power of body and soul.   143–44 **Imagination . . . peccant part**
Imagination disruptively directs the nourishing vital humors to the
already excessive ("peccant") growth of the one ruling passion.

Nature its mother, Habit is its nurse; 145
Wit, Spirit, Faculties, but make it worse;
Reason itself but gives it edge and power;
As Heaven's blest beam turns vinegar more sour;
We, wretched subjects though to lawful sway,
In this weak queen,° some favorite still obey. 150
Ah! if she lend not arms, as well as rules,
What can she more than tell us we are fools?
Teach us to mourn our nature, not to mend,
A sharp accuser, but a helpless friend!
Or from a judge turn pleader, to persuade 155
The choice we make, or justify it made;
Proud of an easy conquest all along,
She but removes weak passions for the strong:
So, when small humors gather to a gout,°
The doctor fancies he has driven them out. 160
    Yes, Nature's road must ever be preferred;
Reason is here no guide, but still a guard:
'Tis hers to rectify, not overthrow,
And treat this passion more as friend than foe:
A mightier Power the strong direction sends, 165
And several men impels to several° ends.
Like varying winds, by other passions tossed,
This drives them constant to a certain coast.°
Let power or knowledge, gold or glory, please,
Or (oft more strong than all) the love of ease; 170
Through life 'tis followed, even at life's expense;
The Merchant's toil, the sage's indolence,
The monk's humility, the hero's pride,
All, all alike, find Reason on their side.
    The Eternal Art educing good from ill, 175
Grafts on this Passion our best principle:
'Tis thus the mercury° of Man is fixed,
Strong grows the virtue with his nature mixed;

150 **weak queen** Reason   159 **gout** supposedly caused by a
gathering into an extremity of redundant humors   166 **several**
different   168 **constant . . . coast** The ruling passions
differentiate men but give each man his distinctive constancy
of nature.   177 **mercury** volatility, changeableness

The dross cements what else were too refined,°
180 And in one interest body acts with mind.
　　As fruits ungrateful° to the planter's care
On savage stocks inserted learn to bear;
The surest virtues thus from passions shoot,
Wild Nature's vigor working at the root.
185 What crops of wit and honesty appear
From spleen, from obstinacy, hate, or fear!
See anger, zeal and fortitude supply;
Even avarice, prudence; sloth, philosophy;
Lust, through some certain strainers well refined,
190 Is gentle love, and charms all womankind:
Envy, to which the ignoble mind's a slave,
Is emulation in the learned or brave:
Nor virtue, male or female, can we name,
But what will grow on pride, or grow on shame.
195 　　Thus Nature gives us (let it check our pride)°
The virtue nearest to our vice allied;
Reason the bias turns to good from ill,
And Nero reigns a Titus,° if he will.
The fiery soul abhorred in Catiline,
200 In Decius charms, in Curtius° is divine.
The same ambition can destroy or save,
And makes a patriot as it makes a knave.
　　IV. This light and darkness in our chaos joined,
What shall divide?° The God within the mind.
205 　　Extremes in Nature equal ends produce,°

179 **The dross . . . refined** i.e., both appetite and aspira-
tion are satisfied at once 181 **ungrateful** unresponsive
195 **pride** the "Stoic's pride" in conquering his passions,
which are in fact necessary; or our pride in noble virtues,
which depend in turn upon our "baser" passions; see II,
231–34 198 **Titus** a virtuous Roman emperor of first cen-
tury A.D. 200 **Decius . . . Curtius** legendary Roman heroes
who gave their lives for their country 204 **divide** As God
divides the light from the darkness in Genesis 1:4, so man
must create order out of the chaos of his nature by an act
of "will" (see line 198). 205 **Extremes . . . produce**
Opposites have comparable ends or, perhaps, cooperate to
the same end.

In Man they join to some mysterious use;
Though each by turns the other's bound invade,
As, in some well-wrought picture, light and shade,
And oft so mix, the difference is too nice
Where ends the virtue, or begins the vice.   *210*
    Fools! who from hence into the notion fall,
That vice or virtue there is none at all.
If white and black blend, soften, and unite
A thousand ways, is there no black or white?
Ask your own heart, and nothing is so plain;   *215*
'Tis to mistake them, costs the time and pain.
    V. Vice is a monster of so frightful mien,
As, to be hated, needs but to be seen;
Yet seen too oft, familiar with her face,
We first endure, then pity, then embrace.°   *220*
But where the extreme of Vice, was ne'er agreed:
Ask where's the North? at York, 'tis on the
        Tweed;°
In Scotland, at the Orcades;° and there,
At Greenland, Zembla, or the Lord knows where:
No creature owns it in the first degree,   *225*
But thinks his neighbor further gone than he.
Even those who dwell beneath its very zone,
Or never feel the rage, or° never own;°
What happier natures shrink at with affright,
The hard inhabitant° contends is right.   *230*
    VI. Virtuous and vicious every Man must be,
Few in the extreme, but all in the degree;
The rogue and fool by fits is fair and wise,
And even the best, by fits, what they despise.
'Tis but by parts we follow good or ill,   *235*
For, vice or virtue, Self directs it still;

219–20 **familiar . . . embrace** Cf. *Paradise Lost,* II, 761–63,
where Sin recalls that "familiar grown, / I pleas'd, and with
attractive graces won / The most averse. . . ."   222 **Tweed** the
river dividing England from Scotland   223 **Orcades** the
Orkney Islands, north of Scotland   228 **Or . . . or** either . . .
or   228 **own** admit it   230 **hard inhabitant** the dweller in an
extreme climate

Each individual seeks a several goal;
But HEAVEN's great view is One, and that the
   Whole.
That counterworks each folly and caprice;
240 That disappoints the effect of every vice:
That happy° frailties to all ranks applied,
Shame to the virgin, to the matron pride,
Fear to the statesman, rashness to the chief,
To kings presumption, and to crowds belief:
245 That virtue's ends from vanity can raise,
Which seeks no interest, no reward but praise;
And build on wants, and on defects of mind,
The joy, the peace, the glory of Mankind.
   Heaven forming each on other to depend,
250 A master, or a servant, or a friend,
Bids each on other for assistance call,
Till one man's weakness grows the strength of all.
Wants, frailties, passions, closer still ally
The common interest, or endear the tie:
255 To these we owe true friendship, love sincere,
Each home-felt joy that life inherits here:
Yet from the same we learn, in its decline,
Those joys, those loves, those interests to resign:
Taught half by Reason, half by mere decay,
260 To welcome death, and calmly pass away.
   Whate'er the passion, knowledge, fame, or pelf,
Not one will change his neighbor with himself.
The learned is happy nature to explore,
The fool is happy that he knows no more;
265 The rich is happy in the plenty given,
The poor contents him with the care of Heaven.
See the blind beggar dance, the cripple sing,
The sot a hero, lunatic a king;
The starving chemist° in his golden views
270 Supremely blest, the poet in his Muse.
   See some strange comfort every state attend,
And Pride bestowed on all, a common friend;

241 **happy** fortunate, useful   269 **chemist** alchemist, hoping to
create gold

See some fit Passion every age supply,
Hope travels through, nor quits us when we die.
   Behold the child, by Nature's kindly law,   275
Pleased with a rattle, tickled with a straw:
Some livelier plaything gives his youth delight,
A little louder, but as empty quite:
Scarfs,° garters, gold, amuse his riper stage;
And beads° and prayer books are the toys of age: 280
Pleased with this bauble still, as that before;
Till tired he sleeps, and Life's poor play is o'er!
   Meanwhile Opinion gilds with varying rays
Those painted clouds that beautify our days;
Each want of happiness by Hope supplied,   285
And each vacuity of sense by Pride:
These build as fast as knowledge can destroy;
In Folly's cup still laughs the bubble,° joy;
One prospect lost, another still we gain;
And not a vanity is given in vain;   290
Even mean Self-love becomes, by force divine,
The scale to measure others' wants by thine.
See! and confess, one comfort still must rise,
'Tis this, though Man's a fool, yet GOD IS WISE.

EPISTLE III

HERE then we rest: "The Universal Cause
Acts to one end,° but acts by various laws."
In all the madness of superfluous health,
The trim of pride, the impudence of wealth,
Let this great truth be present night and day;   5
But most be present, if we preach or pray.
   I. Look round our world; behold the chain of
      love°

279 **Scarfs** badges of the Doctors of Divinity or trophies of
lovers 280 **beads** rosaries 288 **bubble** with secondary
meaning of "deception" 2 **one end** the "general Good" as in
line 14 7 **chain of love** The Chain of Being is here seen as a
unity held together by mutual attention, relatedness, or love,
of which divine love for all creatures is the exemplar.

Combining all below and all above.
See plastic° Nature working to this end,
10 The single atoms each to other tend,
Attract, attracted to, the next in place
Formed and impelled its neighbor to embrace.°
See matter next, with various life endued,·
Press to one center still, the general Good.
15 See dying vegetables life sustain,
See life dissolving vegetate again:
All forms that perish other forms supply,
(By turns we catch the vital breath, and die)
Like bubbles on the sea of matter born,
20 They rise, they break, and to that sea return.
Nothing is foreign: parts relate to whole;
One all-extending all-preserving Soul
Connects each being, greatest with the least;
Made beast in aid of Man, and Man of beast;
25 All served, all serving: nothing stands alone;
The chain holds on, and where it ends, unknown.
 Has God, thou fool! worked solely for thy good,
Thy joy, thy pastime, thy attire, thy food?
Who for thy table feeds the wanton° fawn,
30 For him as kindly spread the flowery lawn.
Is it for thee the lark ascends and sings?
Joy tunes his voice, joy elevates his wings.
Is it for thee the linnet pours his throat?
Loves of his own and raptures swell the note.
35 The bounding steed you pompously bestride,
Shares with his lord the pleasure and the pride.
Is thine alone the seed that strews the plain?
The birds of heaven shall vindicate° their grain.
Thine the full harvest of the golden year?
40 Part pays, and justly, the deserving steer:
The hog, that ploughs not nor obeys thy call,
Lives on the labors of this lord of all.
 Know, Nature's children all divide her care;

---

9 **plastic** forming, creative   12 **embrace** like "attracted" and
"impelled," interpreting the mechanical motions as gestures of
"love"   29 **wanton** untamed   38 **vindicate** lay claim to

The fur that warms a monarch, warmed a bear.
While Man exclaims, "See all things for my use!"   45
"See man for mine!" replies a pampered goose:
And just as short of reason he must fall,
Who thinks all made for one, not one for all.
   Grant that the powerful still the weak control;
Be Man the wit° and tyrant of the whole: 50
Nature that tyrant checks; he only knows,
And helps, another creature's wants and woes.
Say, will the falcon, stooping from above,
Smit with her varying plumage, spare the dove?
Admires the jay the insect's gilded wings?   55
Or hears the hawk when Philomela° sings?
Man cares for all: to birds he gives his woods,
To beasts his pastures, and to fish his floods;
For some his interest prompts him to provide,
For more his pleasure, yet for more his pride: 60
All feed on one vain patron, and enjoy
The extensive blessing of his luxury.
That very life his learnèd° hunger craves,
He saves from famine, from the savage° saves;
Nay, feasts the animal he dooms his feast,   65
And, till he ends the being, makes it blest;
Which sees no more the stroke, or feels the pain,
Than favored° Man by touch ethereal slain.
The creature had his feast of life before;
Thou too must perish, when thy feast is o'er!   70
   To each unthinking being, Heaven a friend,
Gives not the useless knowledge of its end:
To Man imparts it; but with such a view
As, while he dreads it, makes him hope it too:
The hour concealed, and so remote the fear,   75
Death still draws nearer, never seeming near.
Great standing miracle! that Heaven assigned
Its only thinking thing this turn of mind.
   II. Whether with Reason, or with Instinct blest,

---

50 **wit** only intellectual being 56 **Philomela** the night-
ingale 63 **learnèd** artificial, not arising from nature 64
savage wild animal 68 **favored** Those struck by lightning were
held as sacred among some people.

80 Know, all enjoy that power which suits them best;
    To bliss alike by that direction tend,
    And find the means proportioned to their end.
    Say, where full Instinct is the unerring guide,
    What Pope or Council° can they need beside?
85 Reason, however able, cool at best,
    Cares not for service, or but serves when pressed,°
    Stays till we call, and then not often near;
    But honest Instinct comes a volunteer;
    Sure never to o'ershoot, but just to hit,
90 While still too wide or short is human wit;
    Sure by quick Nature happiness to gain,
    Which heavier Reason labors at in vain.
    This too serves always, Reason never long;
    One must go right, the other may go wrong.
95 See then the acting and comparing powers
    One in their nature, which are two in ours,
    And Reason raise o'er Instinct as you can,
    In this 'tis God directs, in that 'tis Man.
       Who taught the nations of the field and wood
100 To shun their poison, and to choose their food?
    Prescient, the tides or tempests to withstand,
    Build on the wave, or arch beneath the sand?°
    Who made the spider parallels design,
    Sure as Demoivre,° without rule or line?
105 Who bid the stork, Columbus-like, explore
    Heavens not his own, and worlds unknown
          before?
    Who calls the council, states the certain day,
    Who forms the phalanx, and who points the way?
       III. God in the nature of each being founds
110 Its proper bliss, and sets its proper bounds:
    But as he framed a Whole, the Whole to bless,
    On mutual wants built mutual happiness:
    So from the first eternal Order ran,

84 **Pope or Council** the latter claiming infallibility   86 **pressed**
forced into service rather than a "volunteer" (line 88)   102
Build . . . sand nesting on the waves, as the halcyon was
believed to do, or in the sand, as the kingfisher does   104
Demoivre an eminent French mathematician

And creature linked to creature, man to man.
Whate'er of life all-quickening aether° keeps,   *115*
Or breathes through air, or shoots beneath the
    deeps,
Or pours profuse on earth, one nature feeds
The vital flame, and swells the genial° seeds.
Not Man alone, but all that roam the wood,
Or wing the sky, or roll along the flood,   *120*
Each loves itself, but not itself alone,
Each sex desires alike, till two are one.
Nor ends the pleasure with the fierce embrace;
They love themselves, a third time, in their race.
Thus beast and bird their common charge attend,   *125*
The mothers nurse it, and the sires defend;
The young dismissed to wander earth or air,
There stops the Instinct, and there ends the care;
The link dissolves, each seeks a fresh embrace,
Another love succeeds, another race.   *130*
A longer care Man's helpless kind demands;
That longer care contracts more lasting bands:
Reflection, Reason, still the ties improve,
At once extend the interest, and the love;
With choice we fix, with sympathy we burn;   *135*
Each Virtue in each Passion takes its turn;
And still new needs, new helps, new habits rise,
That graft benevolence on charities.°
Still as one brood, and as another rose,
These natural love maintained, habitual those: *140*
The last, scarce ripened into perfect Man,
Saw helpless him from whom their life began:
Memory and forecast just returns engage,
That pointed back to youth, this on to age:
While pleasure, gratitude, and hope, combined,   *145*
Still spread the interest, and preserved the kind.
    IV. Nor think, in NATURE'S STATE they
      blindly trod;

115 **all-quickening aether** thought of as the divine breath that
gives life to all things   118 **genial** procreative   138 **benev-
olence on charities** virtuous habits of fellow-feeling on
instinctive or natural affections

The state of Nature° was the reign of God:
Self-love and Social at her birth began,
150 Union the bond of all things, and of Man.
Pride then was not; nor Arts, that Pride to aid;
Man walked with beast, joint tenant of the shade;
The same his table, and the same his bed;
No murder clothed him, and no murder fed.
155 In the same temple, the resounding wood,
All vocal beings hymned their equal° God:
The shrine with gore unstained, with gold undressed,
Unbribed, unbloody,° stood the blameless priest:
Heaven's attribute was Universal Care,
160 And Man's prerogative to rule, but spare.
Ah! how unlike the man of times to come!
Of half that live the butcher and the tomb;°
Who, foe to Nature, hears the general groan,
Murders their species and betrays his own.
165 But just disease to luxury succeeds,
And every death its own avenger breeds;
The Fury-passions from that blood began,
And turned on Man a fiercer savage, Man.
    See him from Nature rising slow to Art!
170 To copy Instinct then was Reason's part;
Thus then to Man the voice of Nature spake—
"Go, from the creatures thy instructions take:
Learn from the birds what food the thickets yield;
Learn from the beasts the physic° of the field;
175 Thy arts of building from the bee° receive;
Learn of the mole to plough, the worm° to weave;
Learn of the little nautilus° to sail,

148 **The state of Nature** rejecting Thomas Hobbes' view of the
original state of nature as a state of war in which each man
was a "wolf to man" and human life was "nasty, brutish, and
short"; social love is not, for Pope, artificial, but natural (line
149).   156 **equal** common, impartial   158 **unbloody** not yet
sacrificing animals or fellowmen   162 **butcher . . . tomb** slayer
and devourer   174 **physic** medicinal herbs   175 **bee** the
architect of honeycombed hives   176 **worm** silkworm   177
nautilus believed to swim on the back of their shells, which
resemble the hulks of ships, to extend a membrane between
as a sail, and to use their other feet as oars

Spread the thin oar, and catch the driving gale.
Here too all forms of social union find,
And hence let Reason, late, instruct Mankind: *180*
Here subterranean works and cities see;
There towns aerial on the waving tree.
Learn each small people's genius, policies,
The Ant's republic, and the realm of Bees;°
How those in common all their wealth bestow,   *185*
And anarchy without confusion know;
And these for ever, though a monarch reign,
Their separate cells and properties maintain.
Mark what unvaried laws preserve each state,
Laws wise as Nature, and as fixed as Fate.   *190*
In vain thy Reason finer webs shall draw,
Entangle Justice in her net of Law,
And right, too rigid, harden into wrong;
Still for the strong too weak, the weak too strong.
Yet go! and thus o'er all the creatures sway,   *195*
Thus let the wiser make the rest obey,
And, for those Arts mere Instinct could afford,
Be crowned as monarchs, or as Gods adored."
    V. Great Nature spoke; observant men obeyed;
Cities were built, societies were made: *200*
Here rose one little state; another near
Grew by like means, and joined, through love or
    fear.
Did here the trees with ruddier burdens bend,
And there the streams in purer rills descend?
What War could ravish, Commerce could bestow,   *205*
And he returned a friend, who came a foe.
Converse and Love mankind might strongly draw,
When Love was Liberty, and Nature Law.
Thus states were formed; the name of King
    unknown,
Till common interest placed the sway in one.   *210*
'Twas Virtue only (or in arts or arms,
Diffusing blessings, or averting harms)

184 **The Ant's . . . Bees** seen as democratic or socialistic and
monarchical respectively, in the next four lines

The same which in a sire the sons obeyed,
A prince the father of a people made.
  VI. Till then, by Nature crowned, each
215   patriarch sate,
King, priest, and parent of his growing state;
On him, their second Providence, they hung,
Their law his eye, their oracle his tongue.
He from the wondering° furrow called the food,
220 Taught to command the fire, control the flood,
Draw forth the monsters of the abyss profound,
Or fetch the aërial eagle to the ground.
Till drooping, sickening, dying they began
Whom they revered as God to mourn as Man:
225 Then, looking up from sire to sire, explored°
One great first father, and that first adored.
Or plain tradition that this All begun,°
Conveyed unbroken faith from sire to son,
The worker from the work distinct was known,
230 And simple Reason never sought but one:
Ere wit oblique° had broke that steady light,
Man, like his Maker, saw that all was right,°
To Virtue, in the paths of Pleasure, trod,
And owned a Father when he owned a God.
235 Love all the faith, and all the allegiance then;
For Nature knew no right divine° in Men,
No ill could fear in God; and understood
A sovereign being but a sovereign good.
True faith, true policy,° united ran,
240 This was but love of God, and this of Man.

219 **wondering** sharing in the amazement of the people   225
explored discovered by inference   227 **this All begun** The
world was created rather than subsisted eternally, a theistic
rather than a pantheistic view (see lines 229–30).   231 **wit
oblique** prismatically breaking the "steady light"; see "Essay
on Criticism"   232 **saw . . . right** Cf. Genesis 1:21: "And God
saw every thing that he had made, and, behold, it was very
good."   236 **right divine** power conferred upon specific men
by God, as was claimed by the divine right of kings   239
policy government

    Who first taught souls enslaved, and realms
        undone,
The enormous° faith of many made for one;°
That proud exception to all Nature's laws,
To invert the world, and counterwork its Cause?°
Force first made Conquest, and that conquest,
        Law;   245
Till Superstition taught the tyrant awe,
Then shared the tyranny, then lent it aid,
And gods of conquerors, slaves of subjects made:
She,° midst the lightning's blaze, and thunder's
        sound,
When rocked the mountains, and when groaned
        the ground,   250
She taught the weak to bend, the proud to pray,
To Power unseen, and mightier far than they:
She, from the rending earth and bursting skies,
Saw Gods descend, and fiends infernal rise:
Here fixed the dreadful, there the blest abodes;   255
Fear made her Devils, and weak Hope her Gods;
Gods partial, changeful, passionate, unjust,
Whose attributes were rage, revenge, or lust;
Such as the souls of cowards might conceive,
And, formed like tyrants, tyrants would believe.° 260
Zeal° then, not charity, became the guide,
And hell was built on spite, and heaven on pride.
Then sacred seemed the ethereal vault no more;

242 **enormous** monstrous 242 **many made for one** "In this
Aristotle placeth the difference between a King and a tyrant,
that the first supposeth himself made for the people, the other
that the people are made for him" (Warburton, citing *Politics*,
V, 10). 244 **To invert . . . Cause** i.e., repudiating God: design
as presented in III, 22–25, 111–12 249 **She** super-
stition 253–60 **She . . . believe** a religion "grounded not on
love but fear." The "superstitious man looks on the great
Father of all as a tyrant. . . . Accordingly he serves his Maker
but as slaves do their tyrants, with a gloomy savage zeal against
his fellow creatures . . . at the same time he trembles with the
dread of being ill-used himself" (Pope, cited by Mack,
Twickenham edition, III, i, 117–18). 261 **Zeal** fanaticism

Altars grew marble then, and reeked with gore:
265 Then first the flamen tasted living food;
Next his grim idol smeared with human blood;°
With Heaven's own thunders shook the world below,
And played the God an engine on his foe.°
    So drives Self-love, through just and through unjust,
270 To one man's power, ambition, lucre, lust:
The same Self-love, in all, becomes the cause
Of what restrains him, Government and Laws.
For, what one likes if others like as well,
What serves one will,° when many wills rebel?
275 How shall he keep, what, sleeping or awake,
A weaker may surprise, a stronger take?
His safety must his liberty restrain:
All join to guard what each desires to gain.
Forced into virtue thus by self-defense,
280 Even kings learned justice and benevolence:
Self-love forsook the path it first pursued,
And found the private in the public good.
    'Twas then, the studious head or generous mind,
Follower of God or friend of humankind,
285 Poet or patriot, rose but to restore
The faith and moral,° Nature gave before;
Relumed her ancient light, not kindled new;
If not God's image, yet his shadow drew:
Taught power's due use to people and to kings,
290 Taught nor to slack, nor strain its tender strings,°
The less, or greater, set so justly true,
That touching one must strike° the other too;
Till jarring° interests of themselves create

266 **smeared . . . blood** Cf. *Paradise Lost,* I, 392–93: "First
Moloch, horrid King, besmear'd with blood / Of human
sacrifice. . . ." 268 **And played . . . foe** i.e., turn God into a
piece of artillery, an instrument of man's will and ven-
geance   274 **What . . . will** Of what force is one will?   286
moral moral principles, as in III, 235–40   290 **its tender strings**
of musical instruments, where harmony was a common figure
for political structure, as in lines 294–95   292 **strike** cause to
reverberate   293 **jarring** conflicting, discordant

The according music of a well-mixed state.°
Such is the world's great harmony, that springs
From order, union, full consent of things!
Where small and great, where weak and mighty, made
To serve, not suffer, strengthen, not invade,
More powerful each as needful to the rest,
And, in proportion as it blesses, blest,
Draw to one point, and to one center bring
Beast, Man, or Angel, Servant, Lord, or King,
For forms of government let fools contest;
Whate'er is best administered is best:°
For modes of faith, let graceless° zealots fight;
His can't be wrong whose life is in the right:
In faith and hope the world will disagree,
But all mankind's concern is charity:°
All must be false that thwart this one great end,
And all of God, that bless mankind or mend.
Man, like the generous vine,° supported lives;
The strength he gains is from the embrace he gives.
On their own axis as the planets run,°
Yet make at once their circle round the sun:
So two consistent motions act the soul;
And one regards itself, and one the Whole.
Thus God and Nature linked the general frame,
And bade Self-love and Social be the same.

295
300
305
310
315

294 **well-mixed state** The mixed state was conceived as a balance of the power of the One (King), the Few (Lords), and the Many (Commons); such a balance was believed to give the state the stability to endure and withstand fluctuations among controlling factions. 303–304 **For forms . . . is best** Pope later explained that these lines did not mean "that no one form of government is, in itself, better than another . . . but that no form of government, however excellent or preferable in itself, can be sufficient to make a people happy, unless it be administered with integrity." 305 **graceless** (1) crude (2) without divine grace 308 **charity** Cf. I Corinthians 13:13. 311 **generous vine** as in traditional fables of the love of vine and elm, "generous" in the giving of oneself to another 313 **run** rotate

EPISTLE IV

OH HAPPINESS! our being's end and aim!
Good, pleasure, ease, content! whate'er thy name:
That something still which prompts the eternal
    sigh,
For which we bear to live or dare to die,
5 Which still so near us, yet beyond us lies,
O'erlooked, seen double,° by the fool, and wise.
Plant of celestial seed! if dropped below,
Say, in what mortal soil thou deignst to grow?
Fair opening to some court's propitious shine,
10 Or deep with diamonds in the flaming mine?°
Twined with the wreaths Parnassian laurels yield,
Or reaped in iron harvests of the field?°
Where grows?—where grows it not? If vain our
    toil,
We ought to blame the culture, not the soil:
15 Fixed to no spot is Happiness sincere,°
'Tis nowhere to be found, or everywhere;
'Tis never to be bought, but always free,
And fled from monarchs, ST. JOHN! dwells with
    thee.
    I. Ask of the learned the way, the learned are
    blind,
20 This bids to serve, and that to shun° mankind;
Some place the bliss in action, some in ease,
Those call it pleasure, and contentment these;
Some sunk to beasts, find pleasure end in pain;
Some swelled to gods, confess even virtue vain;
25 Or indolent, to each extreme they fall,
To trust in every thing, or doubt of all.
    Who thus define it, say they more or less

---

6 **O'erlooked, seen double** neglected where it is to be found,
magnified in other places   10 **deep . . . mine** referring to the
belief that minerals were organisms ripened by the sun, hence
blazing from within beneath the ground   12 **field** battle-
field   15 **sincere** pure, genuine   20 **to serve . . . to shun** as
Stoics or Epicureans might

Than this, that Happiness is Happiness?
  II. Take Nature's path, and mad Opinion's
     leave,
All states can reach it, and all heads conceive;   30
Obvious her goods, in no extreme they dwell,
There needs but thinking right, and meaning well;
And mourn our various portions as we please,
Equal is common sense, and common ease.°
  Remember, Man, "the Universal Cause   35
Acts not by partial, but by general laws;"°
And makes what Happiness we justly call
Subsist not in the good of one, but all.
There's not a blessing individuals find,
But some way leans and hearkens to the kind.   40
No bandit fierce, no tyrant mad with pride,
No caverned hermit, rests self-satisfied.
Who most to shun or hate Mankind pretend,
Seek an admirer, or would fix a friend.
Abstract° what others feel, what others think,   45
All pleasures sicken, and all glories sink;
Each has his share; and who would more obtain,
Shall find, the pleasure pays not half the pain.
  ORDER is Heaven's first law; and this confest,
Some are, and must be, greater than the rest,   50
More rich, more wise; but who infers from hence
That such are happier, shocks all common sense.
Heaven to Mankind impartial we confess,
If all are equal in their Happiness:
But mutual wants this Happiness increase,   55
All Nature's difference keeps all Nature's peace.
Condition,° circumstance is not the thing;
Bliss is the same in subject or in king,
In who obtain defense, or who defend,
In him who is, or him who finds a friend: 60
Heaven breathes through every member of the
     whole

34 **common ease** peace of mind 35–36 **the Universal Cause . . .
general laws** Cf. II, 249–56; III, 1–2, 111–14 45 **Abstract**
remove 57 **Condition** rank, class

One common blessing, as one common soul.
But Fortune's gifts if each alike possessed,
And each were equal, must not all contest?
65 If then to all men Happiness was meant,
God in externals could not place content.
    Fortune her gifts may variously dispose,
And these be happy called, unhappy those;
But Heaven's just balance equal will appear,
70 While those are placed in hope, and these in fear:
Not present good or ill, the joy or curse,
But future views of better, or of worse.
    Oh sons of earth! attempt ye still to rise,
By mountains piled on mountains, to the skies?
75 Heaven still with laughter the vain toil surveys,
And buries madmen in the heaps they raise.°
    III. Know, all the good that individuals find,
Or God and Nature meant to mere Mankind,
Reason's whole pleasure, all the joys of Sense,
Lie in three words, Health, Peace, and
80   Competence.°
But Health consists with Temperance alone;
And Peace, oh Virtue! Peace is all thy own.
The good or bad the gifts of Fortune gain,
But these less taste° them, as they worse obtain.°
85 Say, in pursuit of profit or delight,
Who risk the most, that take wrong means, or
       right?
Of Vice or Virtue, whether blest or curst,
Which meets contempt, or which compassion first?
Count all the advantage prosperous Vice attains,
90 'Tis but what Virtue flies from and disdains:
And grant the bad what happiness they would,

73–76 **Oh sons . . . raise** an allusion to the Titans' war against
the Olympian deities where they heaped Mt. Ossa upon Mt.
Pelion in order to reach heaven; also to the building of the
Tower of Babel, upon which "Great laughter was in Heav'n"
(*Paradise Lost*, XII, 59)   80 **Competence** sufficiency of goods
to support life   84 **taste** enjoy   84 **worse obtain** obtain by
baser means

One they must want,° which is, to pass for good.
  Oh blind to truth, and God's whole scheme
      below,
Who fancy bliss to Vice, to Virtue woe!
Who sees and follows that great scheme the best,   95
Best knows the blessing, and will most be blest.
But fools the Good alone unhappy call,
For ills or accidents that chance to all.
See FALKLAND° dies, the virtuous and the just!
See godlike TURENNE° prostrate on the dust!   100
See SIDNEY° bleeds amid the martial strife!
Was this their Virtue, or contempt of life?
Say, was it Virtue, more though Heaven ne'er
      gave,
Lamented DIGBY!° sunk thee to the grave?
Tell me, if Virtue made the son expire,   105
Why, full of days and honor, lives the sire?
Why drew Marseilles' good bishop° purer breath,
When Nature sickened, and each gale was death?
Or why so long (in life if long can be)
Lent Heaven a parent° to the poor and me?   110
  IV. What makes all physical or moral ill?
There deviates Nature, and here wanders Will.
God sends not ill; if rightly understood,
Or partial ill is universal good,
Or change admits, or Nature lets it fall,°   115
Short and but rare, till Man improved it all.°

---

92 **want** miss   99 **Falkland** Lucius Cary, Second Viscount
Falkland, a man universally admired for his gifts and goodness,
killed fighting for Charles I in 1643   100 **Turenne** the French
marshal and hero slain in battle in 1675   101 **Sidney** Sir Philip
Sidney, courtier, poet, patron, killed at Zutphen in 1586   104
Digby the Hon. Robert Digby who died at forty and was
celebrated in an epitaph by Pope; his father was seventy-four
at the time Pope wrote.   107 **Marseilles' good bishop** François
de Belsunce, who performed notable service in the plague of
1720–21, and who lived on until 1755   110 **a parent** Pope's
mother died in 1734 at the age of ninety-one.   115 **Or change . . .
fall** See I, 145–50.   116 **till Man . . . all** until man increased
the scale of evil through his "will"

We just as wisely might of Heaven complain
That righteous Abel was destroyed by Cain,
As that the virtuous son is ill at ease
120 When his lewd father gave the dire disease.
·Think we, like some weak prince, the Eternal
       Cause,
Prone for his favorites to reverse his laws?
Shall burning Etna, if a sage° requires,
Forget to thunder, and recall her fires?
125 On air or sea new motions be imprest,
Oh blameless Bethel!° to relieve thy breast?
When the loose mountain trembles from on high,
Shall gravitation cease, if you go by?
Or some old temple, nodding to its fall,
130 For Chartres' head° reserve the hanging wall?
   V. But still this world (so fitted for the knave)
Contents us not. A better shall we have?
A kingdom of the Just then let it be:
But first consider how those Just agree.
135 The good must merit God's peculiar care;
But who, but God, can tell us who they are?
One thinks on Calvin Heaven's own spirit fell,
Another deems him instrument of hell;
If Calvin feel Heaven's blessing, or its rod,
140 This cries there is, and that, there is no God.
What shocks one part will edify the rest,
Nor with one system can they all be blest.
The very best will variously incline,
And what rewards your virtue, punish mine.
145 WHATEVER IS, IS RIGHT—This world, 'tis true,
Was made for Caesar—but for Titus too:
And which more blest? who chained his
       country,° say,
Or he° whose Virtue sighed to lose a day?

123 **sage** the philosopher Empedocles, who perished in the crater of Mt. Etna   126 **Bethel** a friend of Pope who suffered from asthma   130 **Chartres' head** a notorious scoundrel of the day   147 **who . . . country** Caesar   148 **he** Titus as quoted by the historian Suetonius; see II, 198.

"But sometimes Virtue starves, while Vice is
    fed."
What then? Is the reward of Virtue bread?   150
That, Vice may merit; 'tis the price of toil;
The knave deserves it, when he tills the soil,
The knave deserves it, when he tempts the main,
Where Folly fights for kings, or dives for gain.
The good man may be weak, be indolent,   155
Nor is his claim to plenty, but content.
But grant him riches, your demand is o'er?
"No—shall the good want health, the good want
    power?"
Add health and power, and every earthly thing;
"Why bounded power? why private? why no
    king?"   160
Nay, why external for internal given?
Why is not Man a God, and Earth a Heaven?
Who ask and reason thus, will scarce conceive
God gives enough, while he has more to give:
Immense the power, immense were the demand;   165
Say, at what part of nature will they stand?
    VI. What nothing earthly gives, or can destroy,
The soul's calm sunshine, and the heartfelt joy,
Is Virtue's prize: a better would you fix?
Then give Humility a coach and six,   170
Justice a conqueror's sword, or Truth a gown,°
Or Public Spirit its great cure,° a Crown.
Weak, foolish man! will Heaven reward us there
With the same trash mad mortals wish for here?
The boy and man an individual makes,   175
Yet sighst thou now for apples and for cakes?
Go, like the Indian,° in another life
Expect thy dog, thy bottle, and thy wife:
As well as dream such trifles are assigned,
As toys and empires, for a godlike mind.   180
Rewards, that either would to Virtue bring

171 **gown** academic or clerical   172 **cure** care, change,
remedy   177 **like the Indian** See I, 99–112.

No joy, or be destructive of the thing:
How oft by these at sixty are undone
The virtues of a saint at twenty-one!
185 To whom can riches give repute, or trust,
Content, or pleasure, but the Good and Just?
Judges and senates have been bought for gold,
Esteem and love were never to be sold.
Oh fool! to think God hates the worthy mind,
190 The lover and the love of humankind,
Whose life is healthful, and whose conscience
      clear;
Because he wants a thousand pounds a year.
   Honor and shame from no condition rise;
Act well your part, there all the honor lies.
195 Fortune in men has some small difference made,
One flaunts in rags, one flutters in brocade,
The cobbler aproned, and the parson gowned,
The friar hooded, and the monarch crowned.
"What differ more" (you cry) "than crown and
      cowl?"
200 I'll tell you, friend! a wise man and a fool.
You'll find, if once the monarch acts the monk,
Or, cobbler-like, the parson will be drunk,
Worth makes the man, and want of it, the fellow;°
The rest is all but leather or prunella.°
   Stuck o'er with titles and hung round with
205   strings,°
That thou mayst be by kings, or whores of kings.
Boast the pure blood of an illustrious race,
In quiet flow from Lucrece° to Lucrece;
But by your fathers' worth if yours you rate,
210 Count me those only who were good and great.°
Go! if your ancient, but ignoble blood
Has crept through scoundrels ever since the flood,
Go! and pretend your family is young;

203 **fellow** rogue   204 **leather or prunella** the cobbler's apron
or the parson's worsted gown   205 **strings** ribbons, dec-
orations   208 **Lucrece** a chaste matron like the Roman victim
of Tarquin's rape who slew herself for shame   210 **good and
great** virtuous as well as in public power

Nor own, your fathers have been fools so long.
What can ennoble sots, or slaves, or cowards?   215
Alas! not all the blood of all the Howards.°
   Look next on Greatness; say where Greatness
     lies?
"Where, but among the heroes and the wise?"
Heroes are much the same, the point's agreed,
From Macedonia's madman° to the Swede;°   220
The whole strange purpose of their lives, to find
Or make, an enemy of all mankind!
Not one looks backward, onward still he goes,
Yet ne'er looks forward farther than his nose.
No less alike the politic and wise,   225
All sly slow things, with circumspective eyes:
Men in their loose unguarded hours they take,
Not that themselves are wise, but others weak.
But grant that those can conquer, these can cheat,
'Tis phrase absurd to call a villain great: 230
Who wickedly is wise, or madly brave,
Is but the more a fool, the more a knave.
Who noble ends by noble means obtains,
Or failing, smiles in exile or in chains,
Like good Aurelius° let him reign, or bleed   235
Like Socrates,° that man is great indeed.
   What's Fame? a fancied life in others' breath,
A thing beyond us, even before our death.
Just what you hear, you have, and what's
     unknown
The same (my Lord) if Tully's° or your own.   240
All that we feel of it begins and ends
In the small circle of our foes or friends;
To all beside as much an empty shade,

216 **Howards** a family of highest rank and great age
220 **Macedonia's madman** Alexander the Great 220 **the
Swede** Charles XII of Sweden, whose short life included
brilliant conquests and ultimate defeat at the hands of Peter
the Great 235 **Aurelius** Marcus Aurelius Antoninus, Roman
emperor, whose *Meditations* is a great work of Stoic
philosophy 236 **Socrates** forced to drink hemlock, not a ruler
but a victim of the state 240 **Tully's** Cicero's

An Eugene° living, as a Caesar dead,
245 Alike or when, or where, they shone, or shine,
Or on the Rubicon, or on the Rhine.
A wit's a feather, and a chief a rod;°
An honest man's the noblest work of God.
Fame but from death a villain's name can save,
250 As Justice tears his body from the grave,°
When what to oblivion better were resigned,
Is hung on high, to poison half mankind.
All fame is foreign, but of true desert;°
Plays round the head, but comes not to the heart:
255 One self-approving hour whole years outweighs
Of stupid starers, and of loud huzzas;
And more true joy Marcellus° exiled feels,
Than Caesar with a senate at his heels.
     In Parts° superior what advantage lies?
260 Tell (for You° can) what is it to be wise?
'Tis but to know how little can be known;
To see all others' faults, and feel our own:
Condemned in business or in arts to drudge
Without a second,° or without a judge:
265 Truths would you teach, or save a sinking land?
All fear, none aid, you, and few understand.
Painful pre-eminence! yourself to view
Above life's weakness, and its comforts too.
     Bring then these blessings to a strict account,
270 Make fair deductions, see to what they mount.
How much of other each is sure to cost;
How each for other oft is wholly lost;
How inconsistent greater goods with these;
How sometimes life is risked, and always ease:

244 **Eugene** Prince Eugene of Savoy, a military hero of the
day, who campaigned on the Rhine against the French   247 **A
wit's . . . rod** A mere wit is no more than his quill, a mere
chief no more than his baton or truncheon.   250 **As Justice . . .
grave** e.g., the bodies of the judges of Charles I were exhumed in
1661 and displayed on gallows.   253 **desert** merit   257 **Marcellus**
banished by Caesar for his loyalty to Pompey   259 **Parts**
abilities   260 **You** Bolingbroke   264 **second** supporter, near-
equal

Think, and if still the things thy envy call,   275
Say, wouldst thou be the man to whom they fall?
To sigh for ribbands° if thou art so silly,
Mark how they grace Lord Umbra,° or Sir Billy:°
Is yellow dirt the passion of thy life?
Look but on Gripus,° or on Gripus' wife: 280
If Parts allure thee, think how Bacon° shined,
The wisest, brightest, meanest of mankind:
Or ravished with the whistling of a name,
See Cromwell,° damned to everlasting fame!
If all, united, thy ambition call,   285
From ancient story learn to scorn them all.
There, in the rich, the honored, famed, and great,
See the false scale of Happiness complete!
In hearts of kings, or arms of queens who lay,
How happy! those to ruin, these betray.°   290
Mark by what wretched steps their glory grows,
From dirt and seaweed as proud Venice rose;
In each how guilt and greatness equal ran,
And all that raised the Hero, sunk the Man.
Now Europe's laurels on their brows behold,   295
But stained with blood, or ill exchanged for gold:
Then see them broke with toils, or sunk in ease,
Or infamous for plundered provinces.
Oh wealth ill-fated! which no act of fame
E'er taught to shine, or sanctified from shame!   300
What greater bliss attends their close of life?
Some greedy minion,° or imperious wife,
The trophied arches, storied halls invade,
And haunt their slumbers in the pompous shade.
Alas! not dazzled with their noontide ray,   305
Compute the morn and evening to the day;
The whole amount of that enormous fame,

277 **ribbands** decorations   278 **Lord Umbra** "Lord Shadow,"
a nonentity   278 **Sir Billy** any foolish nobleman   280 **Gripus**
a miser   281 **Bacon** Sir Francis Bacon, revered as writer and
philosopher, scorned for his dismissal from office on charges of
bribery   284 **Cromwell** Oliver Cromwell as rebel and perhaps
tyrant   290 **these betray** The monarchs are betrayed by the
ambitious careerists.   302 **minion** favorite

A tale, that blends their glory with their shame!
  VII. Know then this truth (enough for Man to
    know)
310 "Virtue alone is Happiness below."
The only point where human bliss stands still,
And tastes the good without the fall to ill,
Where only° Merit constant pay receives,
Is blest in what it takes, and what it gives;
315 The joy unequalled, if its end it gain,
And if it lose, attended with no pain:
Without satiety, though e'er so blessed,
.And but more relished as the more distressed:
The broadest mirth unfeeling Folly wears,
320 Less pleasing far than Virtue's very tears:
Good, from each object, from each place acquired,
For ever exercised, yet never tired;
Never elated, while one man's oppressed;
Never dejected, while another's blessed;
325 And where no wants, no wishes can remain,
Since but to wish more Virtue, is to gain.
    See the sole bliss Heaven could on all bestow!
Which who but feels can taste, but thinks can
    know:
Yet poor with fortune, and with learning blind,
330 The bad must miss; the good, untaught, will find;
Slave to no sect, who takes no private road,
But looks through Nature up to Nature's God;
Pursues that Chain which links the immense
    design,
Joins heaven and earth, and mortal and divine;
335 Sees, that no being any bliss can know,
But touches° some above, and some below;
Learns, from this union of the rising Whole,
The first, last purpose of the human soul;
And knows, where Faith, Law, Morals, all began,
340 All end, in LOVE OF GOD, and LOVE OF MAN.
    For him alone, Hope leads from goal to goal,
And opens still, and opens on his soul,

313 **Where only** where alone

Till lengthened on to Faith, and unconfined,
It pours the bliss that fills up all the mind.
He sees, why Nature plants in Man alone   *345*
Hope of known bliss, and Faith in bliss unknown:
(Nature, whose dictates to no other kind
Are given in vain, but what they seek they find)
Wise is her present; she connects in this
His greatest Virtue with his greatest Bliss,   *350*
At once his own bright prospect to be blest,
And strongest motive to assist the rest.
    Self-love thus pushed to social, to divine,
Gives thee to make thy neighbor's blessing thine.
Is this too little for the boundless heart?   *355*
Extend it, let thy enemies have part:
Grasp the whole worlds of Reason, Life, and
    Sense,
In one close system of Benevolence:
Happier as kinder, in whate'er degree,
And height of Bliss but height of Charity.   *360*
    God loves from whole to parts: but human soul
Must rise from individual to the whole.
Self-love but serves the virtuous mind to wake,
As the small pebble stirs the peaceful lake;
The center moved, a circle straight° succeeds,   *365*
Another still, and still another spreads,
Friend, parent, neighbor, first it will embrace,
His country next; and next all human race;
Wide and more wide, the o'erflowings of the mind
Take every creature in, of every kind;   *370*
Earth smiles around, with boundless bounty blest,
And Heaven beholds its image in his breast.
    Come then, my Friend! my Genius!° come
    along,
Oh master of the poet, and the song!
And while the Muse now stoops, or now ascends,   *375*
To Man's low passions, or their glorious ends,
Teach me, like thee, in various nature wise,

365 **straight** straightway   373 **Genius** Bolingbroke as guardian
spirit

To fall with dignity, with temper rise;
Formed by thy converse, happily to steer
380 From grave to gay, from lively to severe;
Correct with spirit, eloquent with ease,
Intent to reason, or polite to please.
Oh! while along the stream of time thy name
Expanded flies, and gathers all its fame,
385 Say, shall my little bark attendant sail,
Pursue the triumph, and partake the gale?
When statesmen, heroes, kings, in dust repose,
Whose sons shall blush their fathers were thy foes,
Shall then this verse to future age pretend°
390 Thou wert my guide, philosopher, and friend?
That urged by thee, I turned the tuneful art
From sounds to things, from fancy to the heart;
For Wit's false mirror held up Nature's light;
Showed erring Pride, WHATEVER IS, IS RIGHT;
395 That REASON, PASSION, answer one great aim;
That true SELF-LOVE and SOCIAL are the same;
That VIRTUE only makes our Bliss below;
And all our Knowledge is, OURSELVES TO KNOW.

389 **pretend** assert

To Richard Boyle,
Earl of Burlington:°

OF THE USE OF RICHES

(1731)

'Tis strange, the miser should his cares employ
To gain those riches he can ne'er enjoy:
Is it less strange, the prodigal should waste
His wealth, to purchase what he ne'er can taste?
Not for himself he sees, or hears, or eats;   5
Artists must choose his pictures, music, meats:
He buys for Topham,° drawings and designs,
For Pembroke,° statues, dirty gods, and coins;
Rare monkish manuscripts for Hearne° alone,
And books for Mead, and butterflies for Sloane.°   10
Think we all these are for himself! no more

To . . . Burlington Richard Boyle, Third Earl of Burlington
(1695–1753), studied architecture in Italy and upon his re-
turn designed buildings himself, commissioned works by oth-
ers, and published the designs of Inigo Jones and Andrea
Palladio. In opposition to the baroque of Wren and later
Vanbrugh, he promoted a more severe Roman classicism and
spent great sums on public buildings of such design.   7
Topham "A gentleman famous for a judicious collection of
drawings" (Pope)   8 **Pembroke** The Earl of Pembroke had
large collections at Wilton House.   9 **Hearne** an eminent
medievalist and editor of early English chronicles   10
Mead . . . Sloane "Two eminent physicians; the one had an
excellent library, the other the finest collection in Europe of
natural curiosities; both men of great learning and human-
ity" (Pope)

Than his fine wife, alas! or finer whore.
  For what has Virro painted, built, and planted?
Only to show, how many tastes he wanted.°
15 What brought Sir Visto's ill got wealth to waste?
Some demon whispered, "Visto! have a taste."
Heaven visits with a taste the wealthy fool,
And needs no rod° but Ripley° with a rule.°
See! sportive fate, to punish awkward pride,
20 Bids Bubo° build, and sends him such a guide:
A standing sermon, at each year's expense,
That never coxcomb° reached magnificence!°
  You° show us, Rome was glorious, not profuse,
And pompous buildings once were things of use.
25 Yet shall (my Lord) your just, your noble rules
Fill half the land with imitating fools;
Who random drawings from your sheets shall take,
And of one beauty many blunders make;
Load some vain church with old theatric state,°
30 Turn arcs of triumph° to a garden gate;
Reverse your ornaments, and hang them all
On some patched dog-hole eked with ends of wall;
Then clap four slices of pilaster° on't,

14 **wanted** lacked 18 **rod** punishment 18 **Ripley** Thomas
Ripley, a mediocre but politically favored architect; as Pope
put it, "a carpenter, employed by a first Minister who raised
him into an architect, without any genius in the art." 18 **rule**
(1) carpenter's rule, as a form of "rod" (2) misapplied
principle, as in lines 25–26 20 **Bubo** Latin for owl, also a
reference to Bubb Dodingtron who spent £140,000 for a
country house designed by Vanbrugh 22 **coxcomb** fop, vain
fool 22 **magnificence** not merely splendor, but according to
Aristotle (*Nicomachean Ethics,* IV, 2), expenditure on public
objects rather than oneself; tasteful generosity 23 **You**
Burlington, then publishing the *Antiquities of Rome* by the
great Italian architect Palladio and other architectural
drawings, whose "sheets" (line 27) might be pillaged for
decorative details by those without a sense of "use" (line
24). 29 **theatric state** (1) the inappropriate details of a Roman
theatre (2) baroque theatricality based on classical details 30
arcs of triumph Roman triumphal arches reduced in scale as
pompous ornament 33 **pilaster** columns attached to the wall

That, laced with bits of rustic,° makes a front.°
Shall call the winds through long arcades to roar,   35
Proud to catch cold at a Venetian door;°
Conscious they act a true Palladian part,
And, if they starve,° they starve by rules of art.
　Oft have you hinted to your brother peer,
A certain truth, which many buy too dear: 40
Something there is more needful than expense,
And something previous even to taste—'tis sense:
Good sense, which only is the gift of Heaven,
And though no science, fairly worth the seven:
A light, which in yourself you must perceive;   45
Jones° and Le Nôtre° have it not to give.
　To build, to plant, whatever you intend,
To rear the column, or the arch to bend,
To swell the terrace, or to sink the grot;°
In all, let Nature never be forgot.   50
But treat the goddess like a modest fair,
Nor overdress, nor leave her wholly bare;
Let not each beauty everywhere be spied,
Where half the skill is decently° to hide.
He gains all points, who pleasingly confounds,   55
Surprises, varies, and conceals the bounds.°
　Consult the genius of the place° in all;

34 **rustic** rustication, the sharp definition of massive building
stones for an effect of rough strength 34 **front** "frontispiece,"
the formal entrance to a building 36 **Venetian door** Palladio
invented the Venetian window or door, an arched center
opening with two smaller rectangular windows on either
side. 38 **starve** because of (1) cost or (2) the great distances
food had to be brought 46 **Jones** Inigo Jones, the distinguished
English architect of the late Renaissance 46 **Le Nôtre** the great
French designer of formal gardens, including those at
Versailles 49 **grot** grotto, artificial cave 54 **decently** (1)
modestly (2) appropriately 56 **bounds** Pope was one of the
earliest and most influential supporters of the so-called English
garden, which sought to avoid formal symmetry and sharp
geometrical pattern for the sake of greater naturalness.
57 **genius of the place** (1) the character of the natural landscape
(2) the tutelary deity who traditionally inhabited each place
and preserved it from violation

That tells the waters or to rise, or fall;
Or helps the ambitious hill the heavens to scale,
60 Or scoops in circling theatres° the vale;
Calls in the country, catches opening glades,
Joins willing woods, and varies shades from shades;
Now breaks, or now directs, the intending lines;
Paints° as you plant, and, as you work, designs.
65   Still follow sense, of every art the soul,
Parts answering parts shall slide into a whole,
Spontaneous beauties all around advance,
Start even from difficulty, strike from chance;
Nature shall join you; time shall make it grow
70 A work to wonder at—perhaps a Stowe.°
Without it, proud Versailles!° thy glory falls;
And Nero's terraces° desert their walls:
The vast parterres° a thousand hands shall make,
Lo! Cobham° comes, and floats° them with a lake:
75 Or cut wide views through mountains to the plains,°
You'll wish your hill or sheltered seat° again.
Even in an ornament its place remark,
Nor in an Hermitage set Dr. Clarke.°
Behold Villario's ten years' toil complete;

60 **circling theatres** the graceful curves of classical
amphitheatres   64 **Paints** (1) colors (2) shapes into picturesque
composition, like that of landscape paintings   70 **Stowe** the
house and gardens of Lord Cobham, of which Pope wrote,
"If anything under Paradise could set me beyond all earthly
cogitations, Stowe might do it."   71 **Versailles** formal as
opposed to natural gardens   72 **Nero's terraces** the elaborate
works of the Golden House of the Roman Emperor   73
parterres formal terraces   74 **Cobham** as at Stowe   74 **floats**
floods   75 "This was done . . . by a wealthy citizen . . . by
which means (merely to overlook a dead plain) he let in the
north-wind upon his house and parterre, which were before
adorned and defended by beautiful woods" (Pope).   76 **seat**
country house   78 **Hermitage . . . Dr. Clarke** Samuel Clarke
was a liberal theologian and philosopher, rationalistic and
somewhat unorthodox; hence the impropriety of a "hermitage."
But that is also the name of an ornamental building in
Richmond Park, where Queen Caroline placed a bust of her
favorite, Dr. Clarke, as well as of Locke, Newton, and
others.

His quincunx° darkens, his espaliers° meet;   80
The wood supports the plain, the parts unite,
And strength of shade contends with strength of light;
A waving glow the bloomy beds display,
Blushing in bright diversities of day,
With silver-quivering rills meandered o'er—   85
Enjoy them, you! Villario can no more;
Tired of the scene parterres and fountains yield,
He finds at last he better likes a field.
   Through his young woods how pleased
     Sabinus strayed,
Or sat delighted in the thickening shade,   90
With annual joy the reddening shoots to greet,
Or see the stretching branches long to meet!
His son's fine taste an opener vista loves,
Foe to the dryads° of his father's groves;
One boundless green, or flourished carpet° views,   95
With all the mournful family of yews;°
The thriving plants ignoble broomsticks made,
Now sweep those alleys they were born to shade.
   At Timon's Villa let us pass a day,
Where all cry out, "What sums are thrown away!"   100
So proud, so grand; of that stupendous air,
Soft and agreeable come never there.
Greatness, with Timon, dwells in such a draught
As brings all Brobdingnag° before your thought.
To compass this, his building is a town,   105
His pond an ocean, his parterre a down:
Who but must laugh, the master when he sees,
A puny insect, shivering at a breeze!
Lo, what huge heaps of littleness around!

80 **quincunx** a planting of five trees, one in the center of the
square formed by the others   80 **espaliers** trees fastened to a
garden wall   94 **dryads** tree nymphs   95 **flourished carpet** a
terrace elaborated in scrolled beds as opposed to the opposite
vice, the nakedness of the "boundless green"   96 **family of
yews** the typical planting of cemeteries, here forming
"pyramids of dark green continually repeated, not unlike a
funeral procession" (Pope)   104 **Brobdingnag** the land of
giants in the second voyage of Swift's *Gulliver's Travels*

110 The whole, a labored quarry above ground.
    Two cupids squirt before: a lake behind
    Improves the keenness of the northern wind.°
    His gardens next your admiration call,
    On every side you look, behold the wall!
115 No pleasing intricacies intervene,
    No artful wildness to perplex the scene;
    Grove nods at grove, each alley has a brother,
    And half the platform just reflects the other.
    The suffering eye inverted Nature sees,
120 Trees cut to statues, statues thick as trees;°
    With here a fountain, never to be played;
    And there a summerhouse, that knows no shade;
    Here Amphitrite° sails through myrtle bowers;
    There gladiators fight, or die in flowers;
125 Unwatered see the drooping sea-horse mourn,
    And swallows roost in Nilus' dusty urn.°
      My Lord advances with majestic mien,
    Smit with the mighty pleasure, to be seen:
    But soft—by regular approach—not yet—
130 First through the length of yon hot terrace sweat;
    And when up ten steep slopes you've dragged
        your thighs,
    Just at his study door he'll bless your eyes.
      His study! with what authors is it stored?
    In books, not authors, curious is my Lord;
135 To all their dated backs° he turns you round:
    These Aldus° printed, those Du Sueil° has bound.
    Lo, some are vellum, and the rest as good

112 **northern wind** See note to line 75.   120 Referring to the
topiary art of trimming trees or hedges into sculpturesque
shapes and to the common overuse of statuary in gardens
123 **Amphitrite,** a sea nymph, wife of Poseidon and mother of
Triton   126 **Nilus' . . . urn** For the river god's urn, see
"Windsor Forest," line 332 and note.   135 **dated backs** early
editions with dates stamped in gold on the binding: "many
delight chiefly in the elegance of the print or the binding; some
have carried it so far as to cause the upper shelves to be filled
with painted books of wood" (Pope)   136 **Aldus** the great
Venetian printer of the Renaissance   136 **Du Sueil** Parisian
binder of early eighteenth century.

For all his Lordship knows, but they are wood.
For Locke or Milton 'tis in vain to look,
These shelves admit not any modern book.   *140*
   And now the chapel's silver bell you hear,
That summons you to all the pride of prayer:
Light quirks of music, broken and uneven,
Make the soul dance upon a jig to Heaven.
On painted ceilings you devoutly stare,   *145*
Where sprawl the saints of Verrio or Laguerre,°
On gilded clouds in fair expansion lie,
And bring all Paradise before your eye.
To rest, the cushion and soft dean invite,°
Who never mentions Hell to ears polite.   *150*
   But hark! the chiming clocks to dinner call;
A hundred footsteps scrape the marble hall:
The rich buffet well-colored serpents grace,
And gaping tritons° spew to wash your face.
Is this a dinner? this a genial room?   *155*
No, 'tis a temple, and a hecatomb.°
A solemn sacrifice, performed in state,
You drink by measure, and to minutes eat.
So quick retires each flying course, you'd swear
Sancho's dread Doctor and his wand° were there.   *160*
Between each act the trembling salvers ring,
From soup to sweet wine, and God bless the King.°
In plenty starving, tantalized in state,

146 **Verrio or Laguerre** fashionable court painters, here shown in a baroque vein 149 Pope cites an actual Dean of Peterborough Cathedral who referred in a sermon to "a place which he did not think fit to name in that courtly audience." 153–54 **serpents . . . tritons** "Taxes the incongruity of ornaments . . . where an open mouth ejects the water into a fountain, or where the shocking images of serpents, etc., are introduced in grottos or buffets" (Pope). 154 **tritons** sea deities, with a human form in upper part of the body and that of a fish in the lower 156 **hecatomb** slaughter of a hundred oxen 160 **Sancho's . . . wand** Cervantes, *Don Quixote,* Pt. II, Ch. 47, where Sancho's doctor forbids him all the food he ravenously contemplates and causes each dish to be whisked away as he touches it with a wand. 162 that is, from the beginning to the end of the meal, ending with a toast in port

And complaisantly helped to all I hate,
165 Treated, caressed, and tired, I take my leave,
Sick of his civil pride from morn to eve;
I curse such lavish cost, and little skill,
And swear no day was ever passed so ill.
      Yet hence the poor are clothed, the hungry fed;
170 Health to himself, and to his infants bread
The laborer bears: what his hard heart denies,
His charitable vanity supplies.°
      Another age shall see the golden ear°
Embrown the slope, and nod on the parterre,
175 Deep harvests bury all his pride has planned,
And laughing Ceres° reassume° the land.
      Who then shall grace, or who improve the soil?
Who plants like Bathurst,° or who builds like
      Boyle.°
'Tis use alone that sanctifies expense,
180 And splendor borrows all her rays from sense.
      His father's acres who enjoys in peace,
Or makes his neighbors glad, if he increase:
Whose cheerful tenants bless their yearly toil,
Yet to their Lord owe more than to the soil;
185 Whose ample lawns are not ashamed to feed
The milky heifer and deserving steed;
Whose rising forests, not for pride or show,
But future buildings, future navies, grow:
Let his plantations stretch from down to down,
190 First shade a country, and then raise a town.
      You too proceed! make falling arts your care,
Erect new wonders, and the old repair;
Jones and Palladio to themselves restore,
And be whate'er Vitruvius° was before:

169–72 Cf. "Essay on Man," II, 230–37, and "To a Lady," lines
149–50.   173 **ear** of wheat   176 **laughing Ceres** the goddess of
agriculture, (1) cheerfully bounteous (2) scornful of Timon's
unnatural art   176 **reassume** regain possession, as a monarch
reassumes a kingdom   178 **Bathurst** a friend of Pope's and an
enthusiastic landscape gardener   178 **Boyle** Burlington   194
Vitruvius the Roman author of the most influential ancient
work on architecture

Till kings call forth the ideas of your mind,   195
Proud to accomplish what such hands designed,
Bid harbors open, public ways extend,
Bid temples,° worthier of the God, ascend;
Bid the broad arch° the dangerous flood contain,
The mole projected break the roaring main;   200
Back to his bounds their subject sea command,
And roll obedient rivers through the land:
These honors, peace to happy Britain brings,
These are imperial works, and worthy kings.

198 **temples** Some of the new churches had been built on marshy ground and sank dangerously. 199 **broad arch** A proposal to build Westminster Bridge had been rejected, but it was later undertaken with Burlington as a commissioner.

TO A LADY:

OF THE CHARACTERS OF WOMEN

(1735)

NOTHING so true as what you once let fall,
"Most women have no characters at all."
Matter too soft a lasting mark to bear,
And best distinguished by black, brown, or fair.
5   How many pictures of one nymph we view,°
All how unlike each other, all how true!
Arcadia's countess,° here, in ermined pride,
Is, there, Pastora° by a fountain side:
Here Fannia, leering on her own good man,
10 And there, a naked Leda° with a swan.
Let then the fair one beautifully cry,
In Magdalen's loose hair and lifted eye,°
Or dressed in smiles of sweet Cecilia° shine,

5–13 "Attitudes in which several ladies affected to be drawn, and sometimes one lady in them all" (Pope) 7 **Arcadia's countess** suggested by the title of Sir Philip Sidney's romance, *The Countess of Pembroke's Arcadia* (1590) so called in compliment to his sister; here a possible reference to Pope's contemporary Mary Howe 8 **Pastora** a pastoral heroine in contrast with ermined pride (line 7) 10 **naked Leda** a popular Renaissance subject, as in the influential (but now lost) painting by Leonardo da Vinci 12 **loose hair . . . eye** typical attributes of the Magdalen in works of Titian, El Greco, and others; in Titian's work the loose hair partly conceals a bare bosom. 13 **Cecilia** St. Cecilia, as the next line suggests, was the patron saint of music, often shown in her ascent to heaven.

With simpering angels, palms, and harps divine;
Whether the charmer sinner it, or saint it,   15
If folly grow romantic,° I must paint it.
  Come then, the colors and the ground° prepare!
Dip in the rainbow, trick her off° in air,
Choose a firm cloud, before it fall, and in it
Catch, ere she change, the Cynthia° of this minute.   20
  Rufa,° whose eye quick-glancing o'er the park,
Attracts each light gay meteor of a spark,°
Agrees as ill with Rufa studying Locke,°
As Sappho's diamonds with her dirty smock,
Or Sappho° at her toilet's greasy task,   25
With Sappho fragrant at an evening mask:°
So morning insects that in muck° begun,
Shine, buzz, and flyblow in the setting sun.
  How soft is Silia! fearful to offend,
The frail one's advocate, the weak one's friend: 30
To her, Calista proved her conduct nice,°
And good Simplicius° asks of her advice.
Sudden, she storms! she raves! You tip the wink,°
But spare your censure; Silia does not drink.
All eyes may see from what the change arose,   35
All eyes may see—a pimple on her nose.
  Papillia,° wedded to her amorous spark,
Sighs for the shades—"How charming is a park!"°
A park is purchased, but the fair he sees
All bathed in tears—"Oh, odious, odious Trees!"°   40

16 **romantic** extravagant   17 **ground** the painted background
to which colors will be applied   18 **trick her off** sketch her   20
Cynthia Diana, here cited as the fickle goddess of the changing
moon   21 **Rufa** redhead   22 **spark** beau   23 **Locke** the
philosopher John Locke, made a fashionable study by *The
Spectator* of Addison and Steele   25 **Sappho** perhaps an
allusion to the brilliant but notoriously slovenly Lady Mary
Wortley Montagu   26 **mask** masked ball   27 **muck** referring
to the belief that insects were generated by corruption   31
nice foolishly fastidious, overly punctilious   32 **Simplicius** the
name of, among others, the commentator on the Stoic
Epictetus   33 **tip the wink** make a surmise   37 **Papillia** Latin
for butterfly   38 **park** rural estate

hybrids

Ladies, like variegated° tulips, show;
'Tis to their changes half their charms we owe;
Fine by defect, and delicately weak,
Their happy spots the nice° admirer take,
45 'Twas thus Calypso° once each heart alarmed,
Awed without virtue, without beauty charmed;
Her tongue bewitched as oddly as her eyes,
Less wit than mimic, more a wit than wise;
Strange graces still, and stranger flights she had,
50 Was just not ugly, and was just not mad;
Yet ne'er so sure our passion to create,
As when she touched the brink of all we hate.
    Narcissa's° nature, tolerably mild,
To make a wash,° would hardly stew a child;
55 Has even been proved to grant a lover's prayer,
And paid a tradesman once to make him stare;
Gave alms at Easter, in a Christian trim,°
And made a widow happy, for a whim.
Why then declare good-nature is her scorn,
60 When 'tis by that alone she can be borne?
Why pique all mortals, yet affect a name?
A fool to pleasure, yet a slave to fame:
Now deep in Taylor° and the Book of Martyrs,°
Now drinking citron° with his Grace° and
    Chartres:°
65 Now conscience chills her, and now passion burns;
And atheism and religion take their turns;
A very heathen in the carnal part,
Yet still a sad,° good Christian at her heart.
    See Sin in state, majestically drunk;

femme fatale (left margin)
contra variable (left margin)

41 **variegated** Streaked tulips were much cultivated and prized in Pope's day. 44 **nice** discriminating 45 **Calypso** named for the nymph who detained Odysseus for many years 53 **Narcissa** whose name suggests vanity 54 **wash** i.e., for hair or skin 57 **trim** dress 63 **Taylor** Jeremy Taylor's *Holy Living and Holy Dying* was an extremely popular devotional work. 63 **Book of Martyrs** John Foxe's work of 1563 64 **citron** brandy flavored with lemon peel 64 **his Grace** a duke, perhaps her lover 64 **Chartres** a notorious gambler and libertine 68 **sad** sober

Proud as a peeress, prouder as a punk;°   70
Chaste to her husband, frank° to all beside,
A teeming mistress, but a barren bride.
What then? let blood and body bear the fault,
Her head's untouched, that noble seat of thought:
Such this day's doctrine—in another fit   75
She sins with poets through pure love of wit.
What has not fired her bosom or her brain?
Caesar and Tallboy,° Charles° and Charlemagne.
As Helluo,° late dictator of the feast,
The nose of hautgout,° and the Tip of Taste,   80
Critiqued your wine, and analyzed your meat,
Yet on plain pudding deigned at home to eat;
So Philomedé, lecturing all mankind
On the soft passion, and the taste refined,
The address, the delicacy—stoops at once,   85
And makes her hearty meal upon a dunce.

    Flavia's a wit, has too much sense to pray;
To toast our wants and wishes, is her way;
Nor asks of God, but of her stars, to give
The mighty blessing, "while we live, to live."   90
Then all for death, that opiate of the soul!
Lucretia's dagger, Rosamonda's bowl.°
Say, what can cause such impotence of mind?
A spark too fickle, or a spouse too kind.
Wise wretch! with pleasures too refined to please;   95
With too much spirit to be e'er at ease;
With too much quickness ever to be taught;
With too much thinking to have common thought:
You purchase pain with all that joy can give,
And die of nothing but a rage to live.   100

    Turn then from wits; and look on Simo's mate,
No ass so meek, no ass so obstinate.
Or her, that owns her faults, but never mends,
Because she's honest, and the best of friends.

---

70 **punk** prostitute   71 **frank** free   78 **Tallboy** a booby lover
in a popular comedy   78 **Charles** a common name for a
footman   79 **Helluo** Latin for glutton   80 **hautgout** anything
with a strong scent, such as overkept game   92 **Lucretia's . . .
bowl** forms of suicide of wronged women

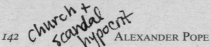

105 Or her, whose life the Church and scandal share,
   For ever in a passion, or a prayer.
   Or her, who laughs at Hell, but (like her Grace)
   Cries, "Ah! how charming, if there's no such place!"
   Or who in sweet vicissitude appears
110 Of mirth and opium, ratafie° and tears,
   The daily anodyne, and nightly draught,
   To kill those foes to fair ones, time and thought.
   Woman and fool are two hard things to hit;
   For true no-meaning puzzles more than wit.
115 But what are these to great Atossa's° mind?
   Scarce once herself, by turns all womankind!
   Who, with herself, or others, from her birth
   Finds all her life one warfare upon earth:
   Shines, in exposing knaves, and painting fools,
120 Yet is, whate'er she hates and ridicules.
   No thought advances, but her eddy brain
   Whisks it about, and down it goes again.
   Full sixty years the world has been her trade,
   The wisest fool much time has ever made.
125 From loveless youth to unrespected age,
   No passion gratified except her rage.
   So much the fury still outran the wit,
   The pleasure missed her, and the scandal hit.
   Who breaks with her, provokes revenge from hell,
130 But he's a bolder man who dares be well.
   Her every turn with violence pursued,
   Nor more a storm her hate than gratitude:
   To that each passion turns, or soon or late;
   Love, if it makes her yield, must make her hate:
135 Superiors? death! and equals? what a curse!
   But an inferior not dependent? worse.
   Offend her, and she knows not to forgive;
   Oblige her, and she'll hate you while you live:
   But die, and she'll adore you—Then the bust°
140 And temple° rise—then fall again to dust.

110 **ratafie** cherry brandy 115 **Atossa** named for the great
Persian princess 139 **bust** funerary monument 140 **temple**
sepulchre

Last night, her Lord was all that's good and great;
A knave this morning, and his will a cheat.
Strange! by the means defeated of the ends,
By spirit robbed of power, by warmth of friends,
By wealth of followers! without one distress,   145
Sick of herself through very selfishness!
Atossa, cursed with every granted prayer,
Childless with all her children, wants an heir.
To heirs unknown descends the unguarded store,
Or wanders, Heaven-directed, to the poor.   150
    Pictures like these, dear Madam, to design,
Asks no firm hand, and no unerring line;
Some wandering touches, some reflected light,
Some flying stroke alone can hit 'em right:
For how should equal° colors do the knack?   155
Chameleons who can paint in white and black?
    "Yet Chloe sure was formed without a spot"—
Nature in her then erred not, but forgot.
"With every pleasing, every prudent part,
Say, what can Chloe want?"—She wants a heart.   160
She speaks, behaves, and acts just as she ought;
But never, never, reached one generous thought.
Virtue she finds too painful an endeavor,
Content to dwell in decencies° for ever.
So very reasonable, so unmoved,   165
As never yet to love, or to be loved.
She, while her lover pants upon her breast,
Can mark the figures on an Indian chest;
And when she sees her friend in deep despair,
Observes how much a chintz exceeds mohair.   170
Forbid it Heaven, a favor or a debt
She e'er should cancel—but she may forget.
Safe is your secret still in Chloe's ear;
But none of Chloe's shall you ever hear.
Of all her dears she never slandered one,   175
But cares not if a thousand are undone.
Would Chloe know if you're alive or dead?
She bids her footman put it in her head.

155 **equal** unvaried   164 **decencies** proprieties

Chloe is prudent—Would you too be wise?
180 Then never break your heart when Chloe dies.
    One certain portrait may (I grant) be seen,
Which Heaven has varnished out, and made a
    Queen:°
The same for ever! and described by all
With truth and goodness, as with crown and ball.°
185 Poets heap virtues, painters gems at will,
And show their zeal, and hide their want of skill.°
'Tis well—but, artists! who can paint or write,
To draw the naked is your true delight.
That robe of quality so struts and swells,
190 None see what parts of nature it conceals:
The exactest traits of body or of mind,
We owe to models of an humble kind.
If Queensbury° to strip there's no compelling,
'Tis from a handmaid we must take a Helen.
195 From peer or bishop 'tis no easy thing
To draw the man who loves his God, or king:
Alas! I copy (or my draught° would fail)
From honest Máhomet,° or plain Parson Hale.°
    But grant, in public men sometimes are shown,
200 A woman's seen in private life alone:
Our bolder talents in full light displayed;
Your virtues open fairest in the shade.
Bred to disguise, in public 'tis you hide;
There, none distinguish twixt your shame or pride,
205 Weakness or delicacy; all so nice,

182 **Queen** with reference to Queen Caroline, who exercised
influence over George II in behalf of Sir Robert Walpole and
favored Lord Hervey, whom Pope presents as Sporus in the
"Epistle to Dr. Arbuthnot." This portrait is in part a satire on
court flattery. 184 **ball** orb (and scepter), symbols of
rule 185–86 Cf. "Essay on Criticism," lines 293–96. 193
Queensbury Catherine Hyde, Duchess of Queensbury, one of
the most beautiful women of her day 197 **draught** sketch
198 **Máhomet** "Servant to the late King, said to be the son of
a Turkish Bassa, whom he took at the siege of Buda, and
constantly kept about his person" (Pope) 198 **Parson Hale**
Dr. Stephen Hales, notable physiologist and admirable parish
priest, a friend of Pope's

That each may seem a virtue, or a vice.
    In men, we various ruling passions find;
In women, two almost divide the kind;
Those, only fixed, they first or last obey,
The love of pleasure, and the love of sway.   210
    That, Nature gives; and where the lesson taught
Is but to please, can pleasure seem a fault?
Experience, this; by man's oppression curst,
They seek the second not to lose the first.
    Men, some to business, some to pleasure take;   215
But every woman is at heart a rake:
Men, some to quiet, some to public strife;
But every lady would be queen for life.
    Yet mark the fate of a whole sex of queens!
Power all their end, but beauty all the means: 220
In youth they conquer, with so wild a rage,
As leaves them scarce a subject in their age:
For foreign glory, foreign joy, they roam,
No thought of peace or happiness at home.
But wisdom's triumph is well-timed retreat,   225
As hard a science to the fair as great!
Beauties, like tyrants, old and friendless grown,
Yet hate repose, and dread to be alone,
Worn out in public, weary every eye,
Nor leave one sigh behind them when they die.   230
    Pleasures the sex, as children birds, pursue,
Still out of reach, yet never out of view;
Sure, if they catch, to spoil the toy at most,
To covet flying, and regret when lost:
At last, to follies youth could scarce defend,   235
It grows their age's prudence to pretend;
Ashamed to own they gave delight before,
Reduced to feign it, when they give no more:
As hags° hold sabbaths, less for joy than spite,
So these their merry, miserable night;°   240
Still round and round the ghosts of beauty glide,
And haunt the places where their honor died.

207 **ruling passions** See "Essay on Man," II, 123 ff.   239 **hags**
witches   240 **night** visiting night

See how the world its veterans rewards!
A youth of frolics, an old age of cards;
245 Fair to no purpose, artful to no end,
Young without lovers, old without a friend;
A fop their passion, but their prize a sot;
Alive, ridiculous, and dead, forgot!

Ah! Friend!° to dazzle let the vain design;
250 To raise the thought, and touch the heart be thine!
That charm shall grow, while what fatigues the
    Ring°
Flaunts and goes down, an unregarded thing:
So when the sun's broad beam has tired the sight,
All mild ascends the moon's more sober light,
255 Serene in virgin modesty° she shines,
And unobserved the glaring orb declines.

Oh! blest with temper, whose unclouded ray
Can make tomorrow cheerful as today;
She, who can love a sister's charms, or hear
260 Sighs for a daughter with unwounded ear;
She, who ne'er answers till a husband cools,
Or, if she rules him, never shows she rules;
Charms by accepting, by submitting sways,
Yet has her humor most, when she obeys;
265 Let fops or fortune fly which way they will;
Disdains° all loss of tickets,° or Codille:°
Spleen, vapors,° or smallpox, above them all,
And mistress of herself, though China° fall.

And yet, believe me, good as well as ill,
270 Woman's at best a contradiction still.
Heaven, when it strives to polish all it can
Its last best work, but forms a softer man;
Picks from each sex, to make the favorite blest,

249 **Friend** Martha Blount, neighbor and close friend of
Pope's 251 **Ring** a fashionable drive in Hyde Park 255 **virgin
modesty** with recollection of Diana as the virgin goddess of
the moon 266 **Disdains** disregards as trifling 266 **tickets** in
lotteries 266 **Codille** a list game of ombre (cf. "Rape of the
Lock," III, 92) 267 **vapors** hypochondria, melancholy 268
China for its double sense, cf. "Rape of the Lock," III, 110,
and III, 159

Your love of pleasure, our desire of rest:
Blends, in exception to all general rules,   275
Your taste of follies, with our scorn of fools:
Reserve with frankness, art with truth allied,
Courage with softness, modesty with pride;
Fixed principles, with fancy ever new;
Shakes all together, and produces—You.   280

  Be this a woman's fame: with this unblest,
Toasts live a scorn, and queens may die a jest.
This Phoebus° promised (I forget the year)
When those blue eyes first opened on the sphere;
Ascendant Phoebus watched that hour with care,   285
Averted half your parents' simple prayer;
And gave you beauty, but denied the pelf
That buys your sex a tyrant o'er itself.
The generous god, who wit and gold° refines,
And ripens spirits as he ripens mines,   290
Kept dross for duchesses, the world shall know it,
To you gave sense, good humor,° and a poet.

---

283 **Phoebus** as god of prophecy 289 **wit and gold** Phoebus
as god of poetry, which fosters true wit, and as god of the sun,
by which gold generates in the earth. 292 **good humor** Cf.
"Rape of the Lock," V, 29–34.

SATIRES AND EPISTLES OF HORACE IMITATED

EPISTLE TO DR. ARBUTHNOT:

BEING THE PROLOGUE TO THE SATIRES

(1735)

P.   Shut, shut the door, good John!° fatigued, I
        said,
Tie up the knocker, say I'm sick, I'm dead.
The dog-star° rages! nay 'tis past a doubt,
All Bedlam, or Parnassus,° is let out:
Fire in each eye, and papers in each hand,   5
They rave, recite, and madden round the land.
   What walls can guard me, or what shades can
        hide?
They pierce my thickets, through my grot° they
        glide;
By land, by water,° they renew the charge;
They stop the chariot, and they board the barge.   10
No place is sacred, not the Church is free;

---

1 **good John** Pope's servant, John Searl   3 **dog-star** Sirius,
which reappears in the season of late summer heat; tradition-
ally a time of satiric rage, occasioned for Juvenal by the read-
ing of pompous epic poems in August (see "Parnassus" in line
4).   4 **Bedlam, or Parnassus** inhabitants of the madhouse or
of Parnassus, the mountain of the Muses   8 **grot** Pope's grotto
at Twickenham was an underground retreat, an artificial cave.
9 **by water** Pope's house was on the Thames; one could be
rowed from London by watermen.

Even Sunday shines no sabbath-day to me:
Then from the Mint° walks forth the man of
    rhyme,
Happy! to catch me just at dinner time.
15   Is there a Parson, much bemused in° beer,
A maudlin poetess, a rhyming peer,
A clerk, foredoomed his father's soul to cross,
Who pens a stanza, when he should *engross*.°
Is there, who, locked from ink and paper, scrawls
20 With desperate charcoal round his darkened walls?°
All fly to TWITNAM, and in humble strain
Apply to me, to keep them mad or vain.
Arthur,° whose giddy son neglects the Laws,
Imputes to me and my damned works the cause:
25 Poor Cornus° sees his frantic wife elope,
And curses wit, and poetry, and Pope.
    Friend to my Life! (which did not you prolong,
The world had wanted many an idle song)
What drop or nostrum° can this plague remove?
30 Or which must end me, a fool's wrath or love?
A dire dilemma! either way I'm sped,
If foes, they write, if friends, they read me dead.
Seized and tied down to judge, how wretched I!
Who can't be silent, and who will not lie;
35 To laugh, were want of goodness and of grace,
And to be grave, exceeds all power of face.
I sit with sad civility, I read
With honest anguish, and an aching head;
And drop at last, but in unwilling ears,
This saving counsel, "Keep your piece nine
40   years."°

13 **Mint** a sanctuary for debtors, who, however, were free of
arrest elsewhere on Sunday   15 **bemused in** rhyming with the
name of Laurence Eusden, a parson and poet laureate much
given to drink   18 **engross** copy a legal document   20
darkened walls i.e., in restful confinement, perhaps Bedlam
23 **Arthur** in fact Arthur Moore, a Member of Parliament; but
the name is generic, like *Cornus* (line 25).   25 **Cornus**
"horned"; a cuckold   29 **drop or nostrum** cures   40 **Keep . . .
years** the advice of Horace, *Ars Poetica,* 386–89

"Nine years!" cries he, who high in Drury Lane,°
Lulled by soft zephyrs through the broken pane,
Rhymes ere he wakes, and prints before Term°
   ~ ends,
Obliged by hunger, and request of friends:°
"The piece, you think, is incorrect? why, take it,   *45*
I'm all submission; what you'd have it, make it."
   Three things another's modest wishes bound,
My friendship, and a prologue,° and ten pound.
   Pitholeon° sends to me: "You know his Grace,
I want a patron; ask him for a place."°   *50*
Pitholeon libelled me—"but here's a letter
Informs you, sir, 'twas when he knew no better.
Dare you refuse him? Curll° invites to dine,
He'll write a Journal, or he'll turn Divine."°
   Bless me! a packet.—" 'Tis a stranger sues,   *55*
A virgin tragedy, an orphan Muse."
If I dislike it, "Furies, death and rage!"
If I approve, "Commend it to the stage."
There (thank my stars) my whole commission
   ends,
The players and I are, luckily, no friends.   *60*
Fired that the house° reject him, " 'Sdeath I'll
   print it,
And shame the fools——Your Interest, sir, with
   Lintot."°
Lintot, dull rogue! will think your price too much:
"Not, sir, if you revise it, and retouch."
All my demurs but double his attacks;   *65*
At last he whispers, "Do; and we go snacks."°

41 **Drury Lane** resort of prostitutes and, here, writers in
garrets   43 **Term** court term, which was also the publishing
season   44 **obliged . . . friends** i.e., covering the first reason
with the second, a frequent apology in prefaces   48 **prologue**
often sought from famous writers to promote a new play   49
Pitholeon a foolish and pretentious poet mentioned by
Horace   50 **place** position, sinecure   53 **Curll** Edmund Curll,
notorious publisher of hacks, might commission another
libel.   54 **Journal . . . Divine** become a party writer in politics
or religion   61 **house** theatre   62 **Lintot** Pope's publisher   66
snacks shares

Glad of a quarrel, straight I clap the door,
"Sir, let me see your works and you no more."
   'Tis sung, when Midas' ears° began to spring,
70 (Midas, a sacred person and a King)
His very Minister who spied them first,
(Some say his Queen) was forced to speak, or
    burst.
And is not mine, my friend, a sorer case,
When every coxcomb perks them in my face?
   "Good friend, forbear! you deal in dangerous
75   things.
I'd never name Queens, Ministers, or Kings;
Keep close to ears, and those let asses prick;
'Tis nothing—" Nothing? if they bite and kick?
Out with it, DUNCIAD! let the secret pass,
80 That secret to each fool, that he's an ass:
The truth once told (and wherefore should we
    lie?)
The Queen of Midas slept, and so may I.
   You think this cruel? take it for a rule,
No creature smarts so little as a fool.
85 Let peals of laughter, Codrus!° round thee break,
Thou unconcerned canst hear the mighty crack:°
Pit, box, and gallery in convulsions hurled,
Thou standst unshook amidst a bursting world.
Who shames a scribbler? break one cobweb
    through,
90 He spins the slight, self-pleasing thread anew:
Destroy his fib or sophistry, in vain,
The creature's at his dirty work° again,
Throned in the center of his thin designs,

[margin handwritten: Spider metaphor]

69 **Midas' ears** the ass's ears given him by Apollo for preferring
Pan's music. Midas' queen whispered it into a hole in the earth
and covered the place, but the reeds which grew there repeated
the message in the wind.   85 **Codrus** a poet ridiculed by Virgil
and Juvenal   86 **mighty crack** This phrase of Addison's
amused Pope by its inadequacy to the conception of a cosmic
catastrophe; here it seems reduced to stage thunder.   92 **dirty
work** The point (as with the spider in Swift's *The Battle of the
Books*) is that he spins a structure out of his excrement.

Proud of a vast extent of flimsy lines!
Whom have I hurt? has poet yet, or peer,   95
Lost the arched eyebrow, or Parnassian sneer?°
And has not Colley still his Lord, and whore?
His butchers Henley,° his Freemasons Moore?°
Does not one table Bavius° still admit?
Still to one bishop Philips° seem a wit?   100
Still Sappho—"Hold! for God's sake—you'll offend,
No names—be calm—learn prudence of a friend:
I too could write, and I am twice as tall;
But foes like these—" One flatterer's worse than
     all.
Of all mad creatures, if the learned are right,   105
It is the slaver kills, and not the bite.
A fool quite angry is quite innocent:
Alas! 'tis ten times worse when they *repent*.
     One dedicates in high heroic prose,
And ridicules beyond a hundred foes: 110
One from all Grubstreet° will my fame defend,
And, more abusive, calls himself my friend.
This prints my *Letters,*° that expects a bribe,
And others roar aloud, "Subscribe, subscribe."°
     There are, who to my person pay their court: 115
I cough like Horace, and, though lean, am short,
Ammon's great son° one shoulder had too high,
Such Ovid's nose, and "Sir! you have an eye"—
Go on, obliging creatures, make me see
All that disgraced my betters, met in me.   120
Say for my comfort, languishing in bed,
"Just so immortal Maro° held his head":

96 **Parnassian sneer** referring to Colley Cibber, the shameless
poet laureate, as in "Dunciad," I   98 **His butchers Henley** See
"Dunciad," III, 199, 209.   98 **Moore** See "Dunciad," II, 50.
Moore used to head Freemasons' processions.   99 **Bavius** the
bad poet of Virgil and Horace's day   100 **Philips** Ambrose
Philips was secretary to the Bishop of Armagh.   111
Grubstreet the center of hack writers   113 **Letters** pirated or
forged   114 **subscribe** Books were published with advance
subscriptions.   117 **Ammon's . . . son** Alexander the
Great   122 **Maro** Virgil

And when I die, be sure you let me know
Great Homer died three thousand years ago.
125 Why did I write? what sin to me unknown
Dipped me in ink, my parents' or my own?
As yet a child, nor yet a fool to fame,
I lisped in numbers,° for the numbers came.
I left no calling for this idle trade,
130 No duty broke, no father disobeyed.
The Muse but served to ease some friend, not
    wife,
To help me through this long disease, my life,
To second, ARBUTHNOT! thy art and care,
And teach the being you preserved to bear.
135 But why then publish? Granville° the polite,
And knowing Walsh, would tell me I could write;
Well-natured Garth inflamed with early praise;
And Congreve loved, and Swift endured my lays;
The courtly Talbot, Somers, Sheffield read,
140 Even mitred Rochester° would nod the head,
And St. John's self° (great Dryden's friends before)
With open arms received one poet more.
Happy my studies, when by these approved!
Happier their author, when by these beloved!
From these the world will judge of men and
145   books,
Not from the Burnets, Oldmixons, and Cookes.°
  Soft were my numbers; who could take offense
While pure description held the place of sense?
Like gentle Fanny's° was my flowery theme,
150 A painted mistress, or a purling stream.
Yet then did Gildon° draw his venal quill;

128 **numbers** verses 135 **Granville** the first of a series of peers, writers, and critics of reputation in contrast to the hacks; see "Windsor Forest," line 6. 140 **mitred Rochester** Francis Atterbury, Bishop of Rochester 141 **St. John's self** Henry St. John, Viscount Bolingbroke 146 **Burnets ... Cookes** "authors of secret and scandalous history" (Pope) 149 **gentle Fanny's** Lord Hervey or some other conventional poet 151 **Gildon** a critic who had attacked Pope personally

I wished the man a dinner, and sat still.
Yet then did Dennis° rave in furious fret;
I never answered—I was not in debt.
If want provoked, or madness made them print,   155
I waged no war with Bedlam or the Mint.
   Did some more sober critic come abroad;
If wrong, I smiled; if right, I kissed the rod.
Pains, reading, study, are their just pretense,
And all they want is spirit, taste, and sense.   160
Commas and points° they set exactly right,
And 'twere a sin to rob them of their mite.
Yet ne'er one sprig of laurel° graced these
      ribalds,°
From slashing Bentley down to pidling Tibalds:°
Each wight, who reads not, and but scans and
      spells,   165
Each word-catcher, that lives on syllables,
Even such small critics some regard may claim,
Preserved in Milton's or in Shakespeare's name.
Pretty! in amber° to observe the forms
Of hairs, or straws, or dirt, or grubs, or worms!   170
The things, we know, are neither rich nor rare,
But wonder how the devil they got there.
   Were others angry? I excused them too;
Well might they rage; I gave them but their due.
A man's true merit 'tis not hard to find;   175
But each man's secret standard in his mind,
That casting-weight° pride adds to emptiness,

153 **Dennis** See note to "Essay on Criticism," lines
585–86.   161 **points** periods   163 **laurel** the crown of the true
poet   163 **ribalds** buffoons   164 **slashing Bentley . . . pidling
Tibalds** Richard Bentley and Lewis Theobald were, among
other things, textual scholars. Bentley's great learning was not
infused with literary sense, and his arrogant handling of
Milton's *Paradise Lost* calls forth the "slashing" (although
Bentley's personality might as well; see "Dunciad," IV, 201).
Theobald made a few great emendations of Shakespeare's text
and many that have been happily forgotten.   169 **in amber** as
flies and other creatures have been decoratively preserved
177 **casting-weight** ballast

This, who can gratify? for who can guess?
The bard° whom pilfered pastorals renown,
180 Who turns a Persian tale for half a crown,°
Just writes to make his barrenness appear,
And strains, from hard-bound brains, eight lines
    a year;
He, who still wanting, though he lives on theft,
Steals much, spends little, yet has nothing left:
185 And he, who now to sense, now nonsense leaning,
Means not, but blunders round about a meaning:
And he, whose fustian's so sublimely bad,
It is not poetry, but prose run mad:
All these, my modest satire bade translate,
190 And owned that nine such poets made a Tate.°
How did they fume, and stamp, and roar, and
    chafe!
And swear, not *Addison*° himself was safe.
    Peace to all such! but were there one whose
    fires
True genius kindles, and fair fame inspires;
195 Blest with each talent and each art to please,
And born to write, converse, and live with ease:
Should such a man, too fond to rule alone,
Bear, like the Turk,° no brother near the throne,
View him with scornful, yet with jealous eyes,
200 And hate for arts that caused himself to rise;
Damn with faint praise, assent with civil leer,
And without sneering, teach the rest to sneer;
Willing to wound, and yet afraid to strike,
Just hint a fault, and hesitate dislike;

179 **bard** Ambrose Philips, author of derivative pastorals and
a book of *Persian Tales* 180 **half a crown** a prostitute's
customary fee 190 **Tate** Nahum Tate, former poet laureate,
"a cold writer of no invention" (Pope) 192 **Addison** who
is clearly meant in the following portrait of Atticus, named
for the friend of Cicero and, later, of Augustus; himself
an author 198 **like the Turk** To forestall rivalry and
assassination, the Turkish rulers often eliminated their close
kinsmen.

Alike reserved to blame, or to commend,   205
A timorous foe, and a suspicious friend;
Dreading even fools, by flatterers besieged,
And so obliging, that he ne'er obliged;
Like Cato,° give his little Senate laws,
And sit attentive to his own applause;   210
While wits and templars° every sentence raise,
And wonder with a foolish face of praise—
Who but must laugh, if such a man there be?
Who would not weep, if Atticus were he?
    What though my name stood rubric° on the
        walls,   215
Or plastered posts, with claps,° in capitals?
Or smoking forth, a hundred hawkers' load,
On wings of wind came flying all abroad?
I sought no homage from the race that write;
I kept, like Asian monarchs,° from their sight: 220
Poems I heeded (now berhymed so long)
No more than thou, great GEORGE! a birthday
        song.°
I ne'er with wits or witlings passed my days,
To spread about the itch of verse and praise;
Nor like a puppy, daggled° through the town,   225
To fetch and carry singsong up and down;
Nor at rehearsals sweat, and mouthed, and cried,
With handkerchief and orange° at my side;
But sick of fops, and poetry, and prate,
To *Bufo* left the whole Castalian state.°   230
    Proud as Apollo on his forkèd hill,

209 **like Cato** the Roman leader of the Senate, the hero of
Addison's famous play   211 **templars** law students, often more
interested in writing than law   215 **stood rubric** was posted in
booksellers' advertisements   216 **with claps** (1) on posters (2)
with advertisements for quack cures for gonorrhea   220
like . . . monarchs Cf. "Elegy to . . . Unfortunate Lady," lines
21–22   222 **birthday song** the official ode of the poet
laureate   225 **daggled** moved in a slovenly way or through
mud   228 **orange** commonly sold at theatres   230 **Castalian
state** poetry, named for the spring on Mt. Parnassus (the *forkèd
hill* of line 231), sacred to Apollo and the Muses

Sat full-blown Bufo,° puffed by every quill;
Fed with soft dedication all day long,
Horace and he° went hand in hand in song.
235 His library (where busts of poets dead
And a true Pindar stood without a head)
Received of wits an undistinguished race,
Who first his judgment asked, and then a place:
Much they extolled his pictures, much his seat,°
240 And flattered every day, and some days eat:
Till grown more frugal in his riper days,
He paid some bards with port, and some with
          praise;
To some a dry rehearsal was assigned,
And others (harder still) he paid in kind.°
245 Dryden alone (what wonder?) came not nigh,
Dryden alone escaped this judging eye:
But still the Great have kindness in reserve,
He helped to bury° whom he helped to starve.
     May some choice patron bless each gray goose
          quill!
250 May every Bavius have his Bufo still!
So, when a statesman wants a day's defense,
Or envy holds a whole week's war with sense,
Or simple pride for flattery makes demands,
May dunce by dunce be whistled off my hands!
255 Blest be the Great! for those they take away,
And those they left me; for they left me GAY,°
Left me to see neglected genius bloom,
Neglected die, and tell it on his tomb:°
Of all thy blameless life the sole return
My Verse, and QUEENSBURY° weeping o'er thy
260   urn!

232 **Bufo** a patron, from the Latin for "toad," a creature that
swells up with air   234 **Horace and he** as a modern Maecenas,
Horace's patron   239 **seat** estate   244 **in kind** with his own
verses   248 **helped to bury** Dryden, although poor much of
his life, was given a lavish funeral.   255–56 Cf. Job: "The Lord
gave and the Lord hath taken away; blessed be the name of
the Lord."   258 **on his tomb** Pope wrote Gay's epitaph.   260
Queensbury with his Duchess patron and friend of Gay

Oh let me live my own, and die so too!
(To live and die is all I have to do:)
Maintain a poet's dignity and ease,
And see what friends, and read what books I please:
Above a patron, though I condescend   *265*
Sometimes to call a Minister my friend.
I was not born for courts or great affairs;
I pay my debts, believe, and say my prayers;
Can sleep without a poem in my head,
Nor know, if Dennis be alive or dead.   *270*
    Why am I asked what next shall see the light?
Heavens! was I born for nothing but to write?
Has life no joys for me? or (to be grave)
Have I no friend to serve, no soul to save?
"I found him close with Swift"—"Indeed? no
      doubt,"   *275*
(Cries prating Balbus) "something will come out."
'Tis all in vain, deny it as I will.
"No, such a Genius never can lie still";
And then for mine obligingly mistakes
The first Lampoon Sir *Will.* or *Bubo*° makes.   *280*
Poor guiltless I! and can I choose but smile,
When every coxcomb knows me by my *style?*
    Cursed be the verse, how well soe'er it flow,
That tends to make one worthy man my foe,
Give Virtue scandal, Innocence a fear,   *285*
Or from the soft-eyed virgin steal a tear!
But he who hurts a harmless neighbor's peace,
Insults fallen worth, or beauty in distress,
Who loves a lie, lame slander helps about,
Who writes a libel, or who copies out: *290*
That fop, whose pride affects a patron's name,
Yet absent, wounds an author's honest fame:
Who can your merit selfishly approve,
And show the sense of it without the love;°
Who has the vanity to call you friend,   *295*

---

280 **Sir Will. or Bubo** Yonge or Bubb Dodington, but any
feeble writers will do.   293–94 **Who can . . . the love** who can
win merit for himself by seeming to approve of ours but
actually placing an invidious interpretation on your words

Yet wants the honor, injured, to defend;
Who tells whate'er you think, whate'er you say,
And, if he lie not, must at least betray:
Who to the *Dean*, and *silver bell* can swear,
300 And sees at *Canons* what was never there;°
Who reads, but with a lust to misapply,
Make Satire a Lampoon, and Fiction, Lie.
A lash like mine no honest man shall dread,
But all such babbling blockheads in his stead.
305   Let *Sporus*° tremble—"What? that thing of silk,
Sporus, that mere white curd of ass's milk?
Satire or sense, alas! can Sporus feel?
Who breaks a butterfly upon a wheel?"°
Yet let me flap this bug with gilded wings,
310 This painted child of dirt that stinks and stings;
Whose buzz the witty and the fair annoys,
Yet wit ne'er tastes, and beauty ne'er enjoys:
So well-bred spaniels civilly delight
In mumbling of the game they dare not bite.
315 Eternal smiles his emptiness betray,
As shallow streams run dimpling all the way.
Whether in florid impotence he speaks,
And, as the prompter breathes, the puppet
            squeaks;
Or at the ear of Eve,° familiar Toad,
320 Half froth, half venom, spits himself abroad,
In puns, or politics, or tales, or lies,
Or spite, or smut, or rhymes, or blasphemies.
His wit all seesaw, between *that* and *this,*
Now high, now low, now master up, now miss,

299–300 **Who . . . never there** who makes false identifications of characters and places in Pope's "Epistle to Burlington." The gossip that linked Timon's villa and the Duke of Chandos's estate, Cannons, was used unjustly to convict Pope of ingratitude.   305 **Sporus** Nero's homosexual favorite; appropriately used for Lord Hervey, prominent in the court of George II and Queen Caroline, of which he left memoirs; a longtime enemy of Pope   308 **wheel** the instrument of torture on which men were disjointed   319 **at the ear of Eve** Cf. *Paradise Lost,* IV, 800, where Satan is found "squat like a Toad, close at the ear of Eve."

And he himself one vile antithesis.   *325*
Amphibious thing! that acting either part,
The trifling head, or the corrupted heart,
Fop at the toilet, flatterer at the board,
Now trips a Lady, and now struts a Lord.
Eve's tempter thus the Rabbins° have exprest,   *330*
A Cherub's face, a reptile all the rest;
Beauty that shocks you, parts that none will trust,
Wit that can creep, and pride that licks the dust.
    Not Fortune's worshipper, nor fashion's fool,
Not lucre's madman, nor ambition's tool,   *335*
Not proud, nor servile; be one poet's praise,
That, if he pleased, he pleased by manly ways:
That flattery, even to kings, he held a shame,
And thought a lie in verse or prose the same.
That not in fancy's maze he wandered long,   *340*
But stooped° to truth and moralized his song:
That not for fame, but virtue's better end,
He stood° the furious foe, the timid friend,
The damning critic, half-approving wit,
The coxcomb hit, or fearing to be hit;   *345*
Laughed at the loss of friends he never had,
The dull, the proud, the wicked, and the mad;
The distant threats of vengeance on his head,
The blow unfelt, the tear he never shed;
The tale revived, the lie so oft o'erthrown,   *350*
The imputed trash, and dulness not his own;
The morals blackened when the writings 'scape,
The libeled person, and the pictured shape;
Abuse, on all he loved, or loved him, spread,
A friend in exile, or a father, dead;   *355*
The whisper,° that to greatness still too near,
Perhaps, yet vibrates on his SOVEREIGN's ear—
Welcome for thee, fair Virtue! all the past:
For thee, fair Virtue! welcome even the *last!*
    "But why insult the poor, affront the great?"   *360*

330 **Rabbins** rabbis, interpreters of the Old Testament   341
stooped as a falcon is said to "stoop" to its prey   343 **stood**
withstood, endured   356 **whisper** by Hervey

A knave's a knave, to me, in every state:
Alike my scorn, if he succeed or fail,
Sporus at court, or Japhet° in a jail,
A hireling scribbler, or a hireling peer,
365 Knight of the post° corrupt, or of the shire;°
If on a pillory, or near a throne,
He gain his Prince's ear, or lose his own.°
    Yet soft by nature, more a dupe than wit,
Sappho° can tell you how this man was bit:°
370 This dreaded satirist Dennis will confess
Foe to his pride, but friend to his distress,°
So humble, he has knocked at Tibbald's door,
Has drunk with Cibber, nay, has rhymed for
      Moore.°
Full ten years slandered, did he once reply?
375 Three thousand suns went down on Welsted's lie.
To please a mistress one aspersed his life;
He lashed him not, but let her be his wife:
Let Budgell charge low Grubstreet° on his quill,
And write whate'er he pleased, except his will;°
380 Let the two Curlls° of town and court, abuse
His father, mother, body, soul, and Muse.
Yet why? that Father held it for a rule,
It was a sin to call our neighbor fool:
That harmless Mother thought no wife a whore:
385 Hear this, and spare his family, *James Moore!*
Unspotted names, and memorable long!
If there be force in virtue, or in song.
    Of gentle blood (part shed in honor's cause,

363 **Japhet** Japhet Crook, a forger   365 **Knight ... post** a false
witness   365 **of the shire** of the county, a legitimate knight
367 **lose his own** as did Japhet Crook, as well as stand in the
pillory   369 **Sappho** Lady Mary Wortley Montagu, to whom
Pope had once been close, after their estrangement joined
Lord Hervey in attacking him.   369 **bit** cheated, deceived   371
his distress Pope had been of help in Dennis' last years.   373
for Moore unintentionally, for Moore plagiarized from Pope
378 **low Grubstreet** contributions to the *Grub Street Journal*
379 **except his will** Budgell seems to have forged a will in which
he displaced a nephew as heir.   380 **two Curlls** the publisher
(line 53) and Lord Hervey

While yet in *Britain* honor had applause)
Each parent sprung—"What fortune, pray?"—
   Their own,   *390*
And better got, than Bestia's° from the throne.
Born to no pride, inheriting no Strife,
Nor marrying discord in a noble wife,
Stranger to civil and religious rage,
The good man walked innoxious through his age. *395*
No courts he saw, no suits would ever try,
Nor dared an oath, nor hazarded a lie.
Unlearned, he knew no schoolman's subtle art,°
No language, but the language of the heart.
By nature honest, by experience wise,   *400*
Healthy by temperance and by exercise;
His life, though long, to sickness passed unknown,
His death was instant, and without a groan.
O grant me, thus to live, and thus to die!
Who sprung from kings shall know less joy than I. *405*
  O Friend!° may each domestic bliss be thine!
Be no unpleasing melancholy mine:
Me, let the tender office long engage,
To rock the cradle of reposing Age,
With lenient arts extend a Mother's breath,°   *410*
Make Languor smile, and smooth the bed of
   Death,
Explore the thought, explain the asking eye,
And keep a while one parent from the sky!
On cares like these if length of days attend,
May Heaven, to bless those days, preserve my
   friend,   *415*
Preserve him social, cheerful, and serene,
And just as rich as when he served a Queen.°
A.   Whether that blessing be denied or given,
Thus far was right, the rest belongs to Heaven.

---

391 **Bestia** a Roman consul bribed with a dishonorable peace
398 **schoolman's . . . art** casuistry   406 **Friend** Arbuthnot   410
Mother's breath Although Pope's mother died before the
"Epistle" was published, this passage had been written during
her illness.   417 **Queen** Anne, to whom Arbuthnot was
physician

THE FIRST SATIRE OF THE
SECOND BOOK OF HORACE

TO MR. FORTESCUE°

(1733)

P.　THERE are (I scarce can think it, but am told),
There are, to whom my satire seems too bold:
Scarce to wise Peter° complaisant enough,
And something said of Chartres° much too rough.
5　The lines are weak, another's pleased to say,
Lord Fanny° spins a thousand such a day.
Timorous by nature, of the rich in awe,
I come to counsel learned in the law:
You'll give me, like a friend, both sage and free,°
10　Advice; and (as you use) without a fee.
　　F.　I'd write no more.
　　P.　　　　　　　　Not write? but then I *think,*
And for my soul I cannot sleep a wink.
I nod in company, I wake at night,

To Mr. Fortescue William Fortescue was a friend and legal
adviser of Pope as well as a friend and supporter of Sir Robert
Walpole. He was later to become Baron of the Exchequer and
Master of the Rolls. He appears in Pope's dialogue as the
celebrated Roman lawyer Trebatius does in Horace's poem.　3
wise Peter Peter Walter, land steward to the Duke of
Newcastle, Member of Parliament, wealthy moneylender to the
aristocracy; cf. "Epilogue to the Satires" I, 121; II, 57.　4
Chartres Cf. "Epistle," I, vi, 120 and note.　6 **Lord Fanny**
Lord Hervey; see note to "Epistle to Dr. Arbuthnot," line
305.　9 **free** generous, open

Fools rush into my head, and so I write.

   F.   You could not do a worse thing for your life.   *15*

Why, if the nights seem tedious, take a wife;

Or rather truly, if your point be rest,

Lettuce and cowslip wine;° *Probatum est.*°

But talk with Celsus,° Celsus will advise

Hartshorn,° or something that shall close your

   eyes.   *20*

Or, if you needs must write, write CAESAR's°

   praise,

You'll gain at least a *knighthood,* or the *bays.*°

   P.   What? like Sir Richard,° rumbling, rough,

   and fierce,

With ARMS, and GEORGE, and BRUNSWICK° crowd

   the verse,

Rend with tremendous sound your ears asunder,   *25*

With gun, drum, trumpet, blunderbuss, and

   thunder?

Or nobly wild, with Budgell's° fire and force,

Paint angels trembling round his falling horse?

   F.   Then all your Muse's softer art display,

Let CAROLINA° smooth the tuneful lay,   *30*

Lull with AMELIA's° liquid name the Nine,

And sweetly flow through all the royal line.

   P.   Alas! few verses touch their nicer° ear;

They scarce can bear their *laureate* twice a year;°

And justly CAESAR scorns the poet's lays,   *35*

It is to *history* he trusts for Praise.

18 **Lettuce . . . wine** inducers of sleep   18 **Probatum est** It is approved.   19 **Celsus** the chief Roman writer on medicine   20 **Hartshorn** ammonia   21 **Caesar** King George II   22 **bays** poet-laureateship   23 **Sir Richard** Blackmore, poet and physician; author of several wretched epics   24 **Brunswick** a German duchy of the Hanoverian George II   27 **Budgell** author of a ludicrous celebration of George II   30 **Carolina** Queen Caroline   31 **Amelia** the third of the royal children   33 **nicer** more delicate   34 **twice a year** at the New Year and the Royal Birthday, occasions for odes. George II, who disliked poetry, was reported to have complained of Pope, "Why will not my subjects write in prose?"

    F.   Better be Cibber, I'll maintain it still,
Than ridicule all taste, blaspheme Quadrille,°
Abuse the City's best good men° in meter,
40 And laugh at Peers that put their trust in Peter.
Even those you touch not, hate you.
    P.   What should ail them?
    F.   A hundred smart in Timon and in Balaam.°
The fewer still you name,° you wound the more;
Bond° is but one, but Harpax° is a score.
45   P.   Each mortal has his pleasure: none deny
Scarsdale his bottle, Darty his ham-pie;
Ridotta° sips and dances, till she see
The doubling lustres° dance as fast as she;
F—— loves the Senate, Hockley Hole° his brother,
50 Like in all else, as one egg to another.
I love to pour out all my self, as plain
As downright SHIPPEN° or as old MONTAIGNE:°
In them, as certain to be loved as seen,
The soul stood forth, nor kept a thought within;
55 In me what spots (for spots I have) appear,
Will prove at least the medium must be clear.
In this impartial glass, my Muse intends
Fair to expose myself, my foes, my friends;
Publish the present age; but where my text
60 Is vice too high, reserve it for the next:
My foes shall wish my life a longer date,
And every friend the less lament my fate.
My head and heart thus flowing through my quill,
Verse-man or prose-man, term me which you will,
65 Papist or Protestant, or both between,
Like good Erasmus in an honest Mean,

38 **Quadrille** a fashionable card game 39 **City . . . men** merchants 42 **Timon . . . Balaam** fictitious characters in earlier satires 43 **name** identify accurately 44 **Bond** See note, "Epilogue to the Satires," I, 121. 44 **Harpax** from Greek for "robber" 47 **Ridotta** a type of society woman 48 **lustres** crystal chandeliers 49 **Hockley Hole** scene of bear-baiting 52 **Shippen** leading Jacobite in Commons, an incorruptible man. 52 **Montaigne** whose *Essays* are candidly self-revealing and self-exploring

In moderation placing all my glory,
While Tories call me Whig, and Whigs a Tory.
Satire's my weapon, but I'm too discreet
To run amuck, and tilt at all I meet;   70
I only wear it in a land of hectors,°
Thieves, supercargoes,° sharpers, and directors.°
Save but our army! and let Jove encrust
Swords, pikes, and guns, with everlasting rust!
Peace is my dear delight—not Fleury's° more: 75
But touch me, and no Minister so sore.
Whoe'er offends, at some unlucky time
Slides into verse, and hitches in a rhyme,
Sacred to Ridicule his whole life long,
And the sad burden of some merry song.   80
    Slander or Poison dread from Delia's rage,
Hard words or hanging, if your judge be Page.
From furious Sappho scarce a milder fate,
P—xed° by her love, or libelled by her hate.
Its proper power to hurt, each creature feels;   85
Bulls aim their horns, and asses lift their heels;
'Tis a bear's talent not to kick, but hug;
And no man wonders he's not stung by Pug.°
So drink with Walters, or with Chartres eat,
They'll never poison you, they'll only cheat.   90
    Then, learnèd sir! (to cut the matter short)
Whate'er my fate, or well or ill at Court,
Whether old age, with faint but cheerful ray,
Attends to gild the evening of my day,
Or death's black wing already be displayed,   95
To wrap me in the universal shade;
Whether the darkened room to muse invite,
Or whitened wall provoke the skewer to write:°

71 **hectors** bullies   72 **supercargoes** officers concerned not with
the sailing of the vessel but only with its trade   72 **directors**
Those of the South Sea Company had been particularly
notorious for fraud.   75 **Fleury** the French cardinal who
pursued, with Walpole, a policy of peace   84 **P—xed** infected
with syphilis   88 **Pug** a common name for a pet dog   97–98
Whether . . . write describing types of confinement, notably in
Bedlam for insanity

In durance, exile, Bedlam, or the Mint,°
100 Like Lee or Budgell,° I will rhyme and print.
        F. Alas, young man! your days can ne'er be
           long,
     In flower of age you perish for a song!
     Plums° and directors, Shylock° and his wife,
     Will club their testers,° now, to take your life!
        P. What? armed for virtue when I point the
105   pen,
     Brand the bold front° of shameless guilty men;
     Dash the proud gamester in his gilded car;
     Bare the mean heart that lurks beneath a Star;°
     Can there be wanting, to defend her cause,
110 Lights of the Church, or guardians of the laws?
     Could pensioned Boileau lash in honest strain
     Flatterers and bigots even in Louis' reign?°
     Could laureate Dryden pimp and friar° engage,
     Yet neither Charles nor James° be in a rage?
115 And I not strip the gilding off a knave,
     Unplaced, unpensioned, no man's heir, or slave?
     I will, or perish in the generous cause:
     Hear this, and tremble! you who 'scape the laws.
     Yes, while I live, no rich or noble knave
120 Shall walk the world, in credit, to his grave.
     TO VIRTUE ONLY AND HER FRIENDS A FRIEND,
     The world beside may murmur, or commend.
     Know, all the distant din that world can keep,
     Rolls o'er my grotto,° and but soothes my sleep.
125 There, my retreat the best companions grace,
     Chiefs out of war, and statesmen out of place.

99 **the Mint** a sanctuary for debtors   100 **Lee or Budgell** both
for a time insane   103 **Plums** sums of £100,000   103 **Shylock**
an adaptation of the name of the Earl of Selkirk   104 **club
their testers** pool their wealth   106 **front** brow   108 **Star** the
decoration for Knight of the Garter   112 **even . . . reign** in
the absolute monarchy of Louis XIV   113 **pimp and friar**
combined in Friar Dominick of Dryden's comedy *The Spanish
Friar*   114 **neither Charles nor James** In fact, James II banned
the play for its satire on the Catholic clergy.   124 **grotto** an
artificial cave on Pope's estate

There St. John° mingles with my friendly bowl
The feast of reason and the flow of soul:
And he, whose lightning pierced the Iberian
    lines,°
Now forms my quincunx,° and now ranks my
    vines,   *130*
Or tames the genius of the stubborn plain,
Almost as quickly as he conquered Spain.
   Envy must own, I live among the Great,
No pimp of pleasure, and no spy of state,
With eyes that pry not, tongue that ne'er repeats, *135*
Fond to spread friendships, but to cover heats;
To help who want, to forward who excel;
This, all who know me, know; who love me, tell;
And who unknown defame me, let them be
Scribblers or Peers, alike are *Mob* to me.   *140*
This is my plea, on this I rest my cause—
What saith my counsel, learnèd in the laws?
   F. Your plea is good; but still I say, beware!
Laws are explained by men—so have a care.
It stands on record, that in Richard's times   *145*
A man was hanged for very honest rhymes.
Consult the Statute: *quart.* I think, it is,
Edwardi sext. or *prim. et quint. Eliz.*
See *Libels, Satires*—here you have it—read.
   P. *Libels* and *satires!* lawless things indeed! *150*
But grave *Epistles,* bringing Vice to light,
Such as a King might read, a Bishop write,
Such as Sir Robert° would approve—
   F.   Indeed?
The case is altered—you may then proceed;
In such a cause the plaintiff will be hissed,   *155*
My Lords the Judges laugh, and you're dismissed.

---

127 **St. John** Bolingbroke, formerly with Harley at the head of
Queen Anne's government.   129 **he . . . Iberian lines** the Earl
of Peterborough, who captured Barcelona and Valencia in
1705–1706   130 **quincunx** a planting of five trees, one at the
center of the square formed by the rest   153 **Sir Robert**
Walpole

THE SECOND SATIRE OF THE SECOND BOOK OF HORACE

TO MR. BETHEL°

(1734)

WHAT, and how great, the virtue and the art
To live on little with a cheerful heart;
(A doctrine sage, but truly none of mine)
Let's talk, my friends, but talk before we dine.
5   Not when a gilt buffet's reflected pride
Turns you from sound philosophy aside;
Not when from plate to plate your eyeballs roll,
And the brain dances to the mantling° bowl.
   Hear Bethel's sermon, one not versed in
      schools,
10 But strong in sense, and wise without the rules.
   Go work, hunt, exercise! (he thus began)
Then scorn a homely dinner, if you can.
Your wine locked up, your butler strolled abroad,
Or fish denied (the river yet unthawed),
15 If then plain bread and milk will do the feat,
The pleasure lies in you, and not the meat.°
   Preach as I please, I doubt our curious men
Will choose a pheasant still before a hen;
Yet hens of Guinea full as good I hold,
20 Except you eat the feathers green and gold.

To Mr. Bethel Hugh Bethel was an old and esteemed friend with
whom Pope maintained "constant, easy, and open commerce."
8 **mantling** sparkling   16 **meat** food in general

Of carps and mullets why prefer the great,
(Though cut in pieces ere my Lord can eat)
Yet for small turbots such esteem profess?
Because God made these large, the other less.
   Oldfield° with more than harpy throat endued,   *25*
Cries "Send me, Gods! a whole hog barbecued!"
Oh blast it, south winds! till a stench exhale
Rank as the ripeness of a rabbit's tail.
By what criterion do ye eat, d' ye think,
If this is prized for sweetness, that for stink?   *30*
When the tired glutton labors through a treat,
He finds no relish in the sweetest meat,
He calls for something bitter, something sour,
And the rich feast concludes extremely poor:
Cheap eggs, and herbs, and olives still we see;   *35*
Thus much is left of old simplicity!
The robin redbreast till of late had rest,
And children sacred held a martin's° nest,
Till *beccaficos*° sold so devilish dear
To one that was, or would have been a Peer.   *40*
Let me extol a cat on oysters fed,
I'll have a party at the Bedford Head;°
Or even to crack live crawfish recommend,
I'd never doubt at court to make a friend.
   'Tis yet in vain, I own, to keep a pother   *45*
About one vice, and fall into the other:
Between excess and famine lies a mean;
Plain, but not sordid; though not splendid, clean.
   Avidien, or his wife (no matter which,
For him you'll call a dog, and her a bitch)   *50*
Sell their presented° partridges, and fruits,
And humbly live on rabbits and on roots:
One half-pint bottle serves them both to dine,
And is at once their vinegar and wine.

25 **Oldfield** a famous glutton   38 **martin** European swallow
39 **beccaficos** Italian name for small migratory birds esteemed
as dainties in the autumn, when they have fattened on figs and
grapes; here, fashionable diet for the socially ambitious   42
Bedford Head a famous eating-house near Covent Garden
51 **presented** those given to them

55 But on some lucky day (as when they found
     A lost bank-bill, or heard their son was drowned)
     At such a feast, old vinegar to spare,
     Is what two souls so generous cannot bear:
     Oil, though it stink, they drop by drop impart,
60 But souse the cabbage with a bounteous heart.
       He knows to live, who keeps the middle state,
     And neither leans on this side, nor on that;
     Nor stops, for one bad cork, his butler's pay,
     Swears, like Albutius, a good cook away;
65 Nor lets, like Naevius, every error pass,
     The musty wine, foul cloth, or greasy glass.
       Now hear what blessings temperance can bring:
     (Thus said our friend, and what he said I sing)
     First health: the stomach (crammed from every
         dish,
70 A tomb of boiled and roast, and flesh and fish,
     Where bile, and wind, and phlegm, and acid jar,
     And all the man is one intestine war)°
     Remembers oft the schoolboy's simple fare,
     The temperate sleeps, and spirits light as air.
75   How pale, each Worshipful and Reverend guest
     Rise from a clergy, or a City feast!°
     What life in all that ample body, say?
     What heavenly particle inspires the clay?
     The soul subsides, and wickedly inclines
80 To seem but mortal, even in sound° divines.
       On morning wings how active springs the mind
     That leaves the load of yesterday behind!
     How easy every labor it pursues!
     How coming to the poet every Muse!
85 Not but we may exceed, some holy time,°
     Or tired in search of truth, or search of rhyme;
     Ill health some just indulgence may engage,
     And more the sickness of long life, old age;

72 **intestine war** punning on civil war as well as digestive
disturbance 76 **City feast** of guild officers, addressed as
"Worshipful" 80 **sound** (1) in body (2) in doctrine 85 **holy
time** holiday

For fainting age what cordial drop remains,
If our intemperate youth the vessel drains?   *90*
  Our fathers praised rank venison. You suppose,
Perhaps, young men! our fathers had no nose.
Not so: a buck was then a week's repast,
And 'twas their point, I ween, to make it last;
More pleased to keep it till their friends could
    come,   *95*
Than eat the sweetest by themselves at home.
Why had I not in those good times my birth,
Ere coxcomb-pies or coxcombs were on earth?
  Unworthy he, the voice of Fame to hear,
That sweetest music to an honest ear;   *100*
(For 'faith, Lord Fanny! you are in the wrong,
The world's good word is better than a song)
Who has not learned, fresh sturgeon and ham pie
Are no rewards for want, and infamy!
When Luxury has licked up all thy pelf,   *105*
Cursed by thy neighbors, thy trustees, thyself,
To friends, to fortune, to mankind a shame,
Think how posterity will treat thy name;
And buy a rope, that future times may tell
Thou hast at least bestowed one penny well.   *110*
  "Right," cries his Lordship, "for a rogue in
      need
To have a Taste is insolence indeed:
In me 'tis noble, suits my birth and state,
My wealth unwieldy, and my heap too great."
Then, like the sun, let Bounty spread her ray,   *115*
And shine that superfluity away.
Oh impudence of wealth! with all thy store,
How dar'st thou let one worthy man be poor?
Shall half the new-built churches° round thee fall?
Make quays, build bridges, or repair Whitehall:°   *120*

119 **the new-built churches** Many of the new churches built
under Queen Anne and George I suffered damage from the
settling of the buildings into marshy ground; the cost of repairs
was a constant concern. 120 **Whitehall** Most of the royal
palace was destroyed by fire in 1698.

Or to thy country let that heap be lent,
As M * * o's was,° but not at five per cent.
  Who thinks that Fortune cannot change her
      mind,
Prepares a dreadful jest for all mankind.
125 And who stands safest? tell me, is it he
That spreads and swells in puffed prosperity,
Or blest with little, whose preventing care
In peace provides fit arms against a war?
  Thus BETHEL spoke, who always speaks his
      thought,
130 And always thinks the very thing he ought:
His equal° mind I copy what I can,
And, as I love, would imitate the man.
In South Sea days° not happier, when surmised
The lord of thousands, than if now excised;°
135 In forest planted by a father's hand,
Than in five acres° now of rented land.
Content with little, I can piddle° here
On broccoli and mutton, round the year;
But ancient friends (though poor, or out of play)°
140 That touch my bell, I cannot turn away.
'Tis true, no turbots dignify my boards,
But gudgeons, flounders, what my Thames affords:
To Hounslow Heath I point and Banstead Down,
Thence comes your mutton, and these chicks my
      own:
145 From yon old walnut tree a shower shall fall;
And grapes, long lingering on my only wall,

122 **As M * * o's was** the Duchess of Marlborough's; the duke
had been notoriously acquisitive and was reported to have
profited greatly from military supplies. 131 **equal** steady 133
South Sea days at the time (1720) when the South Sea Bubble
broke with the plummeting of the company's stocks; Pope lost
heavily. 134 **excised** Walpole introduced what was taken to
be a general excise in 1733 but withdrew it. 136 **five acres** the
extent of Pope's leased property at Twickenham 137 **piddle**
trifle, toy with one's food 139 **out of play** no longer in the
game, i.e., in office

And figs from standard and espalier° join;
The devil is in you if you cannot dine:
Then cheerful healths (your mistress shall have
    place),
And, what's more rare, a poet shall say grace.   *150*
  Fortune not much of humbling me can boast;
Though double taxed,° how little have I lost?
My life's amusements have been just the same,
Before, and after, standing armies° came.
My lands are sold, my father's house is gone;   *155*
I'll hire another's; is not that my own,
And yours, my friends? through whose free-
    opening gate
None comes too early, none departs too late;
(For I, who hold sage Homer's rule the best,
Welcome the coming, speed the going guest.)   *160*
"Pray heaven it last!" (cries SWIFT) "as you go on;
I wish to God this house had been your own:
Pity! to build, without a son or wife:
Why, you'll enjoy it only all your life."
Well, if the use be mine, can it concern one,   *165*
Whether the name belong to Pope or Vernon?°
What's *Property?* dear Swift! you see it alter
From you to me, from me to Peter Walter;°
Or, in a mortgage, prove a lawyer's share;
Or, in a jointure,° vanish from the heir;   *170*
Or in pure equity (the case not clear)
The Chancery° takes your rents for twenty year:
At best, it falls to some ungracious son,
Who cries, "My father's damned, and all's my own."

---

147 **standard and espalier** trees growing naturally and fastened
to a wall or lattice   152 **double taxed** An extra tax was put
upon Catholics' property after the Jacobite Rebellion of
1715.   154 **standing armies** strongly opposed by Tories as an
expense and threat to the state   166 **Vernon** the owner of
Pope's land   168 **Peter Walter** who was buying up estates at
the time; see note to "Satire" I, i, 3   170 **jointure** settlement
of an estate on a widow for her lifetime   172 **Chancery** the
high court of equity, notoriously slow in settling cases

175 Shades, that to Bacon° could retreat afford,
Become the portion of a booby Lord;
And Hemsley, once proud Buckingham's delight,
Slides to a scrivener or a City knight.°
Let lands and houses have what lords they will,
180 Let us be fixed, and our own masters still.

175 **Bacon** Francis Bacon, whose estate near St. Albans finally
passed in Pope's day to a peer much ridiculed as a playwright
178 **scrivener . . . City knight** the estate that once belonged to
the Duke of Buckingham was sold to a London banker (City
knight), Sir Charles Duncombe for £90,000, "the greatest
purchase ever made by any subject of England."

The First Epistle of the First Book of Horace

TO LORD BOLINGBROKE°

(1738)

St. John, whose love indulged my labors past,
Matures my present, and shall bound my last!
Why will you break the sabbath of my days?
Now sick alike of envy and of praise,
Public too long, ah let me hide my age!   5
See, modest Cibber° now has left the Stage:
Our generals now, retired to their estates,
Hang their old trophies o'er the garden gates,
In life's cool evening satiate of applause,
Nor fond of bleeding, even in Brunswick's
    cause.°   10
  A Voice there is, that whispers in my ear,
('Tis Reason's voice, which sometimes one can
    hear)
"Friend Pope! be prudent, let your Muse take
    breath,
And never gallop Pegasus to death;
Lest stiff, and stately, void of fire or force,   15

To Lord Bolingbroke Pope's friend, the brilliant Tory leader
now retired from politics, takes the place of Horace's Maecenas.
Horace was explaining why he had given up the writing of lyric
poetry; he was too old for it and had another, deeper
interest.   **6 modest Cibber** For his immodesty, see "Dunciad," I.
10 Brunswick's cause See note to "Satire," I, i, 24.

You limp, like Blackmore on a Lord Mayor's
    horse."°
  Farewell then verse, and love, and every toy,
The rhymes and rattles of the man or boy;
What right, what true, what fit we justly call.
20 Let this be all my care—for this is all:
To lay this harvest up, and hoard with haste
What every day will want, and most, the last.
  But ask not to what doctors° I apply?
Sworn to no master, of no sect am I:
25 As drives the storm, at any door I knock:
And house with Montaigne now, or now with
    Locke.°
Sometimes a Patriot,° active in debate,
Mix with the world, and battle for the state,
Free as young Lyttleton,° her cause pursue,
30 Still true to virtue, and as warm as true:
Sometimes with Aristippus,° or St. Paul,°
Indulge my candor, and grow all to all;
Back to my native moderation slide,
And win my way by yielding to the tide.
35   Long, as to him who works for debt, the day;
Long as the night to her whose love's away,
Long as the year's dull circle seems to run,
When the brisk minor pants for twenty-one:
So slow the unprofitable moments roll,
40 That lock up all the functions of my soul;
That keep me from myself; and still delay

16 **Blackmore . . . horse** Blackmore's poetry was highly regarded in the City of London if not elsewhere, and his Pegasus is made the slow-paced horse that carries the Lord Mayor. 23 **doctors** teachers, especially dogmatic ones 26 **Montaigne . . . Locke** opposed as extremes of informal and of systematic or regular thought 27 **Patriot** in general sense, but more pointedly a member of the Opposition to Walpole 29 **Lyttleton** a Whig in the Opposition, who tried to gain Pope's public support 31 **Aristippus** the Cyrenaic philosopher who held pleasures of the moment the chief good 31 **St. Paul** Cf. I Corinthians 9:22, "I am made all things to all men," and Philemon 4:5, "Let your moderation be known unto all men."

Life's instant business to a future day:
That task, which as we follow, or despise,
The eldest is a fool, the youngest wise;
Which done, the poorest can no wants endure;° 45
And which not done, the richest must be poor.

Late as it is, I put myself to school,
And feel some comfort, not to be a fool.
Weak though I am of limb, and short of sight,
Far from a lynx, and not a giant quite;° 50
I'll do what Mead and Cheselden° advise,
To keep these limbs, and to preserve these eyes.
Not to go back, is somewhat to advance,
And men must walk at least before they dance.

Say, does thy blood rebel, thy bosom move 55
With wretched avarice, or as wretched love?
Know, there are words, and spells, which can
        control
Between the fits this fever of the soul:
Know, there are rhymes, which fresh and fresh
        applied
Will cure the arrantest puppy of his pride. 60
Be furious, envious, slothful, mad, or drunk,
Slave to a wife, or vassal to a punk,°
A Swiss, a High Dutch, or a Low Dutch bear;
All that we ask is but a patient ear.

'Tis the first virtue, vices to abhor; 65
And the first wisdom, to be fool no more.
But to the world no bugbear is so great,
As want of figure, and a small estate.
To either India see the merchant fly,
Scared at the spectre of pale Poverty! 70
See him, with pains of body, pangs of soul,
Burn through the Tropic, freeze beneath the Pole!
Wilt thou do nothing for a nobler end,
Nothing, to make Philosophy thy friend?
To stop thy foolish views, thy long desires, 75

45 **can . . . endure** can want nothing   50 **Far . . . quite** Pope
was becoming nearsighted, and he was under five feet tall.   51
Mead and Cheselden physician and surgeon, respectively, who
attended Pope   62 **punk** whore

And ease thy heart of all that it admires?
   Here, Wisdom calls: "Seek virtue first, be bold!
As gold to silver, virtue is to gold."
There, London's voice: "Get money, money still!
80 And then let virtue follow, if she will."
This, this the saving doctrine, preached to all,
From low St. James's up to high St. Paul;°
From him whose quills° stand quivered at his ear,
To him who notches sticks° at Westminster.
85   Barnard° in spirit, sense, and truth abounds;
"Pray then, what wants° he?" Fourscore
    thousand pounds,
A pension, or such harness for a slave
As Bug now has, and Dorimant would have.
Barnard, thou art a Cit,° with all thy worth;
90 But wretched Bug, his Honor, and so forth.
   Yet every child another song will sing,
"Virtue, brave boys! 'tis virtue makes a King."
True, conscious honor is to feel no sin,
He's armed without that's innocent within;
95 Be this thy screen, and this thy wall of brass;
Compared to this, a Minister's an ass.
   And say, to which shall our applause belong,
This new court jargon, or the good old song?
The modern language of corrupted Peers,
100 Or what was spoke at CRESSY and POITIERS?°
Who counsels best? who whispers, "Be but great,
With praise or infamy, leave that to fate;
Get place and wealth, if possible, with grace;°
If not, by any means get wealth and place."

82 **From low . . . St. Paul** by both low and high church preachers, also Whigs and Tories   83 **him . . . quills** the city clerk or scrivener   84 **who . . . sticks** the keeper of tallies of debt at the Royal Exchequer   85 **Barnard** M.P. for the City of London, a leader of the Opposition to Walpole, a man of the highest reputation   86 **wants** lacks   89 **Cit** a City man, often used disparagingly   100 **Cressy and Poitiers** the great fourteenth-century English victories in France   103 **grace** with the frequent double reference to manners and to religious salvation

For what? to have a box where eunuchs sing,°   105
And foremost in the circle eye a King.
Or he, who bids thee face with steady view
Proud fortune, and look shallow greatness
    through:
And, while he bids thee, sets the example too?
If such a doctrine, in St. James's air,   110
Should chance to make the well-dressed rabble°
    stare;
If honest S*z° take scandal at a spark,
That less admires the palace than the park:
Faith I shall give the answer Reynard° gave:
"I cannot like, dread Sir, your royal cave: 115
Because I see, by all the tracks about,
Full many a beast goes in, but none come out."
Adieu to virtue, if you're once a slave:
Send her to court, you send her to her grave.
    Well, if a king's a lion, at the least   120
The people are a many-headed beast:°
Can they direct what measures to pursue,
Who know themselves so little what to do?
Alike in nothing but one lust of gold,
Just half the land would buy, and half be sold: 125
Their country's wealth our mightier misers drain,
Or cross, to plunder provinces, the main;
The rest, some farm the poor-box, some the
    pews;°
Some keep assemblies,° and would keep the
    stews;°

---

105 **where . . . sing** at the opera, where *castrati* from Italy
performed; George II often attended.   111 **rabble** Cf. "Mob"
in *Satire* II, i, line 140.   112 **honest S*z** keeper of the Privy
Purse to George II   114 **Reynard** the fox of the fable in reply
to the royal lion   121 **many-headed beast** a term applied by
Socrates in Plato's *Republic*   128 **some farm . . . pews**
Revenues were farmed out to collectors for a percentage of
the yield. Pews were commonly rented at the time. The line
may also allude to embezzlements by officers of the Charitable
Corporation, set up to relieve the poor.   129 **assemblies** public
ballrooms   129 **stews** brothels

130 Some with fat bucks° on childless dotards fawn;
    Some win rich widows by their chine and brawn;
    While with the silent growth of ten per cent,
    In dirt and darkness hundreds stink content.
        Of all these ways, if each pursues his own,
135 Satire be kind, and let the wretch alone:
    But show me one who has it in his power
    To act consistent with himself an hour.
    Sir Job sailed forth, the evening bright and still,
    "No place on earth (he cried) like Greenwich
        hill!"
140 Up starts a palace; lo, the obedient base
    Slopes at its foot, the woods its sides embrace,
    The silver Thames reflects its marble face.
    Now let some whimsy, or that devil within
    Which guides all those who know not what they
        mean,
145 But give the Knight (or give his Lady) spleen;°
    "Away, away! take all your scaffolds down,
    "For snug's the word: My dear! we'll live in
        town."
        At amorous Flavio is the stocking thrown?
    That very night he longs to lie alone.
150 The fool, whose wife elopes some thrice a quarter,
    For matrimonial solace dies a martyr.
    Did ever Proteus,° Merlin,° any witch,
    Transform themselves so strangely as the rich?
    Well, but the poor—The poor have the same itch;
155 They change their weekly barber, weekly news,°
    Prefer a new japanner° to their shoes,
    Discharge their garrets, move their beds, and run
    (They know not whither) in a chaise and one;°
    They hire their sculler,° and when once aboard,
160 Grow sick, and damn the climate—like a Lord.

130 **fat bucks** handsome lovers   145 **spleen** impulse, caprice
152 **Proteus** See note to "Dunciad," I, 37.   152 **Merlin** the
enchanter of King Arthur's court   155 **news** newspaper
156 **japanner** bootblack   158 **chaise and one** light carriage
drawn by one horse   159 **sculler** oarsman

You laugh, half beau, half sloven if I stand,
My wig all powder, and all snuff my band;°
You laugh, if coat and breeches strangely vary,
White gloves, and linen worthy Lady Mary!°
But when no Prelate's lawn° with hairshirt lined,   165
Is half so incoherent as my mind,
When (each opinion with the next at strife,
One ebb and flow of follies all my life)
I plant, root up; I build, and then confound;°
Turn round to square, and square again to round;   170
You never change one muscle of your face,
You think this madness but a common case,
Nor once to Chancery, nor to Hales° apply;
Yet hang your lip, to see a seam awry!
Careless how ill I with myself agree,   175
Kind to my dress, my figure, not to me.
Is this my guide, philosopher, and friend?°
This, he who loves me, and who ought to mend?
Who ought to make me (what he can, or none,)
That man divine whom wisdom calls her own;   180
Great without title, without fortune blessed;
Rich even when plundered, honored while oppressed;
Loved without youth, and followed without power;°
At home, though exiled, free, though in the
    Tower;°

162 **band** neckband   164 **Lady Mary** Lady Mary Wortley
Montagu was notoriously slovenly.   165 **lawn** fine fabric
used in a bishop's attire   169 **confound** destroy   173 **Hales**
physician at Bedlam   177 **my guide . . . friend** Cf. "Essay on
Man," IV, 390.   181–83 **Great . . . power** Bolingbroke's name
was erased from the roll of peers and his estates forfeited
in 1715. He returned from his exile abroad with a pardon in
1723 but was forbidden to resume his seat in the House of
Lords; he became, nevertheless, a leader of the Opposition
to Walpole for the next decade. He remained a close and
much respected friend of Pope, Swift, and Gay.   184 **Tower**
the Tower of London, which Bolingbroke escaped by flight
from England. It should be observed that this portrait is a
general one of the "man divine" Bolingbroke alone can
teach one to become.

185 In short, that reasoning, high, immortal thing,
Just less than Jove, and much above a King,
Nay, half in heaven—except (what's mighty odd)
A fit of vapors° clouds this demigod.

188 **vapors** spleen; hypochondria or melancholy

THE SIXTH EPISTLE OF THE
FIRST BOOK OF HORACE

TO MR. MURRAY°

(1738)

"NOT to admire,° is all the Art I know,
To make men happy, and to keep them so."
(Plain truth, dear MURRAY, needs no flowers of
    speech,
So take it in the very words of Creech.)°
  This vault of air, this congregated ball,°   *5*
Self-centered sun, and stars that rise and fall,
There are, my friend! whose philosophic eyes
Look through, and trust the Ruler with his skies,
To him commit the hour, the day, the year,
And view this dreadful All without a fear.   *10*
  Admire we then what earth's low entrails hold,
Arabian shores, or Indian seas infold;°
All the mad trade of fools and slaves for gold?
Or popularity? or stars and strings?°
The mob's applauses, or the gifts of kings?   *15*
Say with what eyes we ought at courts to gaze,

To Mr. Murray William Murray, later Earl of Mansfield and
Lord Chief Justice, an eloquent orator in Commons, and
pleader at the bar of the House of Lords (line 49). 1 **Not to
admire** Pope's version of Horace's "nil admirari," i.e., be
dazzled by nothing 4 **Creech** Thomas Creech, the pedestrian
translator of Horace, whom Pope adapts in lines 1–2. 5
congregated ball peopled earth 12 **infold** conceal 14 **stars
and strings** medals and ribbons of the knightly orders

And pay the great our homage of amaze?
   If weak the pleasures that from these can
     spring,
The fear to want them is as weak a thing:
20 Whether we dread, or whether we desire,
In either case, believe me, we admire;
Whether we joy or grieve, the same the curse,
Surprised at better, or surprised at worse.
Thus good or bad, to one extreme betray
25 The unbalanced mind, and snatch the man away;
For virtue's self may too much zeal be had;
The worst of madmen is a saint run mad.
   Go then, and if you can, admire the state
Of beaming diamonds, and reflected plate;
30 Procure a TASTE to double the surprise,
And gaze on Parian° charms with learnèd eyes:
Be struck with bright brocade, or Tyrian dye,°
Our birthday nobles' splendid livery.°
If not so pleased, at Council board rejoice,
35 To see their judgments hang upon thy voice;
From morn to night, at Senate, Rolls, and Hall,°
Plead much, read more, dine late, or not at all.
But wherefore all this labor, all this strife?
For fame, for riches, for a noble wife?°
40 Shall one whom nature, learning, birth, conspired
To form, not to admire but be admired,
Sigh, while his Chloe blind to wit and worth
Weds the rich dulness of some son of earth?
Yet time ennobles, or degrades each line;
45 It brightened CRAGGS's,° and may darken thine:°
And what is fame? the meanest have their day;
The greatest can but blaze, and pass away.

31 **Parian** the white marble of which many classical statues
were made   32 **Tyrian dye** Tyre was famous in antiquity for
its dyes.   33 **birthday . . . livery** See notes to "Rape of the
Lock," I, 23, and "Dunciad," IV, 537.   36 **Senate . . . Hall**
Parliament, Chancery, and the High Court of Justice   39 **noble
wife** Cf. "Epistle to Dr. Arbuthnot," line 393.   45 **Craggs** a
prominent statesman of humble birth   45 **darken thine** Murray
was of noble birth.

Graced as thou art, with all the power of words,
So known, so honored, at the House of Lords:
Conspicuous scene! another yet is nigh,   50
(More silent far) where kings and poets lie;°
Where MURRAY (long enough his country's pride)
Shall be no more than TULLY, or than HYDE!°
   Racked with sciatics, martyred with the stone,
Will any mortal let himself alone?   55
See Ward by battered beaux invited over,
And desperate misery lays hold on Dover.°
The case is easier in the mind's disease;
There all men may be cured, whene'er they
    please.
Would ye be blest? despise low joys, low gains;   60
Disdain whatever CORNBURY° disdains;
Be virtuous, and be happy for your pains.
   But art thou one, whom new opinions sway,
One who believes as Tindal° leads the way,
Who virtue and a Church alike disowns,   65
Thinks that but words, and this but brick and
    stones?
Fly then, on all the wings of wild desire,
Admire whate'er the maddest can admire.
Is wealth thy passion? Hence! from Pole to Pole,
Where winds can carry, or where waves can roll,   70
For Indian spices, for Peruvian gold,
Prevent° the greedy, and outbid the bold:
Advance thy golden mountain to the skies;°
On the broad base of fifty thousand rise,
Add one round hundred, and (if that's not fair)   75
Add fifty more, and bring it to a square.

---

51 **where . . . lie** Westminster Abbey 53 **Tully . . . Hyde**
Cicero and the first Earl of Clarendon, men of eloquence of
different ages 56–57 **Ward . . . Dover** two eminent quack
doctors 61 **Cornbury** Henry Hyde, Viscount Cornbury, a
friend of Pope, upon being offered a pension, replied, "How
could you tell, my Lord, that I was to be sold? or, at least,
how could you know my price so exactly?" 64 **Tindal** the
anticlerical deist 72 **Prevent** arrive before 73 **Advance . . .
skies** Cf. "Essay on Man," IV, 73–76.

For, mark the advantage; just so many score
Will gain a wife with half as many more,
Procure her beauty, make that beauty chaste,
80 And then such friends—as cannot fail to last.
A man of wealth is dubbed a man of worth,
Venus shall give him form, and Anstis° birth.
(Believe me, many a German prince is worse,
Who proud of pedigree, is poor of purse.)
85 His wealth brave Timon gloriously confounds;°
Asked for a groat, he gives a hundred pounds;
Or if three ladies like a luckless play,
Takes the whole house upon the poet's day.°
Now, in such exigencies not to need,
90 Upon my word, you must be rich indeed;
A noble superfluity it craves,
Not for yourself, but for your fools and knaves;
Something, which for your honor they may cheat,
And which it much becomes you to forget.
95 If Wealth alone then make and keep us blest,
Still, still be getting, never, never rest.
    But if to power and place your passion lie,
If in the pomp of life consist the joy;
Then hire a slave, or (if you will) a Lord
100 To do the honors, and to give the word;
Tell at your levee,° as the crowds approach,
To whom to nod, whom take into your coach,
Whom honor with your hand: to make remarks,
Who rules in Cornwall,° or who rules in Berks:
105 "This may be troublesome, is near the Chair;
That makes three Members,° this can choose a
      Mayor."
Instructed thus, you bow, embrace, protest,
Adopt him son, or cousin at the least,
Then turn about, and laugh at your own jest.
110   Or if your life be one continued treat,

82 **Anstis** King at Arms   85 **confounds** consumes   88 **poet's
day** the performance for the author's benefit   101 **levee**
morning reception   104 **Who . . . Cornwall** full of pocket
boroughs and of votes easily controlled for a price   106
makes . . . Members controls three pocket boroughs

If to live well means nothing but to eat;
Up, up! cries Gluttony, 'tis break of day,
Go drive the deer, and drag the finny prey;
With hounds and horns go hunt an appetite—
So Russel did, but could not eat at night,   *115*
Called happy dog the beggar at his door,
And envied thirst and hunger to the poor.
   Or shall we every decency confound,
Through taverns, stews, and bagnios° take our
     round,
Go dine with Chartres,° in each vice outdo   *120*
K—l's lewd cargo, or Ty—y's crew,°
From Latian sirens, French Circean feasts,
Return well travelled, and transformed to beasts,°
Or for a titled punk, or foreign flame,°
Renounce our country, and degrade our name?   *125*
   If, after all, we must with Wilmot° own,
The cordial drop of life is love alone,
And SWIFT cry wisely, "Vive la bagatelle!"°
The man that loves and laughs, must sure do well.
Adieu—if this advice appear the worst,   *130*
E'en take the counsel which I gave you first:
Or better precepts if you can impart,
Why do, I'll follow them with all my heart.

---

119 **bagnios** brothels 120 **Chartres** Francis Chartres, gambler, debauchee, supporter of Walpole, "a man infamous for all manner of vices" (Pope) 121 **K—l's . . . crew** The Earl of Kinnoull and the Baron Tyrawley were notoriously immoral; both ambassadors, in Turkey and Portugal. Tyrawley, Horace Walpole reported, returned from Portugal with "three wives and fourteen children." 123 **transformed to beasts** like Odysseus' crew on the island of Circe, where they forgot their homes and were turned into swine 124 **flame** (1) mistress (2) venereal disease 126 **Wilmot** the Earl of Rochester, wrote of love as "That cordial drop Heaven in our cup has thrown, / To make the nauseous draught of life go down." 128 **bagatelle** trifle, joke

EPILOGUE TO THE SATIRES

IN TWO DIALOGUES

(1738)

DIALOGUE I

Fr[iend]. Not twice a twelvemonth you appear
    in print,
And when it comes, the court see nothing in't.
You grow correct, that once with rapture writ,
And are, besides, too *moral* for a wit.
5   Decay of parts, alas! we all must feel—
Why now, this moment, don't I see you steal?
'Tis all from Horace; Horace long before ye
Said, "Tories called him Whig, and Whigs a Tory;"°
And taught his Romans, in much better meter,
10 "To laugh at fools who put their trust in Peter."°
    But Horace, sir, was delicate, was nice;
Bubo° observes, he lashed no sort of *vice:*
Horace would say, Sir Billy° *served the crown,*
Blunt° could *do business,* H—ggins° *knew the town;*

8 Cf. "Satire" II, i, 68.   10 Cf. "Satire" II, i, 40.   12 **Bubo** "Some
guilty person very fond of making such an observation" (Pope)   13
Sir Billy Sir William Yonge, a prominent Whig politician, of whom
Lord Hervey wrote, "His name was proverbially used to express
everything pitiful, corrupt, and contemptible."   14 **Blunt** Sir John,
director of the South Sea Company; upon its collapse he was
compelled to render his estate of almost £200,000.   14 **H—ggins**
John Huggins, warden of Fleet Prison; found guilty of extortion and
cruelty and tried for the murder of a prisoner, he was acquitted
because of the large number of prominent gentlemen who testified
on behalf of his character.

In Sappho° touch the *failings of the sex,*   *15*
In reverend bishops note some *small neglects,*
And own, the Spaniard° did a *waggish thing,*
Who cropped our ears, and sent them to the king.
His sly, polite, insinuating style
Could please at court, and make Augustus smile: *20*
An artful manager, that crept between
His friend and shame, and was a kind of *screen.*°
But 'faith your very friends will soon be sore;
Patriots° there are, who wish you'd jest no more—
And where's the glory? 'twill be only thought   *25*
The Great Man° never offered you a groat.
Go see Sir Robert——
   P.   See Sir Robert!—hum—
And never laugh—for all my life to come?
Seen him I have, but in his happier hour
Of social pleasure, ill-exchanged for power;   *30*
Seen him, uncumbered with the venal tribe,
Smile without art, and win without a bribe.
Would he oblige me? let me only find,
He does not think me what he thinks mankind.°
Come, come, at all I laugh he laughs, no doubt;   *35*
The only difference is, I dare laugh out.
   F.   Why yes: with *Scripture* still you may be free;
A horselaugh, if you please, at *honesty*;
A joke on Jekyl,° or some odd *Old Whig*

15 **Sappho** Cf. "Satire" II, i, 83. 17 **Spaniard** The captain of
a Spanish ship cut off the ear of Jenkins, an English ship
captain, and told him to carry it to his master, the King. This
helped to bring on war with Spain. 22 **screen** "A metaphor
peculiarly appropriated to a certain person in power" (Pope);
i.e., Sir Robert Walpole, who opposed all inquiries of
Parliament into public frauds and was accused of being a
"corrupt and all-screening minister." 24 **Patriots** a term
applied to those in opposition to Walpole and the court
"though some of them . . . had views too mean and interested
to deserve that name" (Pope) 26 **Great Man** a common
phrase for Walpole as first minister 34 **what he . . . mankind**
alluding to Walpole's reputed maxim, "All men have their
price." 39 **Jekyl** "a true Whig in his principles, and a man of
the utmost probity" (Pope)

40 Who never changed his principles, or wig:°
A patriot is a fool in every age,
Whom all Lord Chamberlains° allow the stage:
These nothing hurts; they keep their fashion still,
And wear their strange old virtue, as they will.

45 If any ask you, "Who's the man, so near
His prince, that writes in verse, and has his ear?"
Why, answer, Lyttleton,° and I'll engage
The worthy youth shall ne'er be in a rage:
But were his verses vile, his whisper base,

50 You'd quickly find him in Lord Fanny's° case.
Sejanus, Wolsey,° hurt not honest FLEURY,°
But well may put some statesmen in a fury.

Laugh then at any, but at fools or foes;
These you but anger, and you mend not those.
Laugh at your friends, and, if your friends are
55 sore,
So much the better, you may laugh the more;
To vice and folly to confine the jest,
Sets half the world, God knows, against the rest;
Did not the sneer of more impartial men

60 At sense and virtue, balance all again.
Judicious wits spread wide the ridicule,
And charitably comfort knave and fool.

P. Dear sir, forgive the prejudice of youth:
Adieu distinction, satire, warmth, and truth!

65 Come, harmless characters that no one hit;

40 **wig** The full-bottomed wig, which Jekyl still wore, had fallen
out of fashion among the younger generation. 42 **Lord Cham-
berlains** given power by the Licensing Act (1737) to forbid
performances of politically dangerous plays 47 **Lyttleton** "Sir
George Lyttleton, Secretary of the Prince of Wales, distin-
guished both for his writings and speeches in the spirit of lib-
erty" (Pope), a strong opponent of Walpole and friend of
Pope. 50 **Lord Fanny** Hervey, who appears as Sporus in the
"Epistle to Dr. Arbuthnot," lines 305–33. 51 **Sejanus, Wolsey**
"The one the wicked minister of Tiberius; the other, of Henry
VIII. The writers against the court usually bestowed these and
other odious names on the minister" (Pope) 51 **Fleury**
cardinal and minister to Louis XV of France, whom the Patri-
ots cited for wisdom and honesty

Come, Henley's oratory,° Osborn's wit!°
The honey dropping from Favonio's° tongue,
The flowers of Bubo, and the flow of Y—ng!°
The gracious dew of pulpit eloquence,°
And all the well-whipped cream of courtly sense,   70
That first was H—vy's, F—'s next, and then
The S—te's, and then H—vy's once again.
O come, that easy Ciceronian style,
So Latin, yet so English all the while,
As, though the pride of Middleton and Bland,°   75
All boys may read, and girls may understand!
Then might I sing without the least offense,
And all I sung should be the *Nation's Sense;*°
Or teach the melancholy Muse to mourn,
Hang the sad verse on Carolina's urn,   80

66 **Henley's oratory** John Henley, an eccentric and popular preacher who schooled gentlemen in elocution; cf. "Dunciad," III, 199. 66 **Osborn's wit** James Pitt, a political journalist and party hireling, wrote in defense of Walpole under many names, including Socrates and Francis Osborne. 67 **Favonio's** from Favonius, the gentle west wind 68 **Bubo . . . Y—ng** Bubb Dodington and Sir William Yonge, so coupled in "Epistle to Dr. Arbuthnot," line 280. Dodington was both pretentious and dishonest; Yonge was described by Lord Hervey as "talking eloquently without a meaning and expatiating agreeably upon nothing beyond any man . . . that ever had the gift of speech." 69 In this line and following Pope refers to some florid flattery which he believed Lord Hervey had composed. It was delivered by Henry Fox as a parliamentary address of condolence on Queen Caroline's death and became "The Senate's" (line 72) when Commons accepted and sent it to the King. It reappeared in the form of Hervey's Latin epitaph for the Queen. 75 **Middleton and Bland** Conyers Middleton, Cambridge theologian and librarian, was at work on a *Life of Cicero*, to be dedicated to Hervey in 1741. He helped to correct the Latin of Hervey's epitaph, which Pope described as "between Latin and English." Henry Bland, Provost of Eton, translated the last act of Addison's *Cato* into Latin and had it published through the friendship of Walpole. He may have been consulted on Hervey's epitaph as well. Both would represent men of learning used to give pretentious form to empty court flattery. 78 **Nation's Sense** court phrase for "consensus" or "official line"

And hail her passage to the realms of rest,
All parts performed, and *all* her children blest!°
So—satire is no more—I feel it die—
No *gazetteer*° more innocent than I—
85 And let, a-God's name, every fool and knave
Be graced through life, and flattered in his grave.
     F.   Why so? If satire knows its time and place,
You still may lash the greatest—in disgrace:
For merit will by turns forsake them all.
90 Would you know when? exactly when they fall.
But let all satire in all changes spare
Immortal S——k,° and grave De——re.°
Silent and soft, as saints remove to Heaven,
All ties dissolved, and every sin forgiven,
95 These may some gentle ministerial wing
Receive, and place forever near a king!
There, where no Passion, pride, or shame
        transport,
Lulled with the sweet nepenthe° of a court;
There, where no father's, brother's, friend's
        disgrace
Once break their rest, or stir them from their
100   place:°
But past the sense of human miseries,
All tears are wiped for ever from all eyes;°
No cheek is known to blush, no heart to throb,

---

82 Queen Caroline was reported to die without taking the last
sacrament and without being reconciled to her son, the Prince
of Wales.   84 **gazetteer** a journalist paid by the government
to present its case   92 **Immortal S——k** "A title given to
[Selkirk] by King James II. He was of the Bedchamber to King
William; he was so to King George I; he was so to King George
II" (Pope)   92 **grave De——re** John West, first Earl De La
Warr, an indefatigable supporter of Walpole, "very skillful in
all the forms of the House, in which he discharged himself
with great gravity" (Pope)   98 **nepenthe** a potion that brings
forgetfulness of grief or suffering   100 **place** with a pun upon
political appointment   102 Cf. Isaiah 25:8, "and the Lord God
will wipe away tears from off all faces" Here, as in preceding
lines, the moral obliviousness of the courtier is ironically
celebrated as a state of beatitude.

Save when they lose a question,° or a job.°
   P.   Good Heaven forbid, that I should blast
   their glory,   *105*
Who know how like Whig ministers to Tory,
And when three sovereigns died, could scarce be
   vext,
Considering what a *gracious Prince* was next.
Have I, in silent wonder, seen such things
As pride in slaves, and avarice in kings;   *110*
And at a peer or peeress shall I fret,
Who starves a sister, or forswears a debt?
Virtue, I grant you, is an empty boast;
But shall the dignity of *vice* be lost?
Ye Gods! shall Cibber's son° without rebuke,   *115*
Swear like a lord, or Rich° outwhore a duke?
A favorite's porter with his master vie,
Be bribed as often, and as often lie?
Shall Ward° draw contracts with a statesman's
   skill?
Or Japhet° pocket, like his Grace,° a Will?   *120*
Is it for Bond,° or Peter,° (paltry things)
To pay their debts, or keep their faith, like kings?
If Blount° dispatched himself, he played the man,
And so mayst thou, illustrious Passeran!°

---

104 **question** parliamentary motion 104 **job** opportunity for
personal profit or bribery 115 **Cibber's son** Colley Cibber's
son Theophilus, the actor; cf. "Dunciad," III, 142. 116 **Rich**
John Rich, theater manager; cf. "Dunciad," III, 261 ff. 119
Ward a forger expelled from Parliament; cf. "Dunciad," III,
34 120 **Japhet** Japhet Crook, convicted of forgery and fraud,
condemned to stand in the pillory, have his ears cut off and
his nose slit, forfeit his goods, and to be imprisoned for
life. 120 **his Grace** Archbishop Wake handed the will of
George I to his son, who suppressed it. 121 **Bond** Denis Bond,
who embezzled the funds of the Charitable Corporation
121 **Peter** Peter Walter, the moneylender, controlled many
peers and died leaving £300,000. 123 **Blount** a deist author
and suicide 124 **Passeran** Alberto Radicati, Count of
Passerano, a Piedmontese freethinker who fled to England,
where he wrote a notorious defense of suicide, for which the
translator and bookseller were also taken into custody.

125   But shall a printer,° weary of his life,
        Learn from their books, to hang himself and wife?
        This, this, my friend, I cannot, must not bear;
        Vice thus abused, demands a nation's care:
        This calls the Church to deprecate our Sin,
130   And hurls the thunder of the laws on *gin.*°
          Let modest Foster,° if he will, excel
        Ten metropolitans° in preaching well;
        A simple Quaker, or a Quaker's wife,
        Outdo Landaffe° in doctrine,—yea in life:
135   Let humble Allen,° with an awkward shame,
        Do good by stealth, and blush to find it fame.
        Virtue may choose the high or low degree,
        'Tis just alike to Virtue, and to me;
        Dwell in a monk, or light upon a king,
140   She's still the same, beloved, contented thing.
        Vice is undone, if she forgets her birth,
        And stoops from angels to the dregs of earth:
        But 'tis the *fall* degrades her to a whore;
        Let *greatness* own her, and she's mean no more:
145   Her birth, her beauty, crowds and courts confess,
        Chaste matrons praise her, and grave bishops bless;°
        In golden chains the willing world she draws,
        And hers the gospel is, and hers the laws,
        Mounts the tribunal, lifts her scarlet head,
150   And sees pale Virtue carted° in her stead.

---

125 **printer** as in fact happened in 1732 130 **gin** whose exorbitant use was unsuccessfully restrained by an Act of 1736 131 **Foster** Anabaptist minister and brilliant preacher whom Pope, it was reported, frequently went to hear. 132 **metropolitans** bishops 134 **Landaffe** "A poor bishopric in Wales, as poorly supplied" (Pope) 135 **Allen** Ralph Allen, friend of Pope and Fielding, reformer of postal services, famous for his philanthropy. 145–46 Alluding to Justinian's elevation of the prostitute Theodora as his empress, and perhaps also to Sir Robert Walpole's scandalous marriage in 1738 to Molly Skerrett, his mistress of many years and the mother of two of his children. By the following lines (149) the allusion expands to the Scarlet Whore of Revelations 17. 150 **carted** Prostitutes were punished by being exhibited from a cart.

Lo! at the wheels of her triumphal car,°
Old England's Genius, rough with many a scar,
Dragged in the dust! his arms hang idly round,
His flag inverted° trails along the ground!
Our youth, all liveried o'er with foreign gold,   *155*
Before her dance: behind her, crawl the old!
See thronging millions to the pagod° run,
And offer country, parent, wife, or son!
Hear her black trumpet through the land
    proclaim,
That "Not to be corrupted is the shame."   *160*
In soldier, churchman, patriot, man in power,
'Tis avarice all, ambition is no more!
See, all our nobles begging to be slaves!
See, all our fools aspiring to be knaves!
The wit of cheats, the courage of a whore,   *165*
Are what ten thousand envy and adore.
All, all look up, with reverential awe,
On crimes that 'scape, or triumph o'er the law:
While truth, worth, wisdom, daily they decry—
"Nothing is sacred now but villainy."   *170*
    Yet may this verse (if such a verse remain)
Show there was one who held it in disdain.

DIALOGUE II

    Fr[iend], 'Tis all a libel—Paxton° (sir) will say.
P. Not yet, my friend! tomorrow faith it may;
And for that very cause I print today.
How should I fret to mangle every line,
In reverence to the sins of *Thirty-nine!*   *5*
Vice with such giant strides comes on amain,
Invention strives to be before in vain;

151 **triumphal car** the conqueror's chariot   154 **flag inverted** a reference to Walpole's foreign policy of peace at any price   157 **pagod** (1) pagoda or shrine (2) idol (3) the name of a gold coin used in India   1 **Paxton** an official appointed to scan new publications for libel on the government

Feign what I will, and paint it e'er so strong,
Some rising genius sins up to my song.
10   F.   Yet none but you by name the guilty lash;
Even Guthry° saves half Newgate by a dash.
Spare then the person, and expose the vice.
P.   How, sir! not damn the sharper, but the dice?
Come on then, satire! general, unconfined,
15   Spread thy broad wing, and souse° on all the kind.
Ye statesmen, priests, of one religion all!
Ye tradesmen, vile, in army, court, or hall!°
Ye reverend atheists.   F.   Scandal! name them,
      who?
P.   Why that's the thing you bid me not to do.
20   Who starved a sister, who forswore a debt,
I never named; the town's inquiring yet.
The poisoning dame—   F.   You mean—
      P.   I don't.—   F.   You do.
P.   See, now I keep the secret, and not you!
The bribing statesman—   F.   Hold! too high
      you go.
P.   The bribed elector—   F.   There you stoop
25   too low.
P.   I fain would please you, if I knew with what:
Tell me, which knave is lawful game, which not?
Must great offenders, once escaped the crown,
Like royal harts, be never more run down?
30   Admit your law to spare the knight requires,
As beasts of nature may we hunt the squires?
Suppose I censure—you know what I mean—
To save a bishop, may I name a dean?°
F.   A dean, sir? no: his fortune is not made,
35   You hurt a man that's rising in the trade.
P.   If not the tradesman who set up today,
Much less the prentice who tomorrow may.

11 **Guthry** The chaplain of Newgate Prison, who published the
memoirs or confessions of criminals, often used no more than
the initials of their names. 15 **souse** swooping like a hawk
on its prey   17 **hall** Westminster Hall, the chief law court of
England   33 **dean** chief officer of a cathedral chapter, of lower
rank than a bishop

Down, down, proud satire! though a realm be
    spoiled,°
Arraign no mightier thief than wretched Wild;°
Or, if a court or country's made a job,°   40
Go drench° a pickpocket, and join the mob.
  But, sir, I beg you (for the love of vice!)
The matter's weighty, pray consider twice;
Have you less pity for the needy cheat,
The poor and friendless villain, than the great?   45
Alas! the small discredit of a bribe
Scarce hurts the lawyer, but undoes the scribe,°
Then better sure it charity becomes
To tax directors, who (thank God) have plums;°
Still better, ministers; or, if the thing   50
May pinch even there—why, lay it on a king.
  F.   Stop! stop!
  P.   Must satire, then, nor rise nor fall?
Speak out, and bid me blame no rogues at all.
  F.   Yes, strike that Wild, I'll justify the blow.
  P.   Strike? why, the man was hanged ten
    years ago: 55
Who now that obsolete example fears?
Even Peter° trembles only for his ears.
  F.   What, always Peter? Peter thinks you mad,
You make men desperate, if they once are bad:
Else might he take to virtue some years hence— 60
  P.   As S———k, if he lives, will love the
    Prince.°
  F.   Strange spleen to S———k!
  P.   Do I wrong the man?

38 **spoiled** despoiled   39 **Wild** Jonathan Wild, thief, fence, and
informer; hanged in 1725 (cf. line 55)   40 **made a job** used for
personal profit   41 **drench** a common punishment, either by
ducking or putting under a pump   47 **scribe** scrivener or law
clerk   49 **plums** large round sums, usually £100,000   57 **Peter**
Peter Walter (cf. "Dialogue," I, lines 10, 121), who just escaped
the pillory the year before   61 **As . . . Prince** Cf. "Dialogue,"
I, line 92 ff. Because of the enmity between the King and his
son, Selkirk must now hate the Prince of Wales, but as a true
courtier will love him when he becomes king.

God knows, I praise a courtier where I can.
When I confess, there is who feels for fame,
65 And melts to goodness, need I Scarborough° name?
Pleased let me own, in Esher's peaceful Grove°
(Where Kent° and Nature vie for Pelham's love)
The scene, the master, opening to my view,
I sit and dream I see my Craggs° anew!
70   Even in a bishop I can spy desert;
Secker° is decent, Rundle° has a heart,
Manners with candor are to Benson° given,
To Berkeley,° every virtue under heaven.
     But does the court a worthy man remove?
75 That instant, I declare, he has my love:
I shun his zenith, court his mild decline;
Thus Somers° once, and Halifax,° were mine.
Oft, in the clear, still mirror or retreat,
I studied Shrewsbury,° the wise and great:

65 **Scarborough** a steady adherent of the royal interest but esteemed by all parties for his honor and virtue   66 **Esher's . . . Grove** the estate in Surrey of Henry Pelham, a loyal ministerial Whig   67 **Kent** William Kent improved both the house and gardens at Esher. Kent, a friend of Pope, did much to promote the "natural" garden, and Esher was one of his finest works.   69 **Craggs** until his death in 1721 a neighbor and friend of Pope, who wrote, "There never lived a more worthy nature, a more disinterested mind, a more open and friendly temper."   71 **Secker** Thomas Secker, Bishop of Oxford, later Archbishop of Canterbury, famous for moderation, tolerance, and discretion   71 **Rundle** Thomas Rundle, Bishop of Derry, of whom Pope wrote, "I never saw a man so seldom whom I like so much."   72 **Benson** Martin Benson, Bishop of Gloucester   73 **Berkeley** George Berkeley, Bishop of Cloyne, philosopher, and friend of Swift and Pope   77 **Somers** John Lord Somers, Lord Keeper under William III. Pope knew him after his retirement and found him both "a consummate statesman" and "a man of learning and politeness."   77 **Halifax** Charles Montagu, first Earl of Halifax; statesman, poet, and patron, a supporter of Pope's translation of the *Iliad*   79 **Shrewsbury** Charles Talbot, Duke of Shrewsbury, minister in three reigns, ambassador to France, and Lord Lieutenant of Ireland

Carleton's° calm sense, and Stanhope's° noble flame,   80
Compared, and knew their generous end the same:
How pleasing Atterbury's° softer hour!
How shined the soul, unconquered in the Tower!
How can I Pulteney;° Chesterfield° forget,
While Roman spirit charms, and Attic wit: 85
Argyle,° the state's whole thunder born to wield,
And shake alike the senate and the field:
Or Wyndham,° just to freedom and the throne,
The master of our passions, and his own.
Names, which I long have loved, nor loved in vain,   90
Ranked with their friends, not numbered with
        their train;
And if yet higher° the proud list should end,
Still let me say! No follower, but a friend.
    Yet think not, friendship only prompts my lays;
I follow *virtue; where she shines, I praise:*   95
Point she to priest or elder, whig or tory,
Or round a Quaker's beaver, cast a glory.
I never (to my sorrow I declare)
Dined with the Man of Ross,° or my Lord Mayor.°

80 **Carleton** Henry Boyle, Baron Carleton, held many public offices, including President of the Council under George I.   80 **Stanhope** commander of the British forces in Spain, 1708, and active in foreign policy later   82 **Atterbury** Francis Atterbury, Bishop of Rochester, was imprisoned for correspondence with the Pretender in 1722. Pope testified in his behalf, but Atterbury was banished.   84 **Pulteney** William Pulteney was a leading opponent of Walpole and a brilliant speaker in Commons.   84 **Chesterfield** another opponent of Walpole and friend of Pope; later author of the famous *Letters to his Son*   86 **Argyle** earlier a general, later an influential convert to the opposition against Walpole   88 **Wyndham** a leader of the Tory opposition, a man of "the utmost judgment and temper" (Pope)   92 **yet higher** an allusion to Pope's friendship with the Prince of Wales   99 **Man of Ross** John Kyrle, celebrated by Pope in the "Epistle to Bathurst" (Moral Essay III) for the great public benefits he performed on an income of £500 a year   99 **my Lord Mayor** Sir John Barnard, a religious and modest man, a great example of both private and public virtue

Some, in their choice of friends (nay, look not
100   grave)
Have still a secret bias to a knave:
To find an honest man I beat about,
And love him, court him, praise him, in or out.
     F.   Then why so few commended?
     P.   Not so fierce;
105 Find you the virtue, and I'll find the verse.
But random praise—the task can ne'er be done;
Each mother asks it for her booby son,
Each widow asks it for *the best of men,*
For him she weeps, and him she weds again.
110 Praise cannot stoop, like satire, to the ground;
The number may be hanged, but not be crowned.
Enough for half the greatest of these days,
To scape my censure, not expect my praise.
Are they not rich? what more can they pretend?
115 Dare they to hope a poet for their friend?
What Richelieu° wanted, Louis scarce could gain,
And what young Ammon° wished, but wished in
     vain.
No power the muse's friendship can command;
No power, when virtue claims it, can withstand:
120 To Cato, Virgil paid one honest line;°
O let my country's friends illumine mine!
—What are you thinking?   F.   Faith, the
     thought's no sin,
I think your friends are out, and would be in.
     P.   If merely to come in, sir, they go out,
125 The way they take is strangely round about.
     F.   They too may be corrupted, you'll allow?
     P.   I only call those knaves who are so now.
Is that too little? Come then, I'll comply—

116 **Richelieu** (1585–1642) French cardinal, statesman, author;
principal minister of Louis XIII   117 **Ammon** Alexander the
Great envied Achilles the fame that Homer had given him.
120 **line** *Aeneid,* VIII, 670: "And far apart, the good, and Cato
giving them laws." This is probably Cato Uticensis, who upheld
republican ideals against the first triumvirate.

Spirit of Arnall!° aid me while I lie.
Cobham's° a coward, Polwarth° is a slave,   130
And Lyttleton° a dark, designing knave,
St. John° has ever been a wealthy fool—
But let me add, Sir Robert's° mighty dull,
Has never made a friend in private life,
And was, besides, a tyrant to his wife.   135
    But, pray, when others praise him, do I blame?
Call Verres, Wolsey,° any odius name?
Why rail they then, if but a wreath of mine,
Oh all-accomplished° St. John! deck thy shrine?
    What! shall each spur-galled hackney° of the
        day,   140
When Paxton° gives him double pots° and pay,
Or each new-pensioned sycophant, pretend
To break my windows if I treat a friend?°
Then wisely plead, to me they meant no hurt,
But 'twas my guest at whom they threw the dirt?   145
Sure, if I spare the minister, no rules

129 **Arnall** Cf. "Dunciad," II, 315. 130 **Cobham** a distin-
guished general discharged for protesting Walpole's actions,
thereafter a leading opposition Whig; a friend of Pope, to
whom *Moral Essay* I is addressed 130 **Polwarth** a disinter-
ested and respected statesman, opposed to but admired by
Walpole 131 **Lyttleton** an open leader of the opposition, a
patron of writers, to whom Fielding dedicated *Tom Jones* in
1749 132 **St. John** Henry, Viscount Bolingbroke, friend of
Pope and Swift, leader of the Tory government under Queen
Anne, and of the opposition to Walpole later; a man of learn-
ing and a brilliant orator, to whom Pope addressed the *Essay
on Man* 133 **Sir Robert** Walpole, here ironically dispraised in
the "spirit" of the previous lines; Walpole was personally at-
tractive and totally indifferent to his first wife's infideli-
ties. 137 **Verres, Wolsey** Roman and English models of men
who used their office to gain great personal wealth 139 **all-
accomplished** "Lord Bolingbroke is something superior to any
thing I have seen in human nature" (Pope). 140 **hackney** hack
writer 141 **Paxton** not only a censor (line 1) but director of
Walpole's journalistic campaigns 141 **pots** of ale 143 **treat a
friend** as was done at Twickenham when Pope was entertaining
Bolingbroke and Bathurst

Of honor bind me, not to maul his tools;
Sure, if they cannot cut, it may be said
His saws are toothless, and his hatchet's lead.
150   It angered Turenne,° once upon a day,
To see a footman kicked that took his pay:
But when he heard the affront the fellow gave,
Knew one a man of honor, one a knave;
The prudent general turned it to a jest,
155 And begged, he'd take the pains to kick the rest.
Which not at present having time to do—
    F. Hold, sir! for God's sake, where's the
        affront to you?
Against your worship when had S————k writ?
Or P—ge° poured forth the torrent of his wit?
160 Or grant the bard whose distich all commend
[*In Power a servant, out of Power a friend*]°
To W—le guilty of some venial sin,
What's that to you who ne'er was out nor in?
    The Priest whose flattery bedropped the crown,
165 How hurt he you? he only stained the gown.
And how did, pray, the florid youth offend,
Whose speech you took, and gave it to a friend?°
    P. Faith, it imports not much from whom it came;
Whoever borrowed, could not be to blame,
170 Since the whole House did afterwards the same.
Let courtly wits to wits afford supply,
As hog to hog in huts of Westphaly;
If one, through nature's bounty or his lord's,
Has what the frugal, dirty soil affords,
175 From him the next receives it, thick, or thin,°
As pure a mess almost as it came in;
The blessed benefit, not there confined,
Drops to the third, who nuzzles close behind;
From tail to mouth, they feed and they carouse:

150 **Turenne** (1611–75) Marshal of France   159 **P—ge** Judge
Page; cf. "Satire," II, i, 82.   161 A line from Bubb Dodington's
Epistle to . . . Walpole, published anonymously in 1726.
166–67 Cf. "Dialogue," I, 71–72.   175–80 An earlier couplet
of 1715 reads "Now wits gain praise by copying other wits/As
one hog lives on what another sh——."

The last full fairly gives it to the *House*.   *180*
   F.   This filthy simile, this beastly line,
Quite turns my stomach—
   P.   So does flattery mine;
And all your courtly civet cats can vent,
Perfume° to you, to me is excrement.
But hear me further—Japhet,° 'tis agreed,   *185*
Writ not, and Chartres° scarce could write or read,
In all the courts of Pindus° guiltless quite;
But pens can forge, my friend, that cannot write.
And must no egg in Japhet's face be thrown,
Because the deed he forged was not my own?   *190*
Must never patriot then declaim at gin,
Unless, good man! he has been fairly in?
No zealous pastor blame a failing spouse,
Without a staring reason° on his brows?
And each blasphemer quite escape the rod,   *195*
Because the insult's not on man, but God?
   Ask you what provocation I have had?
The strong antipathy of good to bad.
When truth or virtue an affront endures,
The affront is mine, my friend, and should be
     yours.   *200*
Mine, as a foe professed to false pretense,
Who think a coxcomb's honor like his sense;
Mine, as a friend to every worthy mind;
And mine as man, who feel for all mankind.°
   F.   You're strangely proud.   *205*
   P.   So proud, I am no slave:
So impudent, I own myself no knave:
So odd, my country's ruin makes me grave.
Yes, I am proud; I must be proud to see

---

184 **Perfume** made from a substance extracted from a pouch
near the sexual organs of the civet cat   185 **Japhet** Crook the
forger; cf. "Dialogue," I, 120 and "Epistle to Dr. Arbuthnot,"
line 363.   186 **Chartres,** Francis; debauchee, gambler, usurer;
cf. "Epistle," I, vi, 120.   187 **Pindus** mountain in Thessaly, a
seat of the Muses   194 **staring reason** cuckold's horns   204
From Terence's famous line: "I am a man, and I think nothing
human indifferent to me."

  Men not afraid of God, afraid of me:
210 Safe from the bar, the pulpit, and the throne,
  Yet touched and shamed by ridicule alone.
   O sacred weapon! left for truth's defense,
  Sole dread of folly, vice, and insolence!
  To all but heaven-directed hands denied,
215 The muse may give thee, but the gods must guide.
  Reverent I touch thee! but with honest zeal;
  To rouse the watchmen of the public weal,
  To virtue's work provoke the tardy Hall,°
  And goad the prelate slumbering in his stall.
220 Ye tinsel insects! whom a court maintains,
  That count your beauties only by your stains,
  Spin all your cobwebs o'er the eye of day!
  The muse's wing shall brush you all away:
  All his Grace preaches, all his lordship sings,
225 All that makes saints of queens, and gods of kings,
  All, all but truth, drops deadborn from the press,
  Like the last gazette, or the last address.°
   When black ambition stains a public cause,
  A monarch's sword when mad vainglory draws,
230 Not Waller's wreath° can hide the nation's scar,
  Nor Boileau turn the feather to a star.°
  Not so, when diademed with rays divine,
  Touched with the flame that breaks from virtue's
    shrine,
  Her priestess Muse forbids the good to die,
235 And opes the Temple of Eternity.
  There, other trophies deck the truly brave,
  Than such as Anstis° casts into the grave;

218 **Hall** Westminster Hall, as the seat of justice   227 **address**
the formal reply of Parliament to the King's opening speech
230 **Waller's wreath** Edmund Waller's panegyrics to Oliver
Cromwell   231 **feather . . . star** Boileau, in his celebration of
Louis XIV's conquest of the Lowlands, imitated Pindar's
boldness by making the white feather in Louis's hat into a star
or comet fatal to his enemies. Here the contrast is between
this rhetorical "star" and the "rays divine" of line 232.   237
Anstis the chief herald at arms, who devised symbols of honor
that were often cast into the grave of great peers

Far other stars° than * and * * wear,
And may descend to Mordington from Stair:°
(Such as on Hough's unsullied miter shine,   240
Or beam, good Digby, from a heart like thine).°
Let Envy howl, while Heaven's whole chorus
    sings,
And bark at honor not conferred by kings;
Let Flattery sickening see the incense rise,
Sweet to the world, and grateful to the skies: 245
Truth guards the poet, sanctifies the line,
And makes immortal, verse as mean as mine.
    Yes, the last pen for freedom let me draw,
When truth stands trembling on the edge of law;
Here, last of Britons! let your names be read;   250
Are none, none living? let me praise the dead,
And for that cause which made your fathers shine,
Fall by the votes of their degenerate line.
    F.   Alas! alas! pray end what you began,
And write next winter more *Essays on Man*.   255

238 **stars** symbols of the Order of the Garter; supply the names
of the King and Prince of Wales, George and Frederick   239
to . . . Stair The Earl of Stair was a distinguished soldier and
envoy. Lord Mordington or his wife kept a gambling
house. 240–41 "The one [Bishop Hough] an assertor of the
Church of England in opposition to the false measures of King
James II; the other [Lord Digby] as firmly attached to the
cause of that king; both acting out of principle, and equally
men of honor and virtue" (Pope)

THE DUNCIAD

TO DR. JONATHAN SWIFT

(1727–1743)

BOOK THE FIRST

THE Mighty Mother,° and her Son,° who brings
The Smithfield Muses° to the ear of kings,
I sing. Say you, her instruments the great!°
Called to this work by Dulness, Jove, and Fate;
5   You by whose care, in vain decried and curst,
Still Dunce the Second° reigns like Dunce the
        First;
Say, how the goddess bade Britannia sleep,
And poured her spirit o'er the land and deep.
    In eldest time, ere mortals writ or read,

1 **Mighty Mother** the goddess Dulness, with suggestions of the
Magna Mater, known as Cybele in Asia and associated with
the Greek Rhea; a goddess of the powers of nature, especially
wild nature, she was worshiped in erotic and often ecstatic rites
inducing prophetic rapture and insensibility to pain. 1 **Son**
originally Lewis Theobald, altered to the shamelessly incompe-
tent poet laureate, Colley Cibber, in the final version   2 **Smith-
field Muses** Smithfield was the scene of the popular carnival of
Bartholomew Fair. The poem shows "the taste of the rabble"
brought west (as Troy's culture was borne by Aeneas to Italy)
to rule the arts at the court of George I and II.   3 **great** aristo-
crats, men of influence, particularly the Whigs who helped
bring the Hanoverians to the throne   6 **Dunce the Second**
George II succeeded his father in 1727.

Ere Pallas° issued from the Thunderer's head,   10
Dulness o'er all possessed her ancient right,°
Daughter of Chaos and eternal Night:°
Fate in their dotage this fair idiot gave,
Gross as her sire, and as her mother grave,
Laborious, heavy, busy, bold, and blind,   15
She ruled, in native anarchy, the mind.°
   Still her old empire to restore she tries,
For, born a goddess, Dulness never dies.
   O thou! whatever title please thine ear,
Dean, Drapier, Bickerstaff, or Gulliver!°   20
Whether thou choose Cervantes' serious air,°
Or laugh and shake in Rabelais' easy chair,°
Or praise the court, or magnify° mankind,
Or thy grieved country's copper chains° unbind;
From thy Boeotia° though her power retires,   25
Mourn not, my SWIFT, at aught our realm acquires,
Here pleased behold her mighty wings outspread
To hatch a new Saturnian° age of lead.
   Close to those walls° where Folly holds her
      throne,

10 **Pallas** Athene sprang full-grown from the head of Zeus.
11 **her ancient right** as one of the Titans who ruled before the
sky god, Zeus, gained power and imposed his order upon the
universe   12 **Chaos . . . Night** Chaos was, according to Hesiod,
the progenitor of all the gods. In *Paradise Lost,* II, Chaos and
Night rule that portion of the universe that God has not
ordered.   16 **the mind** Dulness is both an external power and an
internal, the ruler of the mind before it is ordered by reason   20
Dean . . . Gulliver The last three are the guises in which Swift
wrote ironically; he became dean of St. Patrick's Cathedral,
Dublin, in 1713.   21 **Cervantes' . . . air** the ironic style of Don
Quixote   22 **Rabelais' . . . chair** the comic fantasies of
Gargantua and Pantagruel   23 **praise . . . magnify** with ironic
reference to Swift's often scathing satire   24 **copper chains** Swift
wrote *The Drapier's Letters* in 1720 to free Ireland of a debased
and possibly inflationary copper coinage imposed by Sir Robert
Walpole, the Prime Minister of England.   25 **Boeotia** for the
Greeks a land without culture, although the home of a few great
men; here Ireland   28 **Saturnian** traditionally the Golden Age;
but Saturn was also a symbol of lead; see line IV, 16.   29 **those
walls** Bedlam Hospital, the lunatic asylum

And laughs to think Monroe° would take her
30 down,
Where o'er the gates, by his famed father's hand,
Great Cibber's brazen, brainless brothers° stand;
One cell there is, concealed from vulgar eye,
The Cave of Poverty and Poetry.
35 Keen, hollow winds howl through the bleak recess,
Emblem of music° caused by emptiness.
Hence bards, like Proteus° long in vain tied down,
Escape in monsters, and amaze the town.
Hence Miscellanies spring, the weekly boast
40 Of Curll's° chaste press, and Lintot's rubric post.°
Hence hymning Tyburn's° elegiac lines,
Hence Journals,° Medleys, Mercuries, Magazines:
Sepulchral lies,° our holy walls to grace,
And New Year Odes,° and all the Grubstreet°
  race.
45 In clouded majesty here Dulness shone;
Four guardian virtues, round, support her throne:
Fierce champion Fortitude, that knows no fears
Of hisses, blows, or want, or loss of ears:°
Calm Temperance, whose blessings those partake
50 Who hunger and who thirst for scribbling sake:
Prudence, whose glass° presents the approaching
  jail:

30 **Monroe** a physician there 32 **brothers** statues designed by
Colley Cibber's father, a sculptor (actually of stone, not
bronze) 36 **music** explained by an editor as "bowel
music" 37 **Proteus** The old man of the sea, who knew all
things, could assume any shape he wished to elude men's grasp
and questioning. 40 **Curll's** Edmund Curll, fined for
publishing obscene books 40 **Lintot's . . . post** another
bookseller, who posted title pages printed in red letters
41 **Tyburn** the scene of the gallows, where the condemned
criminals might sing psalms; elegies, often satirical, were
published at their death. 42 **Journals,** etc. names of popular
periodicals 43 **lies** flattering epitaphs inscribed on walls of
churches 44 **New Year Odes** composed by the poet
laureate 44 **Grubstreet** center of hack writing 48 **loss of ears**
an old penalty for seditious writing; see I, 103n. 51 **glass**
telescope

Poetic Justice, with her lifted scale,
Where, in nice° balance, truth with gold she
    weighs,
And solid pudding against empty praise.
  Here she beholds the chaos dark and deep,   55
Where nameless somethings° in their causes sleep,
Till genial Jacob,° or a warm third day,°
Call forth each mass, a poem, or a play:
How hints, like spawn, scarce quick° in embryo
    lie,
How newborn nonsense first is taught to cry,   60
Maggots° half-formed in rhyme exactly meet;
And learn to crawl upon poetic feet.°
Here one poor word an hundred clenches° makes,
And ductile° Dulness new meanders takes;
There motley° images her fancy strike,   65
Figures ill paired, and similes unlike.
She sees a mob of metaphors advance,
Pleased with the madness of the mazy dance:
How tragedy and comedy embrace;
How farce and epic get a jumbled race;   70
How Time himself stands still at her command,
Realms shift their place, and ocean turns to land.
Here gay description Egypt° glads with showers,
Or gives to Zembla° fruits, to Barca° flowers;
Glittering with ice here hoary hills are seen,   75
There painted° valleys of eternal green,
In cold December fragrant chaplets° blow,°
And heavy harvests nod beneath the snow.

53 **nice** precise   56 **somethings** unformed things not yet fully
realized   57 **Jacob** Jacob Tonson, the publisher   57 **warm . . .
day** The proceeds of the third performance went to the
playwright. A "warm" third day was a profitable one; but
"warm" also refers to the incubation process. 59 **quick**
alive   61 **Maggots** (1) grubs (2) foolish whimsies   62 **feet** also
referring to versification 63 **clenches** puns 64 **ductile**
fluid   65 **motley** varicolored, like a fool's costume   73 **Egypt**
Egypt has almost no rainfall but depends on the Nile.   74
Zembla Nova Zembla near the Arctic circle   74 **Barca** Libyan
desert   76 **painted** bright-colored   77 **chaplets** garlands
77 **blow** blossom

All these, and more, the cloud-compelling° queen
80 Beholds through fogs, that magnify the scene.
She, tinselled o'er in robes of varying hues,
With self-applause her wild creation views;
Sees momentary monsters rise and fall,
And with her own fool's colors gilds them all.
85   'Twas on the day when * * rich and grave,°
Like Cimon,° triumphed both on land and wave:
(Pomps without guilt, of bloodless swords and
        maces,
Glad chains,° warm furs, broad banners, and
        broad faces)
Now night descending, the proud scene was o'er,
90 But lived, in Settle's° numbers, one day more.
Now mayors and shrieves° all hushed and satiate
        lay,
Yet ate, in dreams, the custard of the day;
While pensive poets painful vigils keep,
Sleepless themselves, to give their readers sleep.
95 Much to the mindful queen the feast recalls
What city swans° once sung within the walls;
Much she revolves their arts, their ancient praise,
And sure succession down from Heywood's° days.
She saw, with joy, the line immortal run,
100 Each sire impressed and glaring in his son:
So watchful Bruin forms, with plastic° care,
Each growing lump, and brings it to a bear.
She saw old Prynne in restless Daniel° shine,

79 **cloud-compelling** Homer's term for Zeus   85 Supply
Thorold, the Lord Mayor of London, whose annual procession
to Westminster by land and water has just taken place.   86
Cimon Athenian victor at Salamis   88 **chains** i.e., of office,
therefore likely to make one "glad"   90 **Settle** Elkanah Settle,
Poet to the City of London (a small-scale counterpart of the
court poet laureate), composed celebrations of the Lord
Mayor.   91 **shrieves** sheriffs   96 **swans** poets   98 **Heywood's**
John Heywood in the reign of Henry VIII   101 **plastic**
shaping   103 **Prynne . . . Daniel** William Prynne (in 1633) and
Daniel Defoe (in 1703) were both pilloried for seditious
writing. Prynne lost his ears.

And Eusden eke out Blackmore's° endless line;
She saw slow Philips creep like Tate's° poor page,   *105*
And all the mighty mad in Dennis° rage.
    In each she marks her image full exprest,
But chief in Bays's° monster-breeding breast;
Bays, formed by nature stage and town to bless,
And act, and be, a coxcomb with success.   *110*
Dulness with transport eyes the lively dunce,
Remembering she herself was Pertness once.
Now (shame to Fortune!) an ill run at play°
Blanked his bold visage, and a thin third day:
Swearing and supperless the hero sate,   *115*
Blasphemed his gods, the dice, and damned his
       fate;
Then gnawed his pen, then dashed it on the
       ground,
Sinking from thought to thought, a vast profound!
Plunged for his sense, but found no bottom there,
Yet wrote and floundered on, in mere despair.°   *120*
Round him much embryo, much abortion lay,
Much future ode, and abdicated play;
Nonsense precipitate,° like running lead,
That slipped through cracks and zigzags of the
       head;
All that on folly frenzy could beget,   *125*
Fruits of dull heat, and sooterkins° of wit.
Next, o'er his books his eyes began to roll,
In pleasing memory of all he stole,

104 **Eusden . . . Blackmore** Laurence Eusden, Cibber's
predecessor as poet laureate and a reputed alcoholic.
Blackmore was court physician to William III and a very
copious poet.   105 **Philips . . . Tate** two weak poets, Ambrose
Philips and Nahum Tate, once poet laureate   106 **Dennis** Not
only a furious critic, John Dennis admired the sublime and the
poet's "divine madness."   108 **Bays's** so called for the bays or
laurel crown 113 **play** gambling 119–20 reminiscent of
Satan's flight through Chaos in *Paradise Lost,* II 123
precipitate in hurried motion 126 **sooterkins** little animals
supposedly bred in ladies by the small stoves placed under
their petticoats in winter

How here he sipped, how there he plundered
  snug°
130 And sucked all o'er, like an industrious bug.
Here lay poor Fletcher's° half-eat scenes, and here
The frippery° of crucified Molière;
There hapless Shakespeare, yet of Tibbald° sore,
Wished he had blotted° for himself before.
135 The rest on outside merit° but presume,
Or serve (like other fools) to fill a room;
Such with their shelves as due proportion hold,
Or their fond parents dressed in red and gold;
Or where the pictures for the page atone,
140 And Quarles° is saved by beauties not his own.
Here swells the shelf with Ogilby° the great,
There, stamped with arms, Newcastle° shines
  complete:
Here all his suffering brotherhood retire,
And 'scape the martyrdom of jakes° and fire:
145 A Gothic library! of Greece and Rome
Well purged, and worthy Settle, Banks, and
  Broome.°
  But, high above, more solid learning shone,
The classics of an age that heard of none;
There Caxton slept, with Wynkyn° at his side,

129 **snug** safely   131 **Fletcher** Sir John Fletcher, the contempo-
rary of Shakespeare   132 **frippery** cast-off clothes or fin-
ery   133 **Tibbald** Lewis Theobald edited Shakespeare and
emended the text heavily.   134 **blotted** The tradition was that
Shakespeare "never blotted a line."   135 **outside merit** not for
use but display, because they fit the shelves (line 137), are
lavishly bound (line 138) or illustrated (line 139)   140 **Quarles**
Francis Quarles designed emblems, others' pictures with his
poetic interpretations. Cf. "Rape of the Lock," I,
148.   141 **Ogilby** voluminous translator of Homer and
Virgil   142 **Newcastle** The Duchess of Newcastle produced
twelve large volumes.   144 **jakes** the privy, where old paper
found its last use   146 **Settle . . . Broome** poetic counterparts
of Cibber   149 **Caxton . . . Wynkyn** William Caxton and Wyn-
kyn de Worde were printers before the full revival of learning
in Tudor England.

One clasped in wood, and one in strong cowhide; *150*
There, saved by spice, like mummies, many a year,
Dry bodies of divinity appear:
De Lyra° there a dreadful front extends,
And here the groaning shelves Philemon° bends.
  Of these, twelve volumes, twelve of amplest
    size,   *155*
Redeemed from tapers and defrauded pies,°
Inspired he seizes: these an altar raise:
An hecatomb° of pure unsullied lays
That altar crowns: a folio commonplace°
Founds the whole pile, of all his works the base: *160*
Quartos, octavos, shape the lessening° pyre;
A twisted Birthday Ode completes the spire.
  Then he: "Great Tamer of all human art!
First in my care, and ever at my heart;
Dulness! whose good old cause I yet defend,   *165*
With whom my Muse began, with whom shall end;
E'er since Sir Fopling's periwig° was praise,
To the last honors of the butt° and bays:
O thou! of business the directing soul!
To this our head like bias to the bowl,°   *170*
Which, as more ponderous, made its aim more
    true,
Obliquely waddling to the mark in view:
O! ever gracious to perplexed mankind,
Still spread a healing mist before the mind;
And lest we err by wit's wild dancing light,°   *175*

153 **De Lyra** His front (an epic term for brow) extends to five
volumes of commentaries. 154 **Philemon** Philemon Holland,
voluminous Elizabethan translator 156 **tapers . . . pies** Old
paper was used to line candlesticks and bakers' tins. 158
hecatomb sacrifice of a hundred oxen 159 **commonplace** book
in which one collected notes and quotations from reading 161
lessening pyramidal, topped by the laureate's birthday ode to
the King (line 162) 167 **periwig** the full wig worn by Cibber
as actor in his first play 168 **butt** The laureate was paid
annually with a butt of wine. 170 **bowl** bowling ball
175 **wild . . . light** The will-o'-the-wisp often led men to
destruction.

Secure us kindly in our native night.
Or, if to wit a coxcomb make pretense,
Guard the sure barrier between that and sense;
Or quite unravel all the reasoning thread,
180 And hang some curious cobweb in its stead!
As, forced from wind-guns,° lead itself can fly,
And ponderous slugs cut swiftly through the sky;
As clocks to weight their nimble motion owe,
The wheels above urged° by the load below:
185 Me emptiness and Dulness could inspire,
And were my elasticity° and fire.
Some demon stole my pen (forgive the offense)
And once betrayed me into common sense:
Else all my prose and verse were much the same,
190 This, prose on stilts, that, poetry fallen lame.
Did on the stage my fops appear confined?°
My life gave ampler lessons to mankind.
Did the dead letter unsuccessful prove?
The brisk example never failed to move.
195 Yet sure had Heaven decreed to save the state,
Heaven had decreed these works a longer date.
Could Troy° be saved by any single hand,
This gray-goose weapon° must have made her
     stand.
What can I now? my Fletcher cast aside,
200 Take up the Bible,° once my better guide?
Or tread the path by venturous heroes trod,
This box° my thunder, this right hand my God?
Or chaired at White's° amidst the doctors° sit,
Teach oaths to gamesters, and to nobles wit?
205 Or bidst thou rather party to embrace?
(A friend to party thou, and all her race;
'Tis the same rope at different ends they twist;

---

181 **wind-guns** air rifles   184 **urged** driven   186 **elasticity** propelling force   191 **confined** restrained   197 **Troy** another echo (see note to I, 2) of the parallel of Cibber and Aeneas   198 **weapon** his quill pen   200 **Bible** Cibber's father meant him for the clergy.   202 **box** dice box   203 **White's** a club for gambling   203 **doctors** a term for loaded dice, with suggestions of Jesus in the temple

To Dulness Ridpath is as dear as Mist.)°
Shall I, like Curtius,° desperate in my zeal,
O'er head and ears plunge for the commonweal?   210
Or rob Rome's ancient geese° of all their glories,
And cackling save the monarchy of Tories?
Hold—to the Minister° I more incline;
To serve his cause, O Queen! is serving thine.
And see! thy very gazetteers° give o'er,   215
Even Ralph repents, and Henley° writes no more.
What then remains? Ourself. Still, still remain
Cibberian° forehead, and Cibberian brain.
This brazen brightness, to the squire so dear;
This polished hardness, that reflects the peer;   220
This arch absurd, that wit and fool delights;
This mess, tossed up of Hockley Hole° and
    White's;
Where dukes and butchers join to wreathe my
    crown,
At once the bear and fiddle° of the town.
    "O born in sin, and forth in folly brought!   225
Works damned, or to be damned! (your father's
    fault)
Go, purified by flames ascend the sky,
My better and more Christian progeny!°
Unstained, untouched, and yet in maiden sheets;
While all your smutty sisters° walk the streets.   230

208 **Ridpath . . . Mist** one a Whig, the other a Tory journalist
209 **Curtius** the legendary hero who leaped into a chasm to
save Rome   211 **geese** They warned the Romans in the
Capitol of the approach of the Gauls.   213 **Minister** Sir Robert
Walpole, the Whig Prime Minister   215 **gazetteers** hireling
political journalists   216 **Ralph . . . Henley** both writers in the
pay of Walpole, against whom James Ralph had turned   218
Cibberian with echoes of Milton's "Cimmerian darkness"; see
note to III, 4.   222 **Hockley Hole** scene of bear-baiting, often
preceded by playing on the fiddle (line 224)   224 **fiddle** also a
jester   228 **more . . . progeny** Cibber wrote: "My muse and my
spouse were equally prolific." His son Theophilus and daughter
Charlotte were both notorious.   230 **smutty sisters** copies of
his works bound and offered for sale

Ye shall not beg, like gratis-given Bland,°
Sent with a pass, and vagrant through the land;
Not sail, with Ward,° to ape-and-monkey climes,
Where vile Mundungus° trucks° for viler rhymes:
235 Not sulphur-tipped emblaze an alehouse fire;
Not wrap up oranges, to pelt your sire!°
O! pass more innocent, in infant state,
To the mild limbo of our father Tate:
Or peaceably forgot, at once be blessed
240 In Shadwell's° bosom with eternal rest!
Soon to that mass of nonsense to return,
Where things destroyed are swept to things
        unborn."
    With that, a tear (portentous sign of grace!)
Stole from the master of the sevenfold° face:
245 And thrice he lifted high the birthday brand,
And thrice he dropped it from his quivering hand;
Then lights the structure, with averted eyes:
The rolling smoke involves° the sacrifice.
The opening clouds disclose each work by turns,
250 Now flames the Cid, and now Perolla burns;
Great Caesar roars, and hisses in the fires;
King John in silence modestly expires:
No merit now the dear Nonjuror claims,
Molière's old stubble in a moment flames.°
255 Tears gushed again, as from pale Priam's eyes
When the last blaze sent Ilion to the skies.
    Roused by the light, old Dulness heaved the
        head,

231 **Bland** His pamphlets for Walpole were sent post-free to
all towns in England. 233 **Ward** Ned Ward's popular works
were widely sold in the colonies. 234 **Mundungus** cheap
tobacco 234 **trucks** is bartered 236 **pelt your sire** Oranges
were sold in theatres and often thrown at actors. 240
Shadwell's Thomas Shadwell, like Tate, was once poet
laureate. Cf. Luke 16:22. 244 **sevenfold** because of (1) actor's
changes (2) shamelessness 248 **involves** enfolds 250–54 **Now
flames . . . flames** a series of references to Cibber's plays, many
of them adaptations

Then snatched a sheet of Thulè° from her bed;
Sudden she flies, and whelms it o'er the pyre;
Down sink the flames, and with a hiss expire.   260
 Her ample presence fills up all the place;
A veil of fogs dilates° her awful face:
Great in her charms! as when on shrieves and
        mayors
She looks, and breathes herself into their airs.
She bids him wait her to her sacred dome:°   265
Well pleased he entered, and confessed his home.
So spirits ending their terrestrial race,
Ascend, and recognize their native place.
This the Great Mother° dearer held than all
The clubs of quidnuncs,° or her own Guildhall:°   270
Here stood her opium, here she nursed her owls,°
And here she planned the imperial seat of fools.
 Here to her chosen all her works she shows;
Prose swelled to verse, verse loitering into prose:
How random thoughts now meaning chance to find,   275
Now leave all memory of sense behind:
How prologues into prefaces° decay,
And these to notes are frittered quite away:
How index learning turns no student pale,
Yet holds the eel of science by the tail:°   280

258 **Thulè** a poem by Ambrose Philips whose title designates
the northernmost region of earth; Pope is alluding to the
"coldness and heaviness" of Philips' writing as well as to the
wet sheets of a newly printed book.   262 **dilates** magnifies, as
in I, 80   265 **dome** the Cave of Poverty and Poetry (I, 34)   269
Great Mother See note to I, 1.   270 **quidnuncs** gossips,
newsmongers; based on *quid nunc*, what news?   270 **her own
Guildhall** any meeting place of a guild; here with reference to
the famous one in the City of London   271 **owls** the bird of
Pallas Athene and a symbol of wisdom; but here, in its other
traditional sense, as a bird of the night, unclean and stupidly
solemn   277 **prologues into prefaces** from verse prologues,
often witty, into prose prefaces, notoriously verbose   279–80
index learning . . . tail "The most accomplished way of using
books at present is . . . to get a thorough insight into the index,
by which the whole book is governed and turned, like fishes
by the tail" (Swift, *A Tale of a Tub,* 1704).

How, with less reading° than makes felons 'scape,
Less human genius than God gives an ape,
Small thanks to France, and none to Rome or
     Greece,
A past, vamped,° future, old, revived, new piece,
'Twixt Plautus, Fletcher, Shakespeare, and
285   Corneille,
Can make a Cibber, Tibbald, or Ozell.°
    The goddess then, o'er his anointed head,
With mystic words, the sacred opium shed.
And lo! her bird (a monster of a fowl,
290 Something betwixt a Heidegger° and owl)
Perched on his crown. "All hail! and hail again,
My son! the promised land expects thy reign.
Know, Eusden° thirsts no more for sack or praise;
He sleeps among the dull of ancient days;
295 Safe, where no critics damn, no duns° molest,
Where wretched Withers, Ward, and Gildon° rest,
And highborn Howard,° more majestic sire,
With fool of quality° completes the quire.°
Thou, Cibber! thou, his Laurel shalt support,°
300 Folly, my son, has still a friend at court.
Lift up° your gates, ye princes, see him come!

281 **less reading** "Benefit of clergy" freed those clergymen who
could prove their ability to read from trial in secular courts
for felonies; this privilege was extended to laymen for many
offenses.   284 **vamped** revamped   286 **Cibber . . . Ozell** all
three minor playwrights given to free but feeble use of others'
works   290 **Heidegger** a Swiss, famous for his ugliness, who
was Master of the Revels under George II and manager of a
London opera house. The not-quiteness of this creature recalls
I, 284.   293 **Eusden** See note to I, 104.   295 **duns** bill collectors
296 **Withers . . . Gildon** minor poets now dead   297 **Howard**
known as "foolish Ned," author of six plays and a much
ridiculed epic poem   298 **quality** aristocratic rank; either
Howard or John Lord Hervey, recently dead (for whom see
notes to "Epistle to Dr. Arbuthnot," line 305)   298 **quire**
choir; but also the collection of pages, since all bad poets are so
much paper   299 **his Laurel . . . support** shall inherit Eusden's
laureateship   301 **Lift up** Cf. Psalms 24:7 "Lift up your heads,
O ye gates; and be ye lift up, ye everlasting doors; and the
King of glory shall come in."

Sound, sound, ye viols; be the catcall dumb!
Bring, bring the madding bay, the drunken
    vine;
The creeping, dirty, courtly ivy° join.
And thou! his aide-de-camp, lead on my sons,   *305*
Light-armed with points,° antitheses, and puns.
Let Bawdry, Billingsgate, my daughters dear,
Support his front, and oaths bring up the rear:
And under his, and under Archer's° wing,
Gaming and Grubstreet skulk behind the King.   *310*
   "O! when shall rise a monarch all our own,
And I, a nursing mother, rock the throne;
'Twixt prince and people close the curtain draw,
Shade him from light, and cover him from law;
Fatten the courtier, starve the learnèd band,   *315*
And suckle armies,° and dry-nurse the land:
Till senates nod to lullabies divine,
And all be sleep, as at an ode of thine."
   She ceased. Then swells the Chapel Royal°
    throat:
"God save King Cibber!" mounts in every note.   *320*
Familiar White's, "God save King Colley!" cries;
"God save King Colley!" Drury Lane° replies:
To Needham's quick the voice triumphal rode,
But pious Needham dropped the name of God;°   *325*
Back to the Devil° the last echoes roll,
And "Coll!" each butcher roars at Hockley Hole.
   So when Jove's block descended from on high

---

304 **ivy** "emblematic of the . . . virtues of a court poet in particular" (Pope) 306 **points** witty turns 309 **Archer** Thomas Archer, as Groom-Porter, presided over gambling at court; he died a very rich man. 316 **armies** George II was criticized for supporting foreign mercenary soldiers. 319 **Chapel Royal** where the laureate's odes were performed to music 322 **Drury Lane** resort of prostitutes 323–24 **Needham's . . . God** Mother Needham, who kept a well-known house of prostitution, protested her hope that she might "get enough by her profession to leave it off in time and make her peace with God." She died as a result of abuse in the pillory. 325 **Devil** the Devil Tavern, where laureate odes were rehearsed

(As sings thy great forefather Ogilby)°
Loud thunder to its bottom shook the bog,
And the hoarse nation croaked, "God save King
330   Log!"

BOOK THE SECOND

HIGH on a gorgeous seat, that far outshone
Henley's gilt tub,° or Flecknoe's Irish throne,°
Or that where on her Curlls the public pours,
All-bounteous, fragrant grains and golden
    showers,°
5   Great Cibber sat:° the proud Parnassian° sneer,
The conscious simper, and the jealous leer,
Mix on his look: all eyes direct their rays
On him, and crowds turn coxcombs as they gaze.
His peers shine round him with reflected grace,
New edge their dulness, and new bronze their
10   face.
So from the sun's broad beam, in shallow urns

328 **Ogilby** as translator of Aesop's *Fables*. When the frogs
begged Zeus for a king, he gave them a log. Later, dissatisfied,
they chose a stork, who devoured them. 2 **Henley's . . . tub**
Orator Henley was a very popular preacher. The dissenter's
pulpit was often called a "tub" (cf. Swift's *A Tale of a Tub*);
but Henley's was richly adorned. Cf. "Dunciad," III, 199. 2
Flecknoe's . . . throne In Dryden's "MacFlecknoe" the former
Irish priest crowns his successor to the throne of Dulness,
Thomas Shadwell, the poet laureate. 3–4 **Curlls . . . showers**
Edmund Curll, bookseller and publisher, stood on a platform
in the pillory, where (Pope suggests) he was pelted with refuse,
malt grains, rotten eggs, or the contents of chamber pots. 1–5
High . . . sat Cf. *Paradise Lost*, II, 1–5: "High on a Throne of
Royal State, which far/Outshone the wealth of Ormus and of
Ind,/Or where the gorgeous East with richest hand/Show'rs on
her Kings Barbaric Pearl and Gold,/Satan exalted sat. . . ." 5
Parnassian as an exalted resident of Parnassus, the mountain
of Apollo and the Muses

Heaven's twinkling sparks draw light, and point
   their horns.°
   Not with more glee, by hands Pontific crowned,
With scarlet hats° wide-waving circled round,
Rome in her capitol saw Querno° sit,   *15*
Throned on seven hills, the Antichrist° of wit.
   And now the queen, to glad her sons, proclaims
By herald hawkers,° high heroic games.
They summon all her race: an endless band
Pours forth, and leaves unpeopled half the land.   *20*
A motley mixture! in long wigs, in bags,°
In silks, in crapes,° in garters,° and in rags,
From drawing rooms, from colleges, from garrets,
On horse, on foot, in hacks, and gilded chariots:
All who true dunces in her cause appeared,   *25*
And all who knew° those dunces to reward.
   Amid that area wide they took their stand,
Where the tall maypole° once o'erlooked the
   Strand,
But now (so Anne and piety ordain)
A church collects the saints° of Drury Lane.   *30*
   With authors, stationers° obeyed the call,
(The field of glory is a field for all.)
Glory, and gain, the industrious tribe provoke;
And gentle Dulness ever loves a joke.
A poet's form she placed before their eyes,   *35*
And bade the nimblest racer seize the prize;

---

12 **horns** of the crescent moon; by analogy, of Venus, the
morning star, which also has phases 14 **scarlet hats** of
cardinals 15 **Querno** A poet made court jester by Pope Leo
X and crowned with laurel. 16 **Antichrist** associated in
Revelations with the power of Rome and the apocalyptic
scarlet beast, whose seven heads can be taken as the seven
hills of Rome 18 **hawkers** Dulness' heralds are newspaper
vendors. 21 **bags** wigs worn in bags, a youthful fashion 22
crapes possibly clerical dress 22 **garters** Order of the Garter,
England's highest decoration, newly revived by Walpole 26
knew knew how 28 **maypole** removed in 1718, replaced by
the new church St. Mary le Strand 30 **saints** the pious; here
applied to the prostitutes of Drury Lane 31 **stationers**
booksellers

No meagre, muse-rid mope, adust° and thin,
In a dun nightgown of his own loose skin;
But such a bulk as no twelve bards could raise,
40 Twelve starveling bards of these degenerate days.
All as a partridge plump, full-fed, and fair,
She formed this image of well-bodied air;
With pert flat eyes she windowed well its head;
A brain of feathers, and a heart of lead;
45 And empty words she gave, and sounding° strain,
But senseless, lifeless! idol void and vain!
Never was dashed out, at one lucky hit,
A fool so just a copy of a wit;
So like, that critics said, and courtiers swore,
50 A wit it was, and called the phantom Moore.°
     All gaze with ardor: some a poet's name,
Others a sword-knot° and laced° suit inflame.
But lofty Lintot in the circle rose:
"This prize is mine; who tempt° it are my foes;
55 With me began this genius, and shall end."
He spoke: and who with Lintot shall contend?
     Fear held them mute. Alone, untaught to fear,
Stood dauntless Curll; "Behold that rival here!
The race by vigor, not by vaunts is won;
60 So take the hindmost, Hell," he said, and run.
Swift as a bard° the bailiff leaves behind,
He left huge Lintot, and outstripped the wind.
As when a dabchick° waddles through the copse
On feet and wings, and flies, and wades, and hops;
65 So laboring on, with shoulders, hands, and head,
Wide as a windmill all his figure spread,

37 **adust** sallow 45 **sounding** resonant, sonorous 50 **Moore**
James Moore Smythe, a young man eager to be recognized as
a wit, who read unpublished works of Arbuthnot and Pope as
his own and tried by any means to fill the theater for his
play 52 **sword-knot** ribbon tied to the hilt 52 **laced**
decorated with lace 54 **tempt** try for. This competition
between rival publishers begins Pope's parody of the epic
games of Homer (*Iliad,* XXIII) and Virgil (*Aeneid,* V). 61
bard i.e., a poet fleeing arrest for debt 63 **dabchick** grebe, an
aquatic bird

With arms expanded Bernard rows his state,
And left-legged Jacob° seems to emulate.
Full in the middle way there stood a lake,
Which Curll's Corinna° chanced that morn to
    make: 70
(Such was her wont, at early dawn to drop
Her evening cates° before his neighbor's shop,)
Here fortuned Curll to slide; loud shout the band,
And "Bernard! Bernard!" rings through all the
    Strand.
Obscene with filth the miscreant lies bewrayed,°   75
Fallen in the plash his wickedness had laid:
Then first (if poets aught of truth declare)
The caitiff vaticide° conceived a prayer.
   "Hear, Jove! whose name my bards and I adore,
As much at least as any God's, or more;   80
And him and his, if more devotion warms,
Down with the Bible,° up with the Pope's Arms."°
   A place there is, betwixt earth, air, and seas,
Where, from ambrosia, Jove retires for ease.
There in his seat two spacious vents appear,   85
On this he sits, to that he leans his ear,
And hears the various vows of fond mankind;
Some beg an eastern, some a western wind:
All vain petitions, mounting to the sky,
With reams abundant this abode supply;   90
Amused he reads, and then returns the bills
Signed with that ichor which from Gods distils.
   In office here fair Cloacina° stands,
And ministers to Jove with purest hands.
Forth from the heap she picked her votary's
    prayer,   95
And placed it next him, a distinction rare!

---

68 **left-legged Jacob** Dryden wrote of Jacob Tonson's "two left
legs." 70 **Corinna** Mrs. Thomas, who sold some of Pope's
letters to Curll for unauthorized publication. She had an
extensive amorous career. 72 **cates** delicacies 75 **bewrayed**
revealed 78 **vaticide** murderer of poets 82 **Bible** Curll's
bookseller's sign 82 **Pope's Arms** Lintot's sign (cross
keys) 93 **Cloacina** goddess of the sewers, or here, the privy

---

Oft had the goddess heard her servant's call,
From her black grottos° near the Temple Wall,
Listening delighted to the jest unclean
100 Of linkboys° vile, and watermen° obscene;
Where as he fished her nether realms for wit,
She oft had favored him, and favors yet.
Renewed by ordure's sympathetic force,
As oiled with magic juices° for the course,
105 Vigorous he rises; from the effluvia strong
Imbibes new life, and scours and stinks along;
Repasses Lintot, vindicates° the race,
Nor heeds the brown dishonors of his face.

    And now the victor stretched his eager hand
Where the tall Nothing° stood, or seemed to
110   stand;
A shapeless shade, it melted from his sight,
Like forms in clouds, or visions of the night.
To seize his papers, Curll, was next thy care;
His papers light fly diverse, tossed in air;
115 Songs, sonnets, epigrams the winds uplift,
And whisk 'em back to Evans, Young, and Swift.°
The embroidered suit at least he deemed his prey;
That suit an unpaid tailor snatched away.
No rag, no scrap, of all the beau, or wit,
120 That once so fluttered, and that once so writ.
    Heavens rings with laughter: of the laughter
     vain,
Dulness, good queen, repeats the jest again.
Three wicked imps, of her own Grubstreet choir,
She decked like Congreve, Addison, and Prior;°
125 Mears, Warner, Wilkins° run: delusive thought!

---

98 **black grottos** coal wharves on the Thames   100 **linkboys** torch-carriers   100 **watermen** ferrymen   104 **oiled . . . juices** as witches use magic ointments to enable them to fly   107 **vindicates** wins   110 **Nothing** the "poet's form" of II, 35   116 **Evans . . . Swift** the original authors   124 **Congreve . . . Prior** three admirable writers, the playwright William Congreve, the essayist and critic Joseph Addison, the poet Matthew Prior   125 **Mears . . . Wilkins** "booksellers and printers of much anonymous stuff" (Pope)

Breval, Bond, Besaleel° the varlets caught.
Curll stretches after Gay, but Gay is gone,
He grasps an empty Joseph for a John:°
So Proteus,° hunted in a nobler shape,
Became, when seized, a puppy, or an ape.   130
    To him the goddess: "Son! thy grief lay down,
And turn this whole illusion on the town:
As the sage dame, experienced in her trade,
By names of toasts retails each battered jade°
(Whence hapless Monsieur much complains at
        Paris   135
Of wrongs from Duchesses and Lady Marys);°
Be thine, my stationer! this magic gift;
Cook shall be Prior, and Concanen, Swift:°
So shall each hostile name° become our own,
And we too boast our Garth and Addison."   140
    With that she gave him (piteous of his case,
Yet smiling at his rueful length of face)
A shaggy tapestry, worthy to be spread
On Codrus'° old, or Dunton's° modern bed;
Instructive work! whose wry-mouthed portraiture   145
Displayed the fates her confessors° endure.
Earless° on high, stood unabashed Defoe,
And Tutchin° flagrant° from the scourge below.

126 **Breval . . . Besaleel** minor authors who had attacked
Pope   128 **Joseph . . . John** Curll published several pamphlets
as by Joseph Gay, hoping that they would be mistaken for the
works of the fine satiric poet John Gay.   129 **Proteus** See note
to I, 37.   134 **jade** prostitute   136 **Duchesses . . . Marys** titles
assumed by (in this case diseased) prostitutes; with a glance at
Pope's enemy, Lady Mary Wortley Montagu   138 **Cook . . .
Swift** Dulness substitutes a feebly scurrilous writer for an
excellent one in each case.   139 **name** Dulness is conquering
the true wits by providing cheap substitutes under the same
name.   144 **Codrus** an impoverished Roman poet in Juvenal's
third satire   144 **Dunton** an abusive satirist and poor
bookseller   146 **confessors** (pronounced with stress on the first
syllable) the adherents of Dulness   147 **Earless** Defoe never
lost his ears; these are prophetic visions, not historical
facts.   148 **Tutchin** sentenced to be whipped through several
towns for libel   148 **flagrant** flaming

There Ridpath, Roper,° cudgelled might ye view,
150 The very worsted still looked black and blue.
Himself among the storied chiefs° he spies,
As, from the blanket,° high in air he flies,
And "Oh!" (he cried) "what street, what lane
    but knows
Our purgings,° pumpings, blanketings, and blows?
155 In every loom our labors shall be seen,
And the fresh vomit run for ever green!"
   See in the circle next, Eliza° placed,
Two babes of love close clinging to her waist;
Fair as before her works she stands confessed,
In flowers and pearls by bounteous Kirkall°
160   dressed.
The goddess then: "Who best can send on high
The salient spout,° far-streaming to the sky;
His be yon Juno of majestic size,
With cow-like udders, and with ox-like eyes.°
165 This china jordan° let the chief o'ercome
Replenish, not ingloriously, at home."
   Osborne° and Curll accept the glorious strife,
(Though this his son dissuades, and that his wife).
One on his manly confidence relies,
170 One on his vigor and superior size.

149 **Ridpath, Roper** authors of scandalous political journals
on opposed sides   151 **among . . . chiefs** Curll sees his story
as Aeneas finds tapestries in Dido's palace representing the
fate of the Trojan heroes, including his own.   152 **blanket**
Curll was tossed in a blanket by the boys of Westminster
School for plagiarism.   154 **purgings** Pope, upon provocation,
secretly administered an emetic to Curll and later wrote an
account of the episode.   157 **Eliza** Eliza Haywood was the
author of two scandalous books.   160 **Kirkall** He engraved
her portrait for her published works.   162 **salient spout**
upward jet (of urine)   164 **cow-like . . . eyes** Pope extends
Homer's "ox-eyed (i.e., bright-eyed) Hera" to include other
bovine attributes.   165 **jordan** chamber pot (as second prize)
167 **Osborne** bookseller who misrepresented his copies of
Pope's works; "a man entirely destitute of shame," according
to Dr. Johnson

First Osborne leaned against his lettered° post;
It rose, and labored to a curve at most.
So Jove's bright bow displays its watery round,
(Sure sign° that no spectator shall be drowned).
A second effort brought but new disgrace: *175*
The wild Meander° washed the artist's face:
Thus the small jet, which hasty hands unlock,
Spurts in the gardener's eyes who turns the cock.
Not so from shameless Curll; impetuous spread
The stream, and smoking flourished o'er his head.   *180*
So (famed like thee for turbulence and horns)°
Eridanus° his humble fountain scorns;
Through half the heavens he pours the exalted urn;
His rapid waters in their passage burn.°
    Swift as it mounts, all follow with their eyes: *185*
Still happy impudence obtains the prize.
Thou triumphst, victor of the high-wrought day,
And the pleased dame, soft-smiling, leadst away.
Osborne, through perfect modesty o'ercome,
Crowned with the jordan, walks contented home.   *190*
    But now for authors nobler palms remain;
Room for my lord! three jockeys in his train;
Six huntsmen with a shout precede his chair:
He grins, and looks broad nonsense with a stare.
His Honor's meaning Dulness thus exprest,   *195*
"He wins this patron, who can tickle° best."
    He chinks his purse, and takes his seat of state:
With ready quills the dedicators wait;
Now at his head the dextrous task commence,
And, instant, fancy feels the imputed sense;°   *200*

---

171 **lettered** covered with advertisements 174 **sign** Jove's
rainbow is a sign to man, as is God's after the deluge in
Genesis 8:12–16. 176 **Meander** the winding river of Asia
Minor 181 **horns** River gods were represented as horned
figures with gushing urns. The horns also suggest Curll's
cuckoldry. 182 **Eridanus** the river that flowed through the
heavens 184 **burn** with the suggestion of venereal disease
196 **tickle** tickling with a feather was a well-known symbol of
flattery 200 **imputed sense** implied praise

Now gentle touches wanton o'er his face,
He struts Adonis,° and affects grimace:
Rolli° the feather to his ear conveys,
Then his nice taste directs our operas:
205 Bentley° his mouth with classic flattery opes,
And the puffed orator bursts out in tropes.
But Welsted° most the poet's healing balm
Strives to extract from his soft, giving palm;
Unlucky Welsted! thy unfeeling master,
210 The more thou ticklest, gripes his fist the faster.
    While thus each hand promotes the pleasing
        pain,
And quick sensations skip from vein to vein;
A youth unknown to Phoebus,° in despair,
Puts his last refuge all in heaven and prayer.
215 What force have pious vows! The Queen of Love
His sister sends, her votaress, from above.
As, taught by Venus, Paris° learnt the art
To touch Achilles' only tender part;
Secure, through her, the noble prize to carry,
220 He marches off, his Grace's secretary.
    "Now turn to different sports" (the goddess
        cries)
"And learn, my sons, the wondrous power of
        noise.
To move, to raise, to ravish every heart,
With Shakespeare's nature, or with Jonson's art,
225 Let others aim: 'tis yours to shake the soul
With thunder° rumbling from the mustard bowl,
With horns and trumpets now to madness swell,

202 **Adonis** the beautiful youth loved by Venus   203 **Rolli** a
poet who taught Italian to gentlemen interested in opera   205
Bentley either Richard Bentley, the great classical scholar, or
(Pope asserts) his nephew Thomas, also an editor of Horace
and a flattering dedicator   207 **Welsted** the poet and
critic   213 **Phoebus** Apollo, god of poetry   217 **Paris** With
Venus' aid, his arrow found Achilles' one vulnerable part, his
heel.   226 **thunder** Stage thunder was produced (like mustard)
by beating in a bowl. The dunces forsake literary art for
spectacular stage effects.

Now sink in sorrows with a tolling bell;
Such happy arts attention can command,
When fancy flags, and sense is at a stand.   230
Improve we these. Three catcalls be the bribe°
Of him, whose chattering shames the monkey tribe:
And his this drum, whose hoarse heroic bass
Drowns the loud clarion of the braying ass."
   Now thousand tongues are heard in one loud
     din: 235
The monkey-mimics rush discordant in.
'Twas chattering, grinning, mouthing, jabbering
     all,
And noise and Norton, brangling and Breval,
Dennis and dissonance,° and captious° art,
And snip-snap short, and interruption smart,   240
And demonstration thin, and theses thick,
And major, minor,° and conclusion quick.
"Hold!" (cried the Queen) "a catcall each shall
     win;
Equal your merits! equal is your din!
But that this well-disputed game may end,   245
Sound forth, my brayers, and the welkin rend."
   As, when the long-eared milky mothers° wait
At some sick miser's triple-bolted gate,
For their defrauded, absent foals they make
A moan so loud, that all the guild° awake;   250
Sore sighs Sir Gilbert, starting at the bray,
From dreams of millions, and three groats to pay.
So swells each windpipe; ass intones to ass,
Harmonic twang! of leather, horn, and brass;
Such as from laboring lungs the enthusiast° blows, 255
High sound, attempered to the vocal nose;
Or such as bellow from the deep divine;

231 **bribe** prize 238–39 **noise . . . dissonance** As W. K.
Wimsatt has observed, these proper names and types of noise
become equivalent and interchangeable. 239 **captious** confusing
242 **major, minor** premises in a syllogism 247 **milky mothers**
Asses' milk was considered medicinal. 250 **guild**
neighborhood of the city 255 **enthusiast** fanatical preacher;
they were famous for loudness and nasal tones.

There Webster! pealed thy voice, and Whitfield!°
   thine.
But far o'er all, sonorous Blackmore's° strain;
260 Walls, steeples, skies, bray back to him again.
In Tottenham fields, the brethren, with amaze,
Prick all their ears up, and forget to graze;
Long Chancery Lane retentive° rolls the sound,
And courts to courts return it round and round;
265 Thames wafts it thence to Rufus' roaring hall,°
And Hungerford° re-echoes bawl for bawl.
All hail him victor in both gifts of song,
Who sings so loudly, and who sings so long.
   This labor past, by Bridewell° all descend,
270 (As morning prayer and flagellation end)
To where Fleet-ditch° with disemboguing streams
Rolls the large tribute of dead dogs to Thames,
The king of dykes!° than whom no sluice of mud
With deeper sable blots the silver flood.
275 "Here strip, my children! here at once leap in,
Here prove who best can dash through thick and
   thin,
And who the most in love of dirt excel,
Or dark dexterity of groping well.
Who flings most filth, and wide pollutes around
280 The stream, be his the Weekly Journals° bound,
A pig° of lead to him who dives the best;
A peck of coals apiece shall glad the rest."
   In naked majesty Oldmixon° stands,

258 **Webster . . . Whitfield** opposed enthusiasts; William
Webster was a bitter anti-Methodist writer, George Whitfield
the celebrated field-preacher and (for a time) companion of
John Wesley. 259 **Blackmore's** mentioned here for his biblical
poetry rather than his six epics 263 **retentive** Chancery cases
were slow in being settled, as a century later in Dickens' *Bleak
House*. 265 **Rufus' . . . hall** Westminster Hall, built by William
Rufus; a scene of legal disputes 266 **Hungerford** the public
market 269 **Bridewell** the house of correction for women
271 **Fleet-ditch** then an open sewer 273 **dykes** canals 280
Journals given to scandal and party politics 281 **pig**
ingot 283 **Oldmixon** an elderly critic and partisan historian

And Milo-like° surveys his arms and hands;
Then, sighing, thus, "And am I now threescore?   285
Ah why, ye Gods! should two and two make four?"
He said, and climbed a stranded lighter's height,
Shot to the black abyss, and plunged downright.
The senior's judgment all the crowd admire,
Who but to sink the deeper, rose the higher.   290
    Next Smedley° dived; slow circles dimpled o'er
The quaking mud, that closed, and oped no more.
All look, all sigh, and call on Smedley lost;
"Smedley" in vain resounds through all the coast.
    Then * * essayed;° scarce vanished out of sight,   295
He buoys up instant, and returns to light:
He bears no token of the sabler streams,
And mounts far off among the swans of Thames.
    True to the bottom, see Concanen° creep,
A cold, long-winded native of the deep: 300
If perseverance gain the diver's prize,
Not everlasting Blackmore this denies:
No noise, no stir, no motion canst thou make,
The unconscious stream sleeps o'er thee like a
    lake.
    Next plunged a feeble but a desperate pack,   305
With each a sickly brother at his back:°
Sons of a day! just buoyant on the flood,
Then numbered with the puppies in the mud.
Ask ye their names? I could as soon disclose
The names of these blind puppies as of those.   310
Fast by, like Niobe° (her children gone)

284 **Milo-like** a famous athlete of antiquity   291 **Smedley** an Irish clergyman, dean of Clogher, who savagely abused Swift and Pope   295 **Then . . . essayed** Pope removed the name of Aaron Hill, a "writer of genius and spirit."   299 **Concanen** an Irish journalist   306 **at his back** Some daily papers printed special issues on their back pages.   311 **Niobe** When she boasted of her seven sons and seven daughters before Leto, who had two, those two (Artemis and Apollo) slew all of Niobe's children. Niobe wept until she was turned into a column of stone.

Sits Mother Osborne,° stupefied to stone!
And monumental brass° this record bears,
"These are,—ah no! these were, the Gazetteers!"
315   Not so bold Arnall;° with a weight of skull,
Furious he dives, precipitately dull.
Whirlpools and storms his circling arm invest,
With all the might of gravitation blest.
No crab more active in the dirty dance,
320 Downward to climb, and backward to advance.
He brings up half the bottom on his head,
And loudly claims the journals and the lead.
    The plunging prelate, and his ponderous
      Grace,°
With holy envy gave one layman place.
325 When lo! a burst of thunder shook the flood:
Slow rose a form,° in majesty of mud;
Shaking the horrors of his sable brows,
And each ferocious feature grim with ooze.
Greater he looks, and more than mortal stares:
330 Then thus the wonders of the deep declares.
    First he relates, how sinking to the chin,
Smit with his mien, the mud-nymphs sucked him
    in:
How young Lutetia,° softer than the down,
Nigrina black, and Merdamante° brown,
335 Vied for his love in jetty bowers below,
As Hylas° fair was ravished long ago.
Then sung, how shown him by the nut-brown
    maids
A branch of Styx here rises from the shades,

312 **Mother Osborne** a term applied to this eldest of journalists 313 **monumental brass** as in church memorial plaques 315 **Arnall** Author of "furious party-papers," he "writ for hire and valued himself upon it" (Pope). 323 **prelate . . . Grace** possibly Thomas Sherlock, Bishop of London, consistent supporter of Walpole, and John Potter, Archbishop of Canterbury 326 **a form** the return of Smedley, lost in II, 293–94 333 **Lutetia** classical name for Paris, perhaps derived from *lutum* (mud) 334 **Merdamante** "filth-loving" 336 **Hylas** "ravished by the water-nymphs and drawn into the river," in Virgil, "Eclogue" VI (Pope)

That tinctured as it runs with Lethe's streams,
And wafting vapors from the land of dreams,   *340*
(As under seas Alpheus'° secret sluice
Bears Pisa's offerings to his Arethuse)
Pours into Thames: and hence the mingled wave
Intoxicates the pert, and lulls the grave:
Here brisker vapors o'er the TEMPLE° creep,   *345*
There, all from Paul's to Aldgate° drink and sleep.
    Thence to the banks where reverend bards
        repose,
They led him soft; each reverend bard arose;
And Milbourn° chief, deputed by the rest,
Gave him the cassock, surcingle,° and vest.   *350*
"Receive" (he said) "these robes which once
        were mine,
Dulness is sacred in a sound divine."
    He ceased, and spread the robe; the crowd
        confess
The reverend flamen in his lengthened dress.
Around him wide a sable army stand,   *355*
A lowborn, cell-bred, selfish, servile band,°
Prompt or to guard or stab, to saint or damn,
Heaven's Swiss,° who fight for any god, or man.
    Through Lud's famed gates,° along the well-
        known Fleet;
Rolls the black troop, and overshades the street, *360*
Till showers of sermons, characters,° essays,
In circling fleeces whiten all the ways:
So clouds replenished from some bog below,

341 **Alpheus** The river runs under the sea at Pisa to mix with
the fountain of Arethuse in Sicily.   345 **Temple** the inns of
court beside the Thames   346 **Paul's to Aldgate** from St.
Paul's Cathedral east through the city to Aldgate   349
Milbourn clergyman and critic who attacked Dryden   350
surcingle girdle or belt for cassock   356 **band** "such only of
the clergy who . . . dedicate themselves for venal and corrupt
ends to that of ministers and factions" (Warburton)   358 **Swiss**
mercenary soldiers   359 **Lud's . . . gates,** gate between Fleet
Street and the western limit of the city, built by King Lud   361
characters The "character" was a distinctive literary form
deriving originally from Theophrastus.

Mount in dark volumes, and descend in snow.
365 Here stopped the goddess; and in pomp proclaims
A gentler exercise to close the games.
   "Ye critics! in whose heads, as equal scales,
I weigh what author's heaviness prevails;
Which most conduce to soothe the soul in
     slumbers,
My H—ley's periods, or my Blackmore's
370   numbers;°
Attend the trial we propose to make:
If there be man, who o'er such works can wake,
Sleep's all-subduing charms who dares defy,
And boasts Ulysses' ear° with Argus' eye;°
375 To him we grant our amplest powers to sit
Judge of all present, past, and future wit;
To cavil, censure, dictate, right or wrong,
Full and eternal privilege of tongue."
   Three college sophs, and three pert templars°
     came,
380 The same their talents, and their tastes the same;
Each prompt to query, answer, and debate,
And smit with love of poesy and prate.
The ponderous books two gentle readers bring;
The heroes sit, the vulgar form a ring.
The clamorous crowd is hushed with mugs of
385   mum,°
Till all, tuned equal, send a general hum.
Then mount the clerks, and in one lazy tone,
Through the long, heavy, painful page drawl on;
Soft, creeping, words on words, the sense
     compose,
390 At every line they stretch, they yawn, they doze.
As to soft gales top-heavy pines bow low
Their heads, and lift them as they cease to blow:
Thus oft they rear, and oft the head decline,
As breathe, or pause, by fits, the airs divine.

370 **periods . . . numbers** prose and verse forms   374 **Ulysses'
ear** as he resisted the song of the Sirens   374 **Argus' eye** He
had a hundred eyes, some always open.   379 **templars** law
students   385 **mum** beer

And now to this side, now to that they nod,   *395*
As verse, or prose, infuse the drowsy god.
Thrice Budgell° aimed to speak, but thrice
    suppressed
By potent Arthur,° knocked his chin and breast.
Toland and Tindal,° prompt at priests to jeer,
Yet silent bowed to Christ's No Kingdom Here.° *400*
Who sat the nearest, by the words o'ercome,
Slept first; the distant nodded to the hum.
Then down are rolled the books; stretched o'er
    'em lies
Each gentle clerk, and muttering seals his eyes.
As what a Dutchman plumps into the lakes,   *405*
One circle first, and then a second makes;
What Dulness dropped among her sons impressed
Like motion from one circle to the rest;
So from the midmost the nutation° spreads
Round and more round, o'er all the sea of heads. *410*
At last Centlivre° felt her voice to fail,
Motteux° himself unfinished left his tale,
Boyer° the state, and Law° the stage gave o'er,
Morgan° and Mandeville° could prate no more;
Norton,° from Daniel and Ostroea° sprung,   *415*
Blessed with his father's front, and mother's
    tongue,

397 **Budgell** a gifted writer, unsettled by losses in the South Sea investment scheme, of which he spoke continually 398 **Arthur** Blackmore's hero in two vast epics, now being read aloud 399 **Toland and Tindal** deistic writers 400 **Christ's ... Here** the title of a long sermon or speech 409 **Nutation** nodding 411 **Centlivre** Susanne Centlivre, a comic dramatist and ardent Whig, friend of Cibber. Prolific writing or talk is the common element in the next few lines. 412 **Motteux** a loquacious man, translator of Rabelais and Cervantes 413 **Boyer** compiler of annals 413 **Law** religious writer, attacker of the theatre. Each man relinquishes his absorbing subject as sleep overtakes him. 414 **Morgan** deistic, self-styled "moral philosopher" 414 **Mandeville** Bernard Mandeville's *The Fable of the Bees* was one of the greatest and most widely criticized books of the age. 415 **Norton** Benjamin Norton Defoe, son of Daniel by **Ostroea,** an oyster-wench

Hung silent down his never-blushing head;
And all was hushed, as Folly's self lay dead.
　　Thus the soft gifts of sleep conclude the day,
420 And stretched on bulks,° as usual, poets lay.
Why should I sing what bards the nightly Muse
Did slumbering visit, and convey to stews;°
Who prouder marched, with magistrates in state,
To some famed roundhouse,° ever open gate!
425 How Henley lay inspired beside a sink,
And to mere mortals seemed a priest in drink:
While others, timely, to the neighboring Fleet°
(Haunt of the Muses) made their safe retreat.

BOOK THE THIRD

But in her temple's last recess inclosed,
On Dulness' lap the anointed head reposed.
Him close she curtains round with vapors blue,
And soft besprinkles with Cimmerian° dew.
5 Then raptures high the seat of sense o'erflow,
Which only heads refined from° reason know.
Hence, from the straw where Bedlam's prophet
　　nods,
He hears loud oracles, and talks with gods:
Hence the fool's paradise, the statesman's scheme,
10 The air-built castle, and the golden dream,
The maid's romantic wish, the chemist's° flame,
And poet's vision of eternal fame.
　　And now, on Fancy's easy wing conveyed,
The King descending views the Elysian shade.°
15 A slipshod Sibyl° led his steps along,

420 **bulks** stalls, shop fronts　422 **stews** brothels　424 **roundhouse** place of detention, lock-up　427 **Fleet** debtors' prison
4 **Cimmerian** as in Homer's mythical land of constant mists and darkness　6 **refined from** purged of　11 **chemist's** alchemist's　14 **Elysian shade** Cibber's fantasies include the epic descent to the underworld.　15 **Sibyl** The Cumaean Sibyl was consulted for her prophetic wisdom by Aeneas before his descent to the lower world.

In lofty madness meditating song;
Her tresses staring from poetic dreams,
And never washed, but in Castalia's streams.°
Taylor,° their better Charon, lends an oar,
(One swan of Thames, though now he sings no
    more.)   20
Benlowes,° propitious still to blockheads, bows;
And Shadwell° nods the poppy on his brows.
Here, in a dusky vale where Lethe rolls,
Old Bavius° sits, to dip poetic souls,
And blunt the sense, and fit it for a skull   25
Of solid proof, impenetrably dull:
Instant, when dipped, away they wing their flight,
Where Brown and Mears° unbar the gates of light,
Demand new bodies, and in calf's array,°
Rush to the world, impatient for the day.   30
Millions and millions on these banks he views,
Thick as the stars of night, or morning dews,
As thick as bees o'er vernal blossoms fly,
As thick as eggs at Ward° in Pillory.

   Wondering he gazed: when lo! a sage appears,   35
By his broad shoulders known, and length of ears,
Known by the band and suit which Settle° wore
(His only suit) for twice three years before:
All as the vest, appeared the wearer's frame,
Old in new state, another yet the same.   40
Bland and familiar as in life, begun
Thus the great father° to the greater son.

   "Oh born to see what none can see awake!
Behold the wonders of the oblivious lake.

---

18 **Castalia's streams** the fountain on Mt. Parnassus   19 **Taylor**
John Taylor, the water poet, was a voluminous writer as well
as boatman. He died in 1654.   21 **Benlowes** a bad poet and
patron of other bad poets   22 **Shadwell** An addict, he died of
an overdose of opium.   24 **Bavius** a bad Roman poet, Virgil's
Cibber   28 **Brown and Mears** "printers . . . for anybody"
(Pope)   29 **calf's array** (1) fool's garb (2) calfskin binding   34
Ward John Ward, expelled from parliament for forgery   37
Settle See note to I, 90.   42 **father** as Anchises in his prophecy
to Aeneas

45 Thou, yet unborn, hast touched this sacred shore;
   The hand of Bavius drenched thee o'er and o'er.
   But blind to former as to future fate,
   What mortal knows his pre-existent state?
   Who knows how long thy transmigrating soul
50 Might from Boeotian° to Boeotian roll?
   How many Dutchmen° she vouchsafed to thrid?°
   How many stages through old monks she rid?
   And all who since, in mild benighted days,
   Mixed the owl's ivy° with the poet's bays?
55 As man's meanders° to the vital spring
   Roll all their tides, then back their circles bring;
   Or whirligigs,° twirled round by skilful swain,
   Suck the thread in, then yield it out again:
   All nonsense thus, of old or modern date,
60 Shall in thee center, from thee circulate.
   For this our Queen unfolds to vision true
   Thy mental eye, for thou hast much to view:
   Old scenes of glory, times long cast behind
   Shall, first recalled, rush forward to thy mind:
65 Then stretch thy sight o'er all her rising reign,
   And let the past and future fire thy brain.
      "Ascend this hill, whose cloudy point
         commands
   Her boundless empire over seas and lands.
   See, round the poles where keener spangles shine,
70 Where spices smoke beneath the burning Line,°
   (Earth's wide extremes) her sable flag displayed,
   And all the nations covered in her shade!
      "Far eastward cast thine eye, from whence the
         sun
   And orient° science their bright course begun:
75 One godlike monarch° all that pride confounds,

50 **Boeotian** See note to I, 25. 51 **Dutchmen** believed to be
heavy and unimaginative 51 **thrid** thread 54 **owl's ivy** the
owl as pedant; cf. "Essay on Criticism," line 706 and note. 55
meanders See note to II, 176. 57 **whirligigs** tops 70 **Line**
equator 74 **orient** rising 75 **One . . . monarch** The Emperor
of China who built the Great Wall destroyed all books and
scholars so that learning would date from his reign.

He, whose long wall the wandering Tartar bounds;
Heavens! what a pile! whole ages perish there,
And one bright blaze turns learning into air.
    "Thence to the south extend thy gladdened
        eyes;
There rival flames with equal glory rise,   *80*
From shelves to shelves see greedy Vulcan° roll,
And lick up all their physic of the soul.
    "How little, mark! that portion of the ball,
Where, faint at best, the beams of science fall:
Soon as they dawn, from hyperborean° skies   *85*
Embodied dark, what clouds of Vandals rise!
Lo! where Macotis° sleeps, and hardly flows
The freezing Tanais° through a waste of snows,
The North by myriads pours her mighty sons,
Great nurse of Goths, of Alans,° and of Huns!   *90*
See Alaric's° stern port! the martial frame
Of Genseric!° and Attila's° dread name!
See the bold Ostrogoths on Latium fall;
See the fierce Visigoths on Spain and Gaul!
See, where the morning gilds the palmy shore   *95*
(The soil° that arts and infant letters bore)
His conquering tribes the Arabian prophet draws,
And saving ignorance enthrones by laws.
See Christians, Jews, one heavy sabbath keep,
And all the western world believe and sleep.   *100*
    "Lo! Rome herself, proud mistress now no
        more
Of arts, but thundering against heathen lore;
Her gray-haired Synods damning books unread,

---

81 **greedy Vulcan** the burning of the great Ptolomean Library
in Egypt (whose inscription was *Medicina Animae,* or the
"physic of the Soul"); ordered by the Caliph Omar I   85
hyperborean of the extreme north   87 **Maeotis** the present Sea
of Azor   88 **Tanais** the river Don   90 **Alans** a Scythian people
from the Caucasus   91 **Alaric** leader of the Visigoth sack of
Rome, A.D. 410   92 **Genseric** King of the Vandals   92 **Attila**
King of the Huns, the so-called Scourge of God   96 **soil** The
Near East, where the alphabet was invented, was the scene of
Mohammed's (the Arabian prophet's) first conquests.

And Bacon° trembling for his brazen head.
105 Padua, with sighs, beholds her Livy° burn,
And even the Antipodes° Virgilius mourn.
See, the Cirque° falls, the unpillared temple nods,
Streets paved with heroes, Tiber choked with
    gods:
Till Peter's keys some christened Jove adorn,
110 And Pan to Moses lends his pagan horn;
See graceless° Venus to a Virgin turned,°
Or Phidias broken, and Apelles° burned.
   "Behold yon isle, by palmers, pilgrims trod,
Men bearded, bald, cowled, uncowled, shod,
    unshod,
Peeled,° patched, and piebald,° linsey-wolsey°
115   brothers,
Grave mummers!° sleeveless some, and shirtless
    others.
That once was Britain—happy! had she seen
No fiercer sons, had Easter° never been.
In peace, great Goddess, ever be adored;
120 How keen the war, if Dulness draw the sword!
Thus visit not thy own! on this blest age
Oh spread thy influence, but restrain thy rage!
   "And see, my son! the hour is on its way,

104 **Bacon** Roger Bacon, the medieval philosopher, was said to have made a brazen head that could speak; he seems to fear persecution for his learning. 105 **Livy** The Roman historian was burned because of his full treatment of pagan rites. 106 **Antipodes** Virgilius, eighth-century bishop, was censured for believing in the existence of the Antipodes. 107 **Cirque** circus, possibly the Colosseum, whose stone was quarried for new buildings 111 **graceless** (1) without the accompanying three Graces (2) unchristian (3) amorous 109–11 **Till Peter's keys . . . Virgin turned** The Popes "spared some of the temples by converting them to churches, and some of the statues by modifying them into images of saints" (Pope). 112 **Phidias . . . Apelles** Marble statues of these Greek sculptors or Roman copies were burned to produce lime. 115 **Peeled** threadbare 115 **piebald** spotted 115 **linsey-wolsey** a mixture of flax and wool; hence "neither one thing nor the other" 116 **mummers** mimes, actors 118 **Easter** The proper date was the subject of wars.

That lifts our goddess to imperial sway;
This favorite isle, long severed from her reign,   *125*
Dove-like,° she gathers to her wings again.
Now look through fate! behold the scene she draws!
What aids, what armies to assert her cause!
See all her progeny, illustrious sight!
Behold, and count them, as they rise to light.   *130*
As Berecynthia,° while her offspring vie
In homage to the mother of the sky,
Surveys around her, in the blest abode,
An hundred sons, and every son a god:
Not with less glory mighty Dulness crowned,   *135*
Shall take through Grubstreet her triumphant
      round;
And her Parnassus glancing o'er at once,
Behold an hundred sons, and each a dunce.
   "Mark first that youth° who takes the
      foremost place,
And thrusts his person full into your face.   *140*
With all thy father's virtues blessed, be born!
And a new Cibber shall the stage adorn.
   "A second see, by meeker manners known,
And modest as the maid that sips alone;
From the strong fate of drams° if thou get free,   *145*
Another Durfey,° Ward! shall sing in thee.
Thee shall each alehouse, thee each gill-house°
      mourn,
And answering gin-shops sourer sighs return.
   "Jacob,° the scourge of grammar, mark with awe,
Nor less revere him, blunderbuss of law.   *150*

126 **Dove-like** Cf. Psalms 91:4 "He shall cover thee with his feathers, and under his wings shalt thou trust." "This is fulfilled in the fourth book" (Pope). 131 **Berecynthia** Cybele, the Mighty Mother of the Gods (i.e., "of the sky," line 132)   139 **that youth** Theophilus Cibber, son of Colley and in most respects his successor as actor and writer   145 **fate of drams** Ned Ward was not only a popular writer but also a tavern keeper; see note to I, 233.   146 **Durfey** popular songwriter and object of ridicule from Dryden's day   147 **gill-house** Gill was a malt liquor treated with ground-ivy.   149 **Jacob** Giles Jacob, poet and biographer of poets, trained in the law.

Lo P—p—le's brow, tremendous to the town,
Horneck's fierce eye, and Roome's funereal frown.
Lo sneering Goode, half malice and half whim,
A fiend in glee, ridiculously grim.°
155 Each cygnet sweet of Bath and Tunbridge race,°
Whose tuneful whistling makes the waters pass:
Each songster, riddler, every nameless name,
All crowd, who foremost shall be damned to fame.
Some strain in rhyme; the Muses, on their racks,
160 Scream like the winding of ten thousand jacks:°
Some free from rhyme or reason, rule or check,
Break Priscian's° head, and Pegasus's° neck;
Down, down they larum,° with impetuous whirl,
The Pindars and the Miltons of a Curll.
    "Silence, ye wolves! while Ralph to Cynthia°
165   howls,
And makes night hideous—answer him, ye owls!
    "Sense, speech, and measure, living tongues
        and dead,
Let all give way—and Morris° may be read.
    "Flow, Welsted, flow! like thine inspirer, beer;
Though stale, not ripe; though thin, yet never
170   clear;
So sweetly mawkish, and so smoothly dull;
Heady, not strong; o'erflowing, though not full.°
    "Ah Dennis! Gildon° ah! what ill-starred rage

151–54 **Lo P—p—le's . . . grim** All of these minor writers (the
first is William Popple) had attacked Pope; they are reduced
here to facial expressions.   155 **Bath . . . race** local poets at
popular spas, whose waters provide one of the senses of line
156   160 **jacks** devices for turning roasting spits   162 **Priscian**
standard Latin grammarian   162 **Pegasus** the steed of po-
etry   163 **larum** rush with cries   165 **Ralph to Cynthia** James
Ralph wrote a bad poem called "Night," thus to Cynthia, the
moon.   168 **Morris** Bezaliel Morris, an inexhaustible
poet   170–72 **Though stale . . . full** a parody of Sir John Den-
ham's famous lines on the Thames in *Cooper's Hill:* "Though
deep, yet clear, though gentle yet not dull,/Strong without
rage, without o'erflowing full."   173 **Dennis . . . Gildon** two
acrimonious critics, worthy of each other's respect

Divides a friendship long confirmed by age?
Blockheads with reason wicked wits abhor,   175
But fool with fool is barbarous civil war.
Embrace, embrace, my sons! be foes no more!
Nor glad vile poets with true critics' gore.

　　"Behold yon pair, in strict embraces joined;
How like in manners, and how like in mind!   180
Equal in wit, and equally polite,
Shall this a Pasquin, that a Grumbler° write;
Like are their merits, like rewards they share,
That shines a consul, this commissioner.

　　"But who is he,° in closet close y-pent,   185
Of sober face, with learnèd dust besprent?
Right well mine eyes arede the myster wight,°
On parchment scraps y-fed, and Wormius hight.
To future ages may thy dulness last,
As thou preservest the dulness of the past!   190

　　"There, dim in clouds, the poring scholiasts°
　　　mark,
Wits, who, like owls, see only in the dark,
A lumberhouse of books in every head,
For ever reading, never to be read!

　　"But, where each science lifts its modern type,° 195
History her pot,° divinity his pipe,
While proud philosophy repines to show,
Dishonest sight! his breeches rent below;
Embrowned with native bronze, lo! Henley°
　　　stands,
Turning his voice, and balancing his hands.   200
How fluent nonsense trickles from his tongue!
How sweet the periods, neither said, nor sung!

182 **Pasquin . . . Grumbler** two weekly journals 185 **he** the
antiquarian Thomas Hearne, whose bookworm nature is
rendered in archaic diction, like Spenser's 187 **myster wight**
"uncouth mortal" (Pope) 191 **scholiasts** commentators,
annotators 195 **type** emblem 196 **pot** of ale 199 **Henley**
Orator Henley preached religion on Sundays, other matters on
Wednesdays, reportedly calling himself the "restorer of ancient
eloquence" and charging a shilling for admission (see line 205).

Still break the benches,° Henley! with thy strain,
While Sherlock, Hare, and Gibson preach in vain.
205 Oh great restorer of the good old stage,
Preacher at once, and zany° of thy age!
Oh worthy thou of Egypt's wise abodes,
A decent° priest, where monkeys were the gods!
But fate with butchers° placed thy priestly stall,
210 Meek modern faith to murder, hack, and maul;
And bade thee live, to crown Britannia's praise,
In Toland's, Tindal's, and in Woolston's days.°
    "Yet oh, my sons! a father's words attend:
(So may the fates preserve the ears you lend)
215 'Tis yours, a Bacon or a Locke to blame,°
A Newton's genius, or a Milton's flame:
But oh! with One, immortal One dispense,
The source of Newton's light, of Bacon's sense!
Content, each emanation of his fires
220 That beams on earth, each virtue he inspires,
Each art he prompts, each charm he can create,
Whate'er he gives, are given for you to hate.
Persist, by all divine in Man unawed,
But, learn, ye Dunces! not to scorn your God."°
225   Thus he, for then a ray of reason stole
Half through the solid darkness of his soul;
But soon the cloud returned—and thus the sire:
"See now, what Dulness and her sons admire!
See what the charms, that smite the simple heart
230 Not touched by nature, and not reached by art."
    His never-blushing head he turned aside,
(Not half so pleased when Goodman° prophesied)

---

203 **benches** referring in part to the bishops (three of them are
cited in line 204) who occupied benches in the House of Lords.
Henley attacked church institutions. 206 **zany** clown 208
decent fitting 209 **butchers** Henley's oratory was in Newport
Market, Butcher Row. 212 **In . . . days** citing three deists;
like Henley, anticlerical 215 **blame** attack, as enemies of
Dulness 224 **But, learn . . . God** i.e., not openly, lest you be
charged with blasphemy 232 **Goodman** who, seeing Cibber in
rehearsal, said, "If he does not make a good actor, I'll be
damned." Cibber reports his exultation at hearing this.

And looked, and saw a sable sorcerer° rise,
Swift to whose hand a wingèd volume flies:
All sudden, gorgons hiss, and dragons glare,   *235*
And ten-horned fiends and giants rush to war.
Hell rises, Heaven descends, and dance on Earth:
Gods, imps, and monsters, music, rage, and mirth,
A fire, a jig, a battle, and a ball,
Till one wide conflagration swallows all.   *240*
   Thence a new world to nature's laws unknown,
Breaks out refulgent, with a heaven its own:
Another Cynthia her new journey runs,
And other planets circle other suns.
The forests dance, the rivers upward rise,   *245*
Whales sport in woods, and dolphins in the skies;
And last, to give the whole creation grace,
Lo! one vast egg° produces human race.
   Joy fills his soul, joy innocent of thought;
"What power," he cries, "what power these
     wonders wrought?"   *250*
"Son, what thou seekest is in thee! Look, and
     find
Each monster meets his likeness in thy mind.
Yet wouldst thou more? In yonder cloud behold,
Whose sarcenet° skirts are edged with flamy gold,
A matchless youth! his nod these worlds controls,   *255*
Wings the red lightning, and the thunder rolls.
Angel of Dulness, sent to scatter round
Her magic charms o'er all unclassic ground:
Yon stars, yon suns, he rears at pleasure higher,
Illumes their light, and sets their flames on fire.   *260*
Immortal Rich!° how calm he sits at ease
Mid snows of paper, and fierce hail of pease;
And proud his mistress' orders to perform,

233 **sorcerer** Dr. Faustus, the hero of a series of popular farces
with elaborate stage effects (as in the next seven lines)   248
one vast egg These theatrical extravagances are a parody of
cosmology, here of the myth of the cosmic egg from which
the universe was hatched.   254 **sarcenet** thin silk   261 **Rich**
theatrical manager in Lincoln's-Inn-Field, deviser of pantomimes

Rides in the whirlwind, and directs the storm.°
265   "But lo! to dark encounter in mid air
New wizards rise; I see my Cibber there!
Booth° in his cloudy tabernacle shrined,
On grinning dragons thou shalt mount the wind.
Dire is the conflict, dismal is the din,
270 Here shouts all Drury, there all Lincoln's Inn;
Contending theatres our empire raise,
Alike their labors, and alike their praise.
   "And are these wonders, Son, to thee
unknown?
Unknown to thee? These wonders are thy own.
275 These Fates reserved to grace thy reign divine,
Foreseen by me, but ah! withheld from mine.
In Lud's old walls though long I ruled, renowned
Far as loud Bow's stupendous bells resound;
Though my own aldermen conferred the bays,
280 To me committing their eternal praise,
Their full-fed heroes, their pacific mayors,
Their annual trophies,° and their monthly wars:°
Though long my party built on me their hopes,
For writing pamphlets, and for roasting popes;°
285 Yet lo! in me what authors have to brag on!
Reduced at last to hiss in my own dragon.°
Avert it, Heaven! that thou, my Cibber, e'er
Shouldst wag a serpent tail in Smithfield fair!
Like the vile straw that's blown about the streets,
290 The needy poet sticks to all he meets,
Coached, carted, trod upon, now loose, now fast,

264 **whirlwind . . . storm** Cf. Nahum 1:3 "The Lord hath his way in the whirlwind and in the storm, and the clouds are the dust of his feet." 267 **Booth** joint-manager with Cibber of the Theatre in Drury Lane, in competition with Rich 282 **annual trophies** on Lord Mayor's Day 282 **monthly wars** military exercises of the City Trainbands 284 **roasting popes** Settle was employed to write anti-Catholic tracts. 286 **my own dragon** in a booth at Smithfield. To another actor's St. George, Settle played the dragon in a costume of green leather that he had devised.

And carried off in some dog's tail at last.
Happier thy fortunes! like a rolling stone,
Thy giddy dulness still shall lumber on,
Safe in its heaviness, shall never stray,   *295*
But lick up every blockhead in the way.
Thee shall the patriot, thee the courtier taste,
And every year be duller than the last.
Till raised from booths, to theatre, to court,
Her seat imperial Dulness shall transport.   *300*
Already opera prepares the way,
The sure forerunner of her gentle sway:
Let her thy heart, next drabs° and dice, engage,
The third mad passion of thy doting age.
Teach thou the warbling Polypheme° to roar,   *305*
And scream thyself° as none e'er screamed
          before!
To aid our cause, if Heaven thou canst not bend,
Hell thou shalt move; for Faustus° is our friend:
Pluto with Cato thou for this shalt join,
And link the Mourning Bride to Proserpine.°   *310*
Grubstreet! thy fall should men and gods conspire,
Thy stage shall stand, ensure it but from fire.°
Another Aeschylus appears! prepare
For new abortions,° all ye pregnant fair!
In flames, like Semele's,° be brought to bed,   *315*
While opening Hell spouts wildfire at your head.

303 **drabs** whores   305 **Polypheme** Cibber translated the
Italian opera *Polifemo*.   306 **scream thyself** Cibber's voice was
shrill and often cracked when he raised it.   308 **Faustus** The
pantomime hero, like Marlowe's, trafficked with the Devil
309–10 **Pluto with Cato . . . Proserpine** alluding to the custom
of coupling a tragedy and a farce in one evening, here
Addison's *Cato* and Congreve's *Mourning Bride* coupled with
the *Love of Pluto and Proserpine*   312 **fire** a favorite if
dangerous effect in pantomime, especially the hellfire of Faustus
314 **new abortions** Aeschylus' tragedy of the Furies threw
children into fits and induced miscarriages; here abortions of
art are also implied.   315 **Semele** When Semele prayed that
Zeus might come to her in all his power, she was consumed
in flames by his lightning; Dionysus was born of her ashes.

"Now, Bavius,° take the poppy from thy brow,
And place it here! here all ye heroes bow!
This, this is he, foretold by ancient rhymes:
320 The Augustus born to bring Saturnian° times.
Signs following signs lead on the mighty year!°
See! the dull stars roll round and reappear.
See, see, our own true Phoebus wears the bays!
Our Midas° sits Lord Chancellor of plays!
325 On poets' tombs see Benson's° titles writ!
Lo! Ambrose Philips° is preferred for wit!
See under Ripley° rise a new Whitehall,°
While Jones' and Boyle's united labors° fall:
While Wren° with sorrow to the grave descends,
330 Gay° dies unpensioned with a hundred friends,
Hibernian politics,° O Swift! thy fate;

317 **Bavius** like Maevius, a bad poet of Virgil's day   320 **Saturnian** See note to I, 28.   321 **mighty year** the great cycle of time in which prophecy will be fulfilled   324 **Midas** who, judging between the performances of Apollo and Pan, gave the prize to Pan; he was rewarded by Apollo with asses' ears.   325 **Benson** William Benson for political reasons displaced Sir Christopher Wren as royal architect; he built a lavish monument to Milton in Westminster Abbey and commissioned a Latin translation of *Paradise Lost;* see IV, 109–12 where he appears as "bold Benson."   326 **Ambrose Philips** a poet of ability but uncertain taste; his verses for children won him the nickname of Namby Pamby.   327 **Ripley** see note to "Epistle to Burlington," line 18   327 **new Whitehall** perhaps the new Admiralty building, but plans for a new royal palace at Whitehall had long been considered   328 **Jones' . . . united labors** The works of Inigo Jones in London had fallen into serious disrepair. Richard Boyle, Earl of Burlington, had restored his Covent Garden church and sponsored the publication of his architectural designs.   329 **Wren** Sir Christopher and Inigo Jones were England's greatest architects up to Pope's day; Wren had built great city churches as well as St. Paul's, but he was dismissed after fifty years' service.   330 **Gay** John Gay, in spite of his friend's efforts, never won a suitable court appointment.   331 **Hibernian politics** Swift resented his failure to win a church office in England and regarded his career in Ireland as exile, although he was deeply involved in Irish politics at times.

And Pope's, ten years° to comment and translate.
   "Proceed, great days! till learning fly the shore,
Till birch° shall blush with noble blood no more,
Till Thames see Eton's sons for ever play,   335
Till Westminster's whole year be holiday,
Till Isis' elders reel, their pupils' sport,
And Alma Mater lie dissolved in Port!"
   "Enough! enough!" the raptured monarch cries;
And through the ivory gate° the vision flies.   340

BOOK THE FOURTH

YET, yet a moment, one dim ray of light
Indulge, dread Chaos, and eternal Night!°
Of darkness visible° so much be lent,
As half to show, half veil, the deep intent.
Ye Powers! whose mysteries restored I sing,   5
To whom Time bears me on his rapid wing,
Suspend a while your force inertly strong,
Then take at once the poet and the song.
   Now flamed the Dog-star's° unpropitious ray,
Smote every brain, and withered every bay;   10
Sick was the sun, the owl forsook his bower,
The moon-struck prophet felt the madding hour:
Then rose the seed of Chaos, and of Night,
To blot out order, and extinguish light,

332 **ten years** Pope's work in translating Homer and editing
Shakespeare lasted from 1713 to 1725.   334 **birch** used for
caning schoolboys. Pope moves up through the public schools
(Eton and Westminster) to the universities (Isis or Oxford),
where the pleasures of the wine cellar replace those of the
library.   340 **ivory gate** through which false dreams pass; the
horn gate releases the true.   2 **Chaos . . . Night** See note to
line I, 12. The "restoration of this empire is the action of the
poem" (Pope and/or Warburton, hereafter P-W; and
Warburton alone, W).   3 **darkness visible** used of Hell in
Paradise Lost, I, 63   9 **Dog-star's** of Sirius, visible in the late,
hot summer

15   Of dull and venal a new world to mold,
    And bring Saturnian days of lead and gold.°
      She mounts the throne: her head a cloud
         concealed,
    In broad effulgence all below revealed;°
    ('Tis thus aspiring Dulness ever shines)
20   Soft on her lap her laureate son reclines.
      Beneath her footstool, *Science* groans in chains,
    And *Wit* dreads exile, penalties, and pains.
    There foamed rebellious *Logic,* gagged and bound,
    There, stripped, fair *Rhetoric* languished on the
         ground;
25   His blunted arms by *Sophistry*° are borne,
    And shameless *Billingsgate* her robes adorn.
    Morality, by her false guardians drawn,
    Chicane in furs, and *Casuistry* in lawn,°
    Gasps, as they straiten° at each end the cord,
30   And dies, when Dulness gives her Page° the word.
    Mad *Máthesis*° alone was unconfined,
    Too mad for mere material chains to bind,
    Now to pure space lifts her ecstatic stare,
    Now running round the circle, finds it square.
35   But held in tenfold bonds the *Muses* lie,
    Watched both by Envy's and by Flattery's eye:
    There to her heart sad Tragedy addrest
    The dagger wont to pierce the tyrant's breast;
    But sober History restrained her rage,
40   And promised vengeance on a barbarous age.
    There sunk Thalia,° nerveless, cold, and dead,
    Had not her sister Satire held her head:

16 **lead and gold** See note to I, 28; here parallel with "dull and venal."   18 **all below revealed** P-W cite the old adage: "The higher you climb, the more you show your arse."   25 **Sophistry** Dulness "admits something *like* each science, or casuistry, sophistry, etc."(P-W)   28 **furs . . . lawn** law (ermine robes of the judge) and church (the fine linen sleeves of a bishop)   29 **straiten** tighten   30 **Page** punning on Sir Francis Page, a famous "hanging judge"   31 **Máthesis** pure mathematics, unlimited by application   41 **Thalia** the Muse of comedy, enervated by the censorship of the Licensing Act, 1737

Nor couldst thou, Chesterfield!° a tear refuse,
Thou weptst, and with thee wept each gentle° Muse.
    When lo! a harlot form° soft sliding by,   45
With mincing step, small voice, and languid eye;
Foreign her air, her robe's discordant pride
In patchwork fluttering, and her head aside.
By singing peers upheld on either hand,
She tripped and laughed, too pretty much to stand;   50
Cast on the prostrate Nine° a scornful look,
Then thus in quaint recitativo spoke.
    "O *Cara! Cara!* silence all that train:
Joy to great Chaos! let Division° reign:
Chromatic tortures° soon shall drive them hence,   55
Break all their nerves, and fritter all their sense:
One trill shall harmonize joy, grief, and rage,
Wake the dull Church, and lull the ranting stage;
To the same notes thy sons shall hum, or snore,
And all thy yawning daughters cry, *encore.*   60
Another Phoebus, thy own Phoebus,° reigns,
Joys in my jigs, and dances in my chains.
But soon, ah soon, rebellion will commence,
If music meanly borrows aid from sense:
Strong in new arms, lo! giant Handel° stands,   65

43 **Chesterfield** who spoke eloquently against the Act   44
gentle as opposed to the lowborn substitutes   45 **harlot form**
Opera, tremendously popular with the importation of Italian
singers, was resented for its tendency to destroy the fusion of
sound and sense in the native English song tradition.   51 **Nine**
the Muses   54 **Division** i.e., breaking up each of a succession
of long notes into a number of short ones, and so dwelling on
a single syllable of the word being sung   55 **Chromatic tortures**
elaborate variations introducing notes which do not belong to
the diatonic scale   61 **thy own Phoebus** referring to the French
term *phebus:* "an appearance of light glimmering over the
obscurity, a semblance of meaning without any real sense"
(Bouhours, cited by P-W)   65 **Handel** whose increase of
"hands" in chorus and orchestra (suggested in the next line)
"proved so much too manly for the fine gentlemen of his age,
that he was obliged to remove his music into Ireland" (P-W).
The *Messiah* was first performed in Dublin in 1741. The power
of Handel's music, as opposed to precious, feminine Opera, is
made clear in line 67 below.

Like bold Briareus,° with a hundred hands;
To stir, to rouse, to shake the soul he comes,
And Jove's own thunders follow Mars's drums.
Arrest him, Empress; or you sleep no more—"
70   She heard, and drove him to the Hibernian shore.
      And now had Fame's posterior trumpet° blown,
And all the nations summoned to the throne.
The young, the old, who feel her inward sway,
One instinct seizes, and transports away.
75   None need a guide, by sure attraction led,
And strong impulsive gravity° of head:
None want° a place, for all their center found,
Hung to the goddess, and cohered around.
Not closer, orb in orb,° conglobed are seen
80   The buzzing bees about their dusky queen.
      The gathering number, as it moves along,
Involves a vast involuntary throng,
Who gently drawn, and struggling less and less,
Roll in her vortex,° and her power confess.
85   Not those alone who passive own her laws,
But who, weak rebels, more advance her cause:
Whate'er of dunce in college or in town
Sneers at another, in toupee or gown;°
Whate'er of mongrel no one class admits,
90   A wit with dunces, and a dunce with wits.
      Nor absent they, no members of her state,
Who pay her homage in her sons, the Great;°
Who, false to Phoebus, bow the knee to Baal;°
Or, impious, preach his word without a call.
95   Patrons, who sneak from living worth to dead,

66 **Briareus** The giant of a hundred hands fought for the
Olympians against the Titans.   71 **posterior trumpet** "her
second or more certain report" (P-W), but cf. also IV, 18.   76
gravity (1) solemnity (2) gravitational attraction, as in lines
81–84   77 **want** lack   79 **orb in orb** Cf. Milton's account of
the angels in *Paradise Lost,* V, 594–96: "Thus when in Orbs/
Of circuit inexpressible they stood,/Orb within Orb"   84
Roll . . . vortex eddy around her   88 **toupee or gown** in curled
periwig (as a man of fashion) or in academic gown   92 **Great**
nobles, men in power   93 **Baal** any false god, presumably
power or wealth

Withhold the pension, and set up the head;°
Or vest dull Flattery in the sacred gown;
Or give from fool to fool the laurel crown.
And (last and worst) with all the cant of wit,
Without the soul, the Muse's hypocrite.°   100
　There marched the bard and blockhead, side
　　by side,
Who rhymed for hire, and patronized for pride.
Narcissus,° praised with all a parson's power,
Looked a white lily sunk beneath a shower.
There moved Montalto° with superior air;   105
His stretched-out arm displayed a volume fair;
Courtiers and patriots in two ranks divide,
Through both he passed, and bowed from side
　　to side:
But as in graceful act, with awful eye
Composed he stood, bold Benson° thrust him by: 110
On two unequal crutches propped he came,
Milton's on this, on that one Johnston's name.
The decent knight retired with sober rage,
Withdrew his hand, and closed the pompous page.
But (happy for him as the times went then)   115
Appeared Apollo's mayor and aldermen,°
On whom three hundred gold-capped youths°
　　await,
To lug the ponderous volume off in state.
　When Dulness, smiling—"Thus revive the wits!
But murder first, and mince them all to bits;   120

96 **Withhold . . . head** i.e., fail to support when alive and
parasitically honor after death   100 **the Muse's hypocrite** "who
thinks the only end of poetry is to amuse" (W)   103 **Narcissus**
Lord Hervey, an epileptic, had a very white face; he was
heavily flattered in the dedication of Dr. Middleton's *Life of
Cicero*.   105 **Montalto** Sir Thomas Hanmer, pompous and
portly, published a lavish edition of Shakespeare at his own
expense.   110 **Benson** See note to III, 325; he published
several editions of Arthur Johnston's Latin version of the
Psalms.   116 **Apollo's . . . aldermen** dignitaries of Oxford,
whose press published Hanmer's Shakespeare   117 **gold-
capped youths** with the gold tassel of the Gentleman-
Commoner

As erst Medea° (cruel, so to save!)
A new edition of old Aeson gave;
Let standard authors, thus, like trophies borne,
Appear more glorious as more hacked and torn,
125 And you, my critics! in the chequered shade,
Admire new light through holes yourselves have
          made.
    "Leave not a foot of verse, a foot of stone,
A page, a grave, that they can call their own;
But spread, my sons, your glory thin or thick,
130 On passive paper, or on solid brick.
So by each bard an alderman° shall sit,
A heavy lord shall hang at every wit,
And while on Fame's triumphal car they ride,
Some slave of mine° be pinioned to their side."
    Now crowds on crowds around the goddess
135   press,
Each eager to present their first address.
Dunce scorning dunce beholds the next advance,
But fop shows fop superior complaisance.°
When lo! a specter° rose, whose index hand
140 Held forth the virtue of the dreadful wand;
His beavered brow a birchen garland wears,
Dropping with infant's blood, and mother's tears.
O'er every vein a shuddering horror runs;
Eton and Winton° shake through all their sons.
145 All flesh is humbled, Westminster's bold race
Shrink, and confess the genius° of the place:

121 **Medea** who had Aeson's daughters cut him up and boil
him in order to restore him to youth; this worked for Aeson
but not Pelias, whom Medea wished to destroy.   131 **alderman**
such as Alderman Barber, the printer, who proudly placed his
own name on the monument he erected to Samuel Butler   134
slave of mine as in Rome, where a slave was chained beside a
triumphant general as he rode through the city   138
complaisance tolerance   139 **specter** Dr. Busby, the famous
headmaster of Westminster School, carrying his birch cane
("dreadful wand") for discipline   144 **Eton and Winton** where
Busby's students are now enrolled   146 **genius** presiding spirit
or deity

The pale boy Senator yet tingling stands,
And holds his breeches close with both his hands.
  Then thus, "Since man from beast by words is
    known,
Words are man's province, words we teach alone.° 150
When reason doubtful, like the Samian letter,°
Points him two ways, the narrower is the better.
Placed at the door of learning, youth to guide,
We never suffer it to stand too wide.
To ask, to guess, to know, as they commence, 155
As fancy opens the quick spring of sense,
We ply the memory, we load the brain,
Bind rebel wit, and double chain on chain,
Confine the thought, to exercise the breath;
And keep them in the pale of words till death. 160
Whate'er the talents, or howe'er designed,
We hang one jingling padlock° on the mind:
A poet the first day he dips his quill;
And what the last? a very poet still.
Pity! the charm works only in our wall, 165
Lost, lost too soon in yonder house or hall.°
There truant Wyndham every Muse gave o'er,
There Talbot° sunk, and was a wit no more!
How sweet an Ovid, Murray° was our boast!
How many martials were in Pulteney° lost! 170
Else sure some bard, to our eternal praise,
In twice ten thousand rhyming nights and days,
Had reached the work, the all that mortal can;

149–50 **Since man . . . teach alone** The humanist view that
eloquence is wisdom expressed is here reduced to a concern
for words to the neglect of thought. 151 **Samian letter** the
letter Y, emblem of the crossroads of choice 162 **jingling
padlock** exercises in composing Greek and Latin verses 166
house or hall Westminster Hall or the House of Commons
167–68 **Wyndham . . . Talbot** two brilliant members of
Parliament 169 **Murray** a student of Busby ("our boast").
Awarded a prize for a Latin poem at Oxford, he became a
distinguished statesman rather than a poet. 170 **Pulteney**
Gifted in epigram like Martial, he used his skill as political
writer and orator in opposition to Walpole.

And South° beheld that masterpiece of man."
   "Oh" (cried the goddess) "for some pedant
175   reign!
Some gentle James,° to bless the land again;
To stick the doctor's° chair into the throne,
Give law to words, or war with words alone,
Senates and courts with Greek and Latin rule,
180 And turn the Council to a grammar school!
For sure, if Dulness sees a grateful day,
'Tis in the shade of arbitrary sway.°
O! if my sons may learn one earthly thing,
Teach but that one, sufficient for a king:
185 That which my priests, and mine alone, maintain,
Which as it dies, or lives, we fall, or reign:
May you, may Cam and Isis,° preach it long!
The RIGHT DIVINE of kings to govern wrong."
   Prompt at the call, around the goddess roll
190 Broad hats, and hoods, and caps, a sable shoal:
Thick and more thick the black blockade extends,
A hundred head of Aristotle's friends.
Nor went thou, Isis! wanting to the day,
Though Christ Church° long kept prudishly away.
195 Each staunch polemic, stubborn as a rock,
Each fierce logician, still expelling Locke,°
Came whip and spur, and dashed through thin
    and thick
On German Crousaz, and Dutch Burgersdyck.°

174 **South** "Dr. South declared a perfect epigram as difficult a
performance as an epic poem, and the critics say, 'an epic
poem is the greatest work human nature is capable of' " (P-W).
The epigram becomes the culmination of Busby's and Dulness'
verbalism.   176 **James** James I was a famous pedant and the
first English monarch to espouse the divine right of kings.   177
doctor's teacher's   181–82 **For sure . . . sway** "no branch of
learning thrives well under arbitrary government but verbal"
(W).   187 **Cam and Isis** the universities of Cambridge and
Oxford   194 **Christ Church** the college at Oxford whose dons
resisted Dulness most successfully   196 **Locke** actually
censured in 1703 by the heads of Oxford, where Aristotelian
philosophy was still strong   198 **Crousaz . . . Burgersdyck**
two logicians

As many quit the streams that murmuring fall
To lull the sons of Margaret and Clare Hall,°   200
Where Bentley° late tempestuous wont to sport
In troubled waters, but now sleeps in port.
Before them marched that awful Aristarch;°
Ploughed was his front with many a deep remark:
His hat, which never vailed° to human pride,   205
Walker° with reverence took, and laid aside.
Low bowed the rest: he, kingly, did but nod;
So upright° Quakers please both man and God.
"Mistress! dismiss that rabble from your throne:
Avaunt——is Aristarchus yet unknown?   210
Thy mighty scholiast, whose unwearied pains
Made Horace dull, and humbled Milton's strains.°
Turn what they will to verse, their toil is vain,
Critics like me shall make it prose again.
Roman and Greek grammarians! know your
      better: 215
Author of something yet more great than letter;°
While towering o'er your alphabet, like Saul,°
Stands our Digamma,° and o'ertops them all.
'Tis true, on words is still our whole debate,
Disputes of *Me* or *Te*, of *aut* or *at*,   220
To sound° or sink in *cano*, O or A,
Or give up Cicero° to C or K.
Let Freind affect to speak as Terence spoke,

200 **Margaret and Clare Hall** St. John's and Clare College in
Cambridge 201 **Bentley** As master of Trinity College,
Cambridge, Richard Bentley had been at odds with his Fellows
but was now at rest; but see III, 338. 203 **Aristarch** Bentley,
here named for Aristarchus, Homeric commentator and
corrector 205 **vailed** yielded 206 **Walker** the vice-master of
Trinity 208 **upright** (1) honest (2) not bowing in prayer, as
Aristarchus will not bow before Dulness 212 **Milton's strains**
which Bentley, as editor, arrogantly corrected on the pretext
that Milton's blindness allowed numerous errors to appear
216 **letter** the invention of a single letter by other gram-
marians 217 **Saul** taller than any of his people 218 **Digamma**
a letter restored by Bentley in his projected edition of Homer;
taller than ordinary letters 221 **sound** stress 222 **Cicero** the
pronunciation of whose name was disputed

And Alsop° never but like Horace joke:
225 For me, what Virgil, Pliny may deny,
Manilius or Solinus shall supply:°
For Attic phrase in Plato let them seek,
I poach in Suidas° for unlicensed Greek.
In ancient sense if any needs will deal,
230 Be sure I give them fragments, not a meal:
What Gellius or Stobaeus° hashed before,
Or chewed by blind old scholiasts o'er and o'er.
The critic eye, that microscope of wit,
Sees hairs and pores, examines bit by bit;
235 How parts relate to parts, or they to whole,
The body's harmony, the beaming soul,°
Are things which Kuster, Burman, Wasse° shall
      see,
When man's whole frame is obvious to a *flea*.
    "Ah, think not, Mistress! more true Dulness lies
240 In folly's cap, than wisdom's grave disguise.
Like buoys, that never sink into the flood,
On learning's surface we but lie and nod.
Thine is the genuine head of many a house,
And much divinity without a Νοῦς.°
245 Nor could a Barrow work on every block,
Nor has one Atterbury° spoiled the flock.
See! still thy own, the heavy canon° roll,
And metaphysic smokes involve the pole.
For thee we dim the eyes, and stuff the head

223–24 **Freind . . . Alsop** two scholars who catch the spirit of
the ancients 226 **Manilius . . . supply** As a philologist,
Bentley is not interested in literature but in words; for his
purposes minor authors are as useful as major. 228 **Suidas** a
dictionary writer and collector of strange words 231 **Gellius
or Stobaeus** who collected fragments of ancient writers in their
works 236 **beaming soul** the soul irradiating the body with
form 237 **Kuster . . . Wasse** editors and philologists 244
without a Νοῦς "Νόυς was the Platonic word for mind, or the
first cause, and that system of divinity is here hinted at which
terminates in blind nature without a νοῦς" (P–W) 245–46
Barrow . . . Atterbury both eloquent preachers, Isaac Barrow a
fine mathematician, Francis Atterbury a classical scholar 247
canon (1) churchman (2) artillery (cannon)

With all such reading as was never read: 250
For thee explain a thing till all men doubt it,
And write about it, Goddess, and about it:
So spins the silkworm small its slender store,
And labors till it clouds itself all o'er.
      "What though we let some better sort of fool   255
Thrid° every science, run through every school?
Never by tumbler through the hoops was shown
Such skill in passing all, and touching none.
He may indeed (if sober all this time)
Plague with dispute, or persecute with rhyme.   260
We only furnish what he cannot use,
Or wed to what he must divorce, a Muse:
Full in the midst of Euclid dip at once,
And petrify a genius to a dunce:
Or set on metaphysic ground to prance,   265
Show all his paces, not a step advance.
With the same cement, ever sure to bind,
We bring to one dead level every mind.
Then take him to develop, if you can,
And hew the block off, and get out the man.°   270
But wherefore waste I words? I see advance
Whore, pupil, and laced governor° from France.
Walker! our hat"———nor more he deigned to
      say,
But, stern as Ajax' specter,° strode away.
      In flowed at once a gay embroidered race,   275
And tittering pushed the pedants off the place:
Some would have spoken, but the voice was
      drowned
By the French horn, or by the opening° hound.
The first came forwards, with as easy mien,
As if he saw St. James'° and the Queen.   280
When thus the attendant orator° begun:

256 **thrid** thread   270 **And hew . . . man** the traditional notion
that in every block of stone there is a statue waiting to be
freed   272 **governor** tutor   274 **Ajax' specter** which turns
sullenly from Ulysses, *Odyssey*, XI   278 **opening** giving
tongue   280 **St. James'** the royal palace   281 **orator** the
"governor" of line 272

"Receive, great Empress! thy accomplished son,
Thine from the birth, and sacred° from the rod,
A dauntless infant! never scared with God.
285 The sire saw, one by one, his virtues wake:
The mother begged the blessing of a rake.
Thou gav'st that ripeness, which so soon began,
And ceased so soon, he ne'er was boy, nor man.
Through school and college, thy kind cloud
         o'ercast,
290 Safe and unseen° the young Aeneas past:
Thence bursting glorious, all at once let down,°
Stunned with his giddy larum° half the town.
Intrepid then, o'er seas and lands he flew:°
Europe he saw, and Europe saw him too.
295 There all thy gifts and graces we display,
Thou, only thou, directing all our way!
To where the Seine, obsequious as she runs,
Pours at great Bourbon's feet her silken sons;°
Or Tiber, now no longer Roman, rolls,
300 Vain of Italian arts, Italian° souls:
To happy convents, bosomed deep in vines,
Where slumber abbots, purple as their wines:
To isles of fragrance, lily-silvered vales,
Diffusing languor in the panting gales:
305 To lands of singing, or of dancing slaves,
Love-whispering woods, and lute-resounding
         waves.
But chief her shrine where naked Venus keeps,
And Cupids ride the Lion of the Deeps;°
Where, eased of fleets, the Adriatic main

283 **sacred** exempt 290 **unseen** as Aeneas enters Carthage
veiled in cloud by his mother, Venus 291 **let down** revealed,
freed 292 **larum** alarm, commotion 293 **he flew** on the
Grand Tour 298 **Bourbon's feet . . . sons** France is seen as
an absolute monarchy encouraging courtly luxury or ef-
feminacy. 300 **Italian** i.e., in place of Roman 308 **the Lion
of the Deeps** the winged lion, emblem of Venice, no longer a
great naval and mercantile power, famous instead as the
brothel of Europe

Wafts the smooth eunuch and enamored swain.   *310*
Led by my hand, he sauntered Europe round,
And gathered every vice on Christian ground;
Saw every court, heard every king declare
His royal sense, of operas or the fair;°
The stews° and palace equally explored,   *315*
Intrigued with glory, and with spirit whored;
Tried all *hors d'oeuvres,* all *liqueurs* defined,
Judicious drank, and greatly daring dined;
Dropped the dull lumber of the Latin store,°
Spoiled his own language, and acquired no more;   *320*
All classic learning lost on classic ground;
And last turned *air,* the echo of a sound!
See now, half-cured,° and perfectly well-bred,
With nothing but a solo° in his head;
As much estate, and principle, and wit,   *325*
As Jansen, Fleetwood, Cibber° shall think fit;
Stolen° from a duel, followed by a nun,
And, if a borough choose him,° not undone;
See, to my country happy I restore
This glorious youth, and add one Venus more.   *330*
Her too receive (for her my soul adores)°
So may the sons of sons of sons of whores,
Prop thine, O Empress! like each neighbor throne,
And make a long posterity thy own."
Pleased, she accepts the hero, and the dame,   *335*
Wraps in her veil, and frees from sense of shame.
     Then looked, and saw a lazy, lolling sort,
Unseen at church, at senate, or at court,
Of ever-listless loiterers, that attend

314 **of operas or the fair** The royal conversations recall the
interests of George II.   315 **stews** brothels   319 **Dropped . . .
store** forgot his Latin   323 **half-cured** of a venereal disease
324 **solo** like "air" (line 322), the reduction of substance to
sound; see IV, 159–60   326 **Jansen . . . Cibber** all gamblers, the
last two theatre-managers, hence tutors to youth   327 **Stolen**
escaped   328 **borough choose him** Members of Parliament
could not be arrested for debt.   331 **my soul adores** Both tutor
and pupil seem attached to the former nun.

340 No cause, no trust, no duty, and no friend.
    Thee too, my Paridel!° she marked thee there,
    Stretched on the rack of a too easy chair,
    And heard thy everlasting yawn confess
    The pains and penalties of idleness.
345 She pitied! but her pity only shed
    Benigner influence on thy nodding head.
        But Annius,° crafty seer, with ebon wand,
    And well-dissembled emerald on his hand,
    False as his gems, and cankered° as his coins,
350   Came, crammed with capon, from where Pollio°
        dines.
    Soft, as the wily fox is seen to creep,
    Where bask on sunny banks the simple sheep,
    Walk round and round, now prying here, now
        there;
    So he; but pious, whispered first his prayer.
        "Grant, gracious Goddess! grant me still to
355   cheat,
    O may thy cloud still cover the deceit!
    Thy choicer mists on this assembly shed,
    But pour them thickest on the noble head.
    So shall each youth, assisted by our eyes,
360 See other Caesars, other Homers° rise;
    Through twilight ages hunt the Athenian fowl,°
    Which Chalcis gods, and mortals call an owl,
    Now see an Attys, now a Cecrops° clear,
    Nay, Mahomet!° the pigeon at thine ear;
365 Be rich in ancient brass, though not in gold,

341 **Paridel** Spenser's name for a wandering courtly squire
347 **Annius** named for an early collector, monk of Viterbo,
and a famous forger of antiquities   349 **cankered** corrupt   350
Pollio named for the Roman patron   360 **other Caesars . . .
Homers** possibly forged manuscripts; more tellingly, substitute
models, i.e., the heroics of collecting and the supreme value of
rarity   361 **Athenian fowl** Athenian coins were stamped with
an owl.   363 **Attys . . . Cecrops** forged coins professedly issued
by the ancient king of Lydia or the mythical founder of
Athens   364 **Mahomet** Mohammed, who forbade all images,
here represented on a coin or medal with the white pigeon he
claimed (according to legend) was the angel Gabriel.

And keep his Lares,° though his house be sold;
To headless Phoebe° his fair bride postpone,
Honor a Syrian prince° above his own;
Lord of an Otho,° if I vouch it true;
Blest in one Niger,° till he knows of two."   370
   Mummius° o'erheard him; Mummius, fool-
      renowned,°
Who like his Cheops stinks above the ground,
Fierce as a startled adder, swelled, and said,
Rattling an ancient sistrum° at his head.
   "Speakst thou of Syrian princes? Traitor base!   375
Mine, Goddess! mine is all the hornèd race.°
True, he had wit, to make their value rise;
From foolish Greeks to steal them, was as wise;
More glorious yet, from barbarous hands to keep,
When Sallee rovers° chased him on the deep.   380
Then taught by Hermes,° and divinely bold,
Down his own throat he risked the Grecian gold;
Received each demigod,° with pious care,
Deep in his entrails—I revered them there,
I bought them, shrouded in that living shrine,   385
And, at their second birth, they issue mine."
   "Witness, great Ammon!° by whose horns I
      swore,"

366 **Lares** statues of household gods   367 **headless Phoebe** a mutilated statue of Diana, which preempts the place of a living bride   368 **Syrian prince** presumably as represented on a rare medal   369 **Otho** coin of a Roman Emperor who ruled very briefly   370 **Niger** another Emperor of short reign, whose coins would be very rare   371 **Mummius** dealer in Egyptian antiquities   371 **fool-renowned** "a compound epithet in the Greek manner, *renowned by fools,* or *renowned for making fools*" (Pope)   374 **sistrum** Egyptian musical instrument   376 **hornèd race** the successors of Alexander, supposedly born of the gods, represented with horns on their medals   380 **Sallee rovers** pirate ships from Morocco   381 **Hermes** god of commerce but also the patron of thieves   383 **demigod** coins of emperors who claimed that status; with suggestions of the eucharist, sustained by "pious care" and culminating in the Second Coming of line 386   387 **Ammon** Jupiter Ammon, from whom Alexander and his heirs claimed descent; cf. line 376.

(Replied soft Annius) "this our paunch before
Still bears them, faithful; and that thus I eat,
390 Is to refund the medals with the meat.
To prove me, Goddess! clear of all design,
Bid me with Pollio sup, as well as dine:
There all the learned shall at the labor stand,
And Douglas° lend his soft, obstetric hand."
395   The goddess smiling seemed to give consent;
So back to Pollio, hand in hand, they went.
    Then thick as locusts blackening all the ground,
A tribe, with weeds and shells fantastic crowned,
Each with some wondrous gift approached the
        Power,
400 A nest, a toad, a fungus, or a flower.
But far the foremost, two, with earnest zeal,
And aspect ardent to the throne appeal.
    The first thus opened: "Hear thy suppliant's
        call,
Great Queen, and common Mother of us all!
405 Fair from its humble bed I reared this flower,°
Suckled and cheered, with air, and sun, and
        shower,
Soft on the paper ruff its leaves° I spread,
Bright with the gilded button tipped its head,
Then throned in glass, and named it Caroline:°
Each maid cried, charming! and each youth,
410   divine!
Did nature's pencil° ever blend such rays,
Such varied light in one promiscuous blaze?
Now prostrate! dead! behold that Caroline:
No maid cries, charming! and no youth, divine!
415 And lo the wretch! whose vile, whose insect lust
Laid this gay daughter of the spring in dust.

394 **Douglas** a famous obstetrician and collector of editions of
Horace   405 **flower** a reference to the efforts in the age to
produce a perfect carnation   407 **leaves** petals   409 **Caroline**
for the Queen, an ardent gardener; P-W pursue the theme of
idolatry of lines 359–86 by citing a gardener who advertised
his favorite flower as "*my* Queen Caroline."   411 **pencil**
paintbrush

Oh punish him, or to the Elysian shades
Dismiss my soul, where no carnation fades!"
  He ceased, and wept. With innocence of mien,
The accused stood forth, and thus addressed the
      queen.   420
  "Of all the enamelled race,° whose silvery wing
Waves to the tepid zephyrs of the spring,
Or swims along the fluid atmosphere,
Once brightest shined this child of heat and air.
I saw, and started from its vernal bower   425
The rising game,° and chased from flower to
      flower.
It fled, I followed; now in hope, now pain;
It stopped, I stopped; it moved, I moved again.°
At last it fixed, 'twas on what plant it pleased,
And where it fixed, the beauteous bird° I seized: 430
Rose or carnation was below my care;
I meddle, Goddess! only in my sphere.
I tell the naked fact without disguise,
And, to excuse it, need but show the prize;
Whose spoils this paper° offers to your eye,   435
Fair even in death! this peerless *butterfly*."
  "My sons!" (she answered) "both have done
      your parts:
Live happy both, and long promote our arts!
But hear a mother, when she recommends
To your fraternal care, our sleeping friends.°   440
The common soul, of Heaven's more frugal make,
Serves but to keep fools pert, and knaves awake:
A drowsy watchman, that just gives a knock,
And breaks our rest, to tell us what's a-clock.
Yet by some object every brain is stirred;   445

421 **enamelled race** colorful butterflies   425–26 **started . . .
game** the idiom of the huntsman   427–28 Cf. Eve's words
(*Paradise Lost,* IV, 462–63) on first seeing her reflection in
water and, without recognizing what it is, adoring it: "I started
back,/It started back; but pleased I soon returned,/Pleased it
returned as soon."   430 **bird** any winged creature; here the
butterfly 435 **this paper** on which the butterfly is
mounted   440 **sleeping friends** Cf. line IV, 345.

The dull may waken to a hummingbird;
The most recluse, discreetly opened find
Congenial matter in the cockle kind;°
The mind, in metaphysics at a loss,
450 May wander in a wilderness of moss;°
The head that turns at superlunar things,
Poised with a tail, may steer on Wilkins' wings.°
  "O! would the sons of men once think their eyes
And reason given them but to study *flies!*
455 See nature in some partial narrow shape,
And let the author of the whole escape:
Learn but to trifle; or, who most observe,
To wonder at their maker, not to serve!"°
  "Be that my task (replies a gloomy clerk,
460 Sworn foe to mystery,° yet divinely dark;
Whose pious hope aspires to see the day
When moral evidence° shall quite decay,
And damns implicit faith,° and holy lies,
Prompt to impose,° and fond to dogmatize:)
465 "Let others creep by timid steps, and slow,
On plain experience lay foundations low,
By common sense to common knowledge bred,
And last, to Nature's Cause through Nature led.°
All-seeing in thy mists, we want no guide,
470 Mother of arrogance, and source of pride!
We nobly take the high priori road,°
And reason downward, till we doubt of God:

448 **cockle kind** collections of scallop shells   450 **moss** of which
300 species had been identified   452 **Wilkins' wings** John
Wilkins in the seventeenth century proposed flights to the
moon.   458 **wonder. . . serve** to lose themselves in natural
wonder and neglect divine laws of morality   460 **mystery**
religious mysteries   462 **moral evidence** the probability of the
historical facts of the Bible, believed by some to decay as the
events became more remote   463 **implicit faith** belief upon
authority, unquestioning adherence   464 **Prompt to impose**
the freethinker seen as dogmatically rejecting dogma, self-
deceiving while he attacks "holy lies"   468 **Nature's Cause . . .
led** For this empirical, inductive procedure cf. "Essay on Man,"
IV, 332.   471 **high priori road** the deductive or a priori
method, such as Descartes takes in his *Meditations*

Make Nature still encroach° upon his plan;
And shove him off as far as e'er we can:
Thrust some mechanic cause into his place,   475
Or bind in matter, or diffuse in space.°
Or, at one bound o'erleaping° all his laws,
Make God man's image, man the final cause,°
Find virtue local, all relation scorn,°
See all in *self,*° and but for self be born: 480
Of naught so certain as our *reason* still,
Of naught so doubtful as of *soul* and *will.*°
Oh hide the God still more! and make us see
Such as Lucretius° drew, a God like Thee:
Wrapped up in self, a God without a thought,   485
Regardless of our merit or default.
Or that bright image to our fancy draw,

473 **Nature . . . encroach** explain away Providence by natural
("mechanic") causes, or create some metaphysical natural
principle (such as Ralph Cudworth's plastic nature) to displace
or limit a theistic God   475–76 **Thrust . . . space** "the first of
these follies is that of Descartes; the second of Hobbes; the
third of some succeeding Philosophers" (P-W). The last may
include Henry More, the Cambridge Platonist, who separated
extension from materiality in order to attribute extension or
pure space to spirit; space for More is "an obscure re-
presentation of the essential presence of the divine being."
More in turn influenced Newton's conception of absolute
space. (See E. L. Burtt, *The Metaphysical Foundations of
Modern Science.*)   477 **o'erleaping** like Satan overleaping the
walls of Paradise (*Paradise Lost,* IV, 181)   478 **Make God . . .
cause** as in the "Essay on Man," see human happiness as the end
of the universe and God as subservient to that end   479 **Find
virtue . . . scorn** make morality relative to local customs rather
than absolute, universal, or dependent upon God's will   480
self the final contraction of scale, in contrast to the opening
movement of "Essay on Man," IV, 361ff   482 **soul and will**
The metaphysical and moral principle of human nature are
neglected by the dogmatic rationalism of the freethinkers.   484
Lucretius whose philosophical poem *De Rerum Natura*
(following Epicurean thought) seeks to free man of his fears
of anthropomorphic gods and presents nature as an impartial
divine force free of the limitations and narrow human concerns
(therefore, for the "gloomy clerk," like Dulness, sublimely
indifferent to all distinctions of value)

Which Theocles° in raptured vision saw,
While through poetic scenes the Genius roves,
490 Or wanders wild in academic groves;
That NATURE our society° adores,
Where Tindal° dictates, and Silenus° snores."
      Roused at his name, up rose the bousy sire,
And shook from out his pipe the seeds of fire;°
Then snapped his box,° and stroked his belly
495   down:
Rosy and reverend, though without a gown.°
Bland and familiar to the throne he came,
Led up the Youth, and called the goddess *Dame.*
Then thus. "From priestcraft happily set free,
500 Lo! every finished son returns to thee:
First slave to words, then vassal to a name,°
Then dupe to party; child and man the same;
Bounded by nature, narrowed still by art,
A trifling head, and a contracted heart.
505 Thus bred, thus taught, how many have I seen,
Smiling on all, and smiled on by a queen.
Marked out for honors, honored for their birth,
To thee the most rebellious things on earth:
Now to thy gentle shadow all are shrunk,
510 All melted down, in pension, or in punk!°
So K——, so B——° sneaked into the grave,

488 **Theocles** the philosophical visionary in Shaftesbury's *The Moralists,* here taken as an enthusiastic worshiper of nature (his "Genius"), cultivating Platonic ecstasy in the natural landscape 491 **our society** the association of free-thinkers 492 **Tindal** the deist; see II, 399; III, 212. 492 **Silenus** the fat, drunken, and debauched companion of Dionysius who appears in Virgil's Sixth Eclogue; here associated with Thomas Gordon, a political writer whom Walpole made Commissioner of the Wine Licenses 494 **seeds of fire** par- odying Epicurean language for atoms 495 **box** snuffbox 496 **without a gown** not a priest 501 **name** reputation 510 **punk** whore 511 **So K——, so B——** Kent, Berkeley; two noblemen, both holders of the highest royal honor, Knight of the Garter; possibly indebted to one of George I's mistresses ("harlot's slave")

A monarch's half, and half a harlot's slave.
Poor W——° nipped in folly's broadest bloom,
Who praises now? his chaplain on his tomb.
Then take them all, oh take them to thy breast!   515
Thy *Magus,*° Goddess! shall perform the rest."
    With that, a WIZARD OLD his *Cup* extends;
Which whoso tastes, forgets his former friends,
Sire, ancestors, himself. One casts his eyes
Up to a *star,*° and like Endymion° dies: 520
A *feather,*° shooting from another's head,
Extracts his brain; and principle is fled;
Lost is his God, his country, everything;
And nothing left but homage to a king!
The vulgar herd turn off to roll with hogs,°   525
To run with horses, or to hunt with dogs;
But, sad example! never to escape
Their infamy, still keep the human shape.
But she, good goddess, sent to every child
Firm impudence, or stupefaction mild;   530
And straight succeeded, leaving shame no room,
Cibberian forehead, or Cimmerian° gloom.
    Kind self-conceit to some her glass applies,
Which no one looks in with another's eyes:
But as the flatterer or dependent paint,   535
Beholds himself a patriot, chief, or saint.
    On others Interest her gay livery° flings,
Interest that waves on party-colored° wings:
Turned to the sun, she casts a thousand dyes,

513 **W——** Wharton or Warwick, both of whom died
young 516 **Magus** adept in occult arts, high priest, the wizard
of the next line; Sir Robert Walpole "is suggested, whose use
of bribery is embodied in the 'Cup of Self-love'" (P-W). 520
star worn by Knights of the Garter or of the Bath 520
Endymion Loved by the Moon, he was thrown into perpetual
sleep and visited by her each night. 521 **feather** worn in the
cap of Knights of the Garter 525 **roll with hogs** with
suggestion of those transformed by Circe's enchantment 532
Cimmerian See note to III, 4. 537 **livery** costume worn by
retainers, whether courtiers or servants 538 **party-colored** a
pun on "party" and "vari-colored"

540 And, as she turns, the colors fall or rise.
    Others the Siren Sisters° warble round,
And empty heads console with empty sound.
No more, alas! the voice of fame they hear,
The balm of Dulness trickling in their ear.
545 Great C——, H——, P——, R——, K——,°
Why all your toils? your sons have learned to sing.
How quick ambition hastes to ridicule!
The sire is made a peer, the son a fool.
    On some, a priest succinct in amice white°
550 Attends; all flesh is nothing in his sight!
Beeves, at his touch, at once to jelly turn,
And the huge boar is shrunk into an urn:°
The board with specious° miracles he loads,
Turns hares to larks, and pigeons into toads.
555 Another (for in all what one can shine?)
Explains the *sève* and *verdeur*° of the vine.
What cannot copious sacrifice atone?°
Thy truffles, Perigord! thy hams, Bayonne!
With French libation, and Italian strain,
560 Wash Bladen white, and expiate Hays's° stain.
Knight° lifts the head, for what are crowds undone

541 **Siren Sisters** perhaps the muses of opera, but see note to IV, 324. 545 **Great . . . K**—— noblemen ambitious for their families 549 **priest . . . white** a chef dressed in a white cap, counterpart of the priestly "amice" worn over head and shoulders with white vestments 551–52 **Beeves . . . urn** culinary miracles, where beef is reduced (a form of transubstantiation) to jelly, or boned meats are given decorative or amusing shapes as in the ingenious transformations in line 554 553 **specious** striking, showy 556 **sève . . . verdeur** fineness of flavor and briskness of sparkling wines 557 **sacrifice atone** the yield of luxuries by famous French districts (Perigord, Bayonne) seen as religious offerings (libations accompanied by operatic music, as in line 559) 560 **Bladen . . . Hays** two notorious gamblers who "lived with utmost magnificence at Paris and kept open table frequented by persons of the first quality of England and even by princes of the blood of France" (P-W) The form of Bladen's name suggests the proverbial "wash blackamoors white." 561 **Knight** the cashier of the South Sea Company, who fled England at its collapse in 1720

To three essential partridges in one?°
Gone every blush, and silent all reproach,
Contending princes mount them in their coach.
Next bidding all draw near on bended knees,   565
The Queen confers her *titles* and *degrees*.
Her children first of more distinguished sort,
Who study Shakespeare at the Inns of Court,°
Impale a glowworm, or virtú° profess,
Shine in the dignity of F.R.S.°   570
Some, deep Freemasons,° join the silent race
Worthy to fill Pythagoras's place:°
Some botanists, or florists at the least;
Or issue members of an annual feast.°
Nor passed the meanest unregarded; one   575
Rose a Gregorian, one a Gormogon.°
The last, not least in honor or applause,
Isis and Cam° made Doctors of her Laws.
Then, blessing all, "Go, children of my care!
To practice now from theory repair.   580
All my commands are easy, short, and full:
My sons! be proud, be selfish, and be dull.
Guard my prerogative,° assert my throne:
This nod confirms each privilege your own.

562 **three essential . . . one** two partridges dissolved with sauce
for a third, with clear reference to the mystery of the Trinity
(three persons in one essence)   568 **Shakespeare . . . Court**
lawyers who neglect their proper tasks to dabble in Shakes-
peare criticism   569 **virtú** amateur pursuit of arts or sciences
(hence "virtuosity")   570 **F.R.S.** Fellow of the Royal Society,
a title often granted at the time to untrained noblemen.   571
Freemasons "where taciturnity is the *only* essential qual-
ification, as it was the *chief* of the disciples of Pythagoras"
(P-W)   572 **Pythagoras's place** referring to the ascetic
brotherhood of Pythagoras which pursued mathematical and
religious mysteries at Croton in southern Italy, *ca.* 600–450 B.C.
(see IV, 31)   574 **annual feast** held by various groups, such as
the Freemasons and the Royal Society   576 **Gregorian . . .
Gormogon** members of societies founded in ridicule of the
Freemasons 578 **Isis and Cam** Oxford and Cambridge
bestowed honorary degrees.   583 **prerogative** royal powers
unlimited by law or accountability, sometimes used tyrannically

585 The cap and switch° be sacred to his Grace;
With staff and pumps° the Marquis lead the race;
From stage to stage° the licensed° Earl may run,
Paired with his fellow charioteer the sun;
The learnèd Baron butterflies design,°
590 Or draw to silk Arachne's subtile line,°
The Júdge to dance his brother Sergeant° call;
The Senator at cricket urge the ball;
The Bishop stow (pontific luxury!)°
An hundred souls of turkeys in a pie;
595 The sturdy Squire to Gallic masters° stoop,
And drown his lands and manors in a soup.
Others import yet nobler arts from France,
Teach kings to fiddle, and make senates dance.°
Perhaps more high some daring son may soar,°
600 Proud to my list to add one monarch more;
And nobly conscious, princes are but things
Born for first ministers, as slaves for kings,
Tyrant supreme! shall three estates° command,
And MAKE ONE MIGHTY DUNCIAD OF THE LAND!"
        More she had spoke, but yawned—all nature
605   nods:

585 **cap and switch** of a jockey; here awarded to a lord devoted
to horseracing   586 **staff and pumps** the equipment of grooms
or footmen   587 **stage to stage** driving a stagecoach, as the Earl
of Salisbury did   587 **licensed** as coach-owners were; also
"privileged"   589 **design** study and draw   590 **draw ... line** try
to obtain silken thread from spiders' webs (see Swift, *Gulliver's
Travels*, III, Ch. 5)   591 **Sergeant** barrister; the "call of
sergeants" involved ceremonies much like a dance   593
pontific luxury such as was in fact enjoyed by the Bishop of
Durham in Pope's day   595 **Squire to Gallic masters** the
cultivation of fashionable foreign tastes (here a costly "soup")
by traditionally conservative country squires   598 **dance** "either
after their Prince" or, banished, "to Siberia" (P-W). In
Gulliver's Travels, I, Ch. 3, courtiers are chosen for office in
Lilliput for their agility in dancing on a rope.   599 **more high ...
soar** Walpole, as First Minister, had virtually ruled England from
1721 until his fall in 1742, shortly before this was published.   603
three estates Walpole controlled through appointment, bribery,
and appeal to interest the nobility, the clergy, and the merchants.

What mortal can resist the yawn of gods?°
Churches and chapels° instantly it reached;
(St. James's first, for leaden G——° preached)
Then catched the schools;° the hall scarce kept
    awake;
The convocation gaped, but could not speak: *610*
Lost was the nation's sense, nor could be found,
While the long solemn unison went round:
Wide, and more wide, it spread o'er all the realm;
Even Palinurus° nodded at the helm:
The vapor mild o'er each committee crept;   *615*
Unfinished treaties in each office slept;
And chiefless armies dozed out the campaign;
And navies yawned for orders on the main.
  O Muse! relate (for you can tell alone,
Wits have short memories, and dunces none)   *620*
Relate, who first, who last resigned to rest;
Whose heads she partly, whose completely
    blessed;
What charms could faction, what ambition lull,
The venal quiet, and entrance the dull;
Till drowned was sense, and shame, and right,
    and wrong—   *625*
O sing, and hush the nations with thy song!

606 **the yawn of gods** "The Great Mother composes all, in
the same manner as Minerva at the period of the Odyssey"
(P-W). 607 **chapels** place of dissenters' worship 608 **leaden
G——** Bishop Gilbert was eloquent; for the point of "leaden"
see IV, 16. 609 **Then catched the schools** "The progress of
this yawn is judicious, natural, and worthy to be noted. First
it seizeth the churches and chapels; then catcheth the schools,
where, though the boys be unwilling to sleep, the masters are
not; next Westminster Hall [the chief law courts], much more
hard indeed to subdue, and not totally put to silence even by
the Goddess; then the Convocation [of the clergy], which
though extremely desirous to speak yet cannot; even the House
of Commons, justly called, the Sense of the Nation [see line
611] is *lost* (that is to say *suspended*) during the yawn"
(P-W). 614 **Palinurus** the pilot of the ship of Aeneas; here
Walpole, pilot of the ship of state

*   *   *   *   *   *   *

In vain, in vain—the all-composing hour
Resistless falls: the Muse obeys the power.
She comes! she comes! the sable throne behold
630 Of *Night* primeval, and of *Chaos* old!
Before her, *Fancy's* gilded clouds decay,
And all its varying rainbows die away.
Wit shoots in vain its momentary fires,
The meteor drops, and in a flash expires.
635 As one by one, at dread Medea's strain,°
The sickening stars fade off the ethereal plain;
As Argus' eyes° by Hermes' wand opprest,
Closed one by one to everlasting rest;
Thus at her felt approach, and secret might,
640 *Art* after *Art* goes out, and all is night.
See skulking *Truth* to her old cavern° fled,
Mountains of casuistry heaped o'er her head!
Philosophy, that leaned on Heaven before,
Shrinks to her second cause,° and is no more.
645 *Physic* of *Metaphysic*° begs defense,
And *Metaphysic* calls for aid on *Sense!*°
See *Mystery* to *Mathematics*° fly!
In vain! they gaze, turn giddy, rave, and die.
Religion blushing veils her sacred fires,

635 **dread Medea's strain** In Seneca's *Medea,* the enchantress, seeking revenge for Jason's desertion, calls back to life all the monstrous serpents and sings an incantation that causes the sun to halt and the stars to fall.   637 **Argus' eyes** placed all over his body so that some might always remain open   641 **Truth . . . cavern** "alludes to the saying of Democritus, that truth lay at the bottom of a deep well" (P-W)   643–44 **leaned on Heaven . . . second cause** as in IV, 471–82, explains away all divinity by natural causation   645 **Physic of Metaphysic** natural science turning to traditional speculative metaphysics for its ground (Pope had originally written "the Stagirite's defense")   646 **Metaphysic . . . Sense** metaphysics in turn depending upon sense data, creating in line 645 a vicious circle   647 **Mystery to Mathematics** religious mystery seeking deductive mathematical demonstration, perhaps infecting mathematics with an occult and mystical strain such as that of the Pythagoreans

And unawares *Morality* expires.   650
Nor public flame, nor private, dares to shine;
Nor human spark is left, nor glimpse divine!
Lo! thy dread empire, CHAOS! is restored;
Light dies before thy uncreating word:°
Thy hand, great anarch! lets the curtain fall;   655
And universal darkness buries all.

654 **uncreating word** referring to the terms (based on the
Greek *logos*) "wisdom" and "word," applied to the Son, that
is, to Christ as creator and orderer

Afterword:
Why Pope?

Alexander Pope thinks in couplets. But what is a couplet?

In part, it's a traditional two-line verse form requiring a lot of technical skill. As a verse form, it distinguishes hacks from virtuosi; it tests the mettle of poets and displays their limitations unforgivingly. Thus it's no surprise that Pope was a master craftsman of this particular form. He was always up for a scrap and always eager to display his stunning technical command of versification.

But more broadly, the couplet is an organizing metaphor, a dynamic juxtaposition of concepts within a restricted domain. Circumscribed tension is another way of describing the couplet—a form of limited space bursting with restless energy. The form is dynamic, teasing, nuancing; it zooms from microscopic to cosmic and, within one breathless line, from plaintive longing to bitter scorn; it builds productive oppositions and suggests innovative pairings. Pope's verse is not, it must be said, a mere stacking up of two-line granules of Enlightenment reason. In order to understand Pope—and to approach an answer to my titular question—we have to begin by seeing the couplet as more than a verse form: seeing it instead as the key organizing metaphor of Pope's art and his life.

Pope lived in couplets. He was at once a celebrity and

an outcast, a master creator and an imperfect creature, the spirit of his age and a hopelessly belated neoclassicist. Pope was politically and physically disabled, and despite these apparent setbacks, he became synonymous with the literature of his era, such that for many generations the first half of the eighteenth century was known as the Age of Pope. He was probably the first literary celebrity in the modern sense of that word, and his life as much as his work was the subject of intense public fascination. Describing his visits to English aristocratic households, Voltaire remarked that he saw in every house some image of Pope (usually a portrait or a bust), and more than two hundred portraits of the poet appeared during his lifetime. His quarrels, his humiliations, his achievements, and his quirks were all on display—a fact he both lamented and exploited throughout his long career. He was a virtuoso of a brand-new media culture—print was his element—who turned his satirist's pen on himself and his enemies with equal vigor.

In one famous episode, Pope's unrequited infatuation with Lady Mary Wortley Montagu crumbled disastrously into a bitter feud. At his declaration of passion, Lady Mary collapsed in uncontrollable laughter at the thought of becoming the lover of a short, hunchbacked, socially awkward, Roman Catholic, professional poet. Naturally Pope was crushed; he blasted "MWM" in verse only to receive some searing, contemptuous lines from her pen: "And with the emblem of thy Crooked Mind, / Mark'd on thy Back, like Cain, by God's own hand; / Wander like him, accursed through the Land." Appropriating this sort of violent language directed at his deformed body became a regular tactic of Pope's in the volatile world of London print culture. In that milieu, Pope would turn his personal celebrity into a work of satirical art; in many different works, he mocks his own high-handed pose as a learned scourge of hypocrisy even as he savages his enemies.

"The Epistle to Dr. Arbuthnot" is one example of such a balancing act between attacking his enemies and poking fun at himself. Much of the poem outlines the pain that accompanies Pope's literary fame; he earns

public humiliation, suffers from critical pedantry, and is
smothered by the fawning attention of would-be poets
and parasites. But a good deal of Pope's suffering is
inward and personal, and often self-authored. His poetic
vocation is not a choice but a destiny: some "sin to me
unknown / Dipped me in ink" and "As yet a child, nor
yet a fool to fame / I lisped in numbers, for the numbers
came" (ll. 125–28). An Achilles dipped in ink rather than
the fortifying waters of the Styx, Pope is propelled by
destiny into an arena of violent struggle for reputation
and glory, namely poetry, which turns out to aid him
"through this long disease, my life" (l. 132).

The gentle joshing of this self-referential moment
contrasts with the violent rage on display in Pope's sub-
sequent portrait of Sporus (a stand-in for Lord John
Hervey, the aristocratic toady of his now-rival Lady Mary
Wortley Montagu. Hervey is, in Pope's account, a "painted
child of dirt that stinks and stings," a satanic fop, a vacuous,
giggling conniver, and a bisexual opportunist. Here is the
end of the portrait:

> Amphibious thing! that acting either part,
> The trifling head, or the corrupted heart,
> Fop at the toilet, flatterer at the board,
> Now trips a Lady, now struts a Lord.
> Eve's tempter thus the Rabbins have exprest,
> A Cherub's face, a reptile all the rest;
> Beauty that shocks you, parts that none will trust,
> Wit that can creep, and pride that licks the dust.   (ll. 326–33)

Immediately following this litany of brutal descriptions
of Hervey's bestial corruption is a long portrait of the
poet himself. In exaggerated contrast to the lubricious
flip-flopper Hervey, the poet is a "manly" and dis-
interested intellectual:

> Not Fortune's worshipper, nor fashion's fool,
> Not lucre's madman, nor ambition's tool,
> Not proud, nor servile; be one poet's praise,
> That, if he pleased, he pleased by manly ways. (ll. 334–37)

At first glance, the long verse character of Pope—of which the above lines are the opening gambit—seems like plain old self-congratulatory preening. In this view, the poet is an upright model of moderation whose verse is bent toward the cultivation of moral virtue despite the slings and arrows of a slanderous public culture.

Yet unlike the frontal assault on Hervey, Pope defines himself by negation and deferral. Most certainly he is not Hervey, but it's hard to take those repetitive "nots" and "nors" as evidence of confident self-fashioning. The distance between self and hated other is uncomfortably close here; Hervey contaminates the portrait of Pope, crowding him out until a final and redemptive flourish in line 337; that assertion of pleasing by manly ways means to drive the wedge suddenly between the manly poet and the vile creature Sporus. It is a brilliant strategy of avoidance and deferral that suddenly resolves with a decisive virtuoso twist, but even that twist does little to dispel the tension, the dynamic bond between these two figures contained in one portrait.

This tense pairing, in which apparently opposed concepts gain increased significance from their entanglement, is descriptive of Pope's poetic method. Here as elsewhere, we see not a crude antithesis—the comparison of vice to virtue—but rather a cascade of affiliations and the bundling together of tensions, ironies, and bonds between apparent opponents. Pope and Hervey are knit together in a corrosive rivalry; Pope may come out ahead, but he is contaminated by the very contrast he himself orchestrates. Even that decisive last line can do little to wash away the stink and the sting of Hervey.

Despite his satirical bent, Pope took seriously the idea that there might be something called a "national poet," and he flirted with the role of the English Poet throughout his career. Pope did little to dispel the sense that he "wrote for his own age, and his own nation," as Samuel Johnson would remark in his *Life of Pope*. While Pope saw satire as a literary technique that might help regenerate a self-interested and undereducated public, he was always tinkering and never finish-

ing a serious epic poem describing the mythic origins of
the English people. This was *Brutus*, an English *Aeneid*
built on the historically ludicrous myth that the nation
had been founded by the Trojan Felix Brutus (a grand-
son of Aeneas). The verse fragment and the notes and
outlines of this poem tell us something of Pope's priori-
ties, especially when juxtaposed with an undoubtedly
influential predecessor text: John Dryden's 1697 transla-
tion of the *Aeneid*. Here is Pope's opening for *Brutus*:

> The patient Chief, who lab'ring long, arriv'd
> On Britains shore and brought with fav'ring Gods
> Arts Arms and Honour to her Ancient Sons
> Daughter of Memory! From elder Time
> Recall; and me, with Britains Glory fir'd,
> Me far from meaner care or meaner Song,
> Snatch to thy Holy Hill of Spotless Bay,
> My Countrys Poet, to record her Fame.

Dryden is not as free to improvise with Virgil's original
text, of course, but his careful version of the *Aeneid*'s
opening lines do point the contrast:

> Arms, and the Man I sing, who forc'd by Fate,
> And haughty Juno's unrelenting Hate;
> Expell'd and exil'd, left the Trojan shoar;
> Long Labours, both by Sea and land he bore;
> . . .
> O Muse! The Causes and the Crimes relate,
> What Goddess was provok'd, and whence her hate:
> For what Offence the Queen of Heav'n began
> To persecute so brave, so just a Man!

Pope's Brutus lacks a divine adversary dispensing hate
and the propulsive urgency of exile and persecution. He is,
instead, a custodian of "Arms, Arts, and Honor" whose
movement is patient and labored—Brutus is a lucky but
shuffling avatar of tradition rather than a heroic refugee
trailing energy. But the most obvious difference between
epic invocations lies in the poet's own self-presentation.

Where Dryden echoes Virgil's attenuated first-person *canto*—"I sing"—Pope announces his literary ambition to become through his exalted song "my Countrys Poet." For this poet, "Britains Glory" is an occasion for elaborate self-creation, a chance to shun the meaner song of the quotidian. The *Aeneid* is an epic designed to glorify the nation through a triumphant founding narrative; Pope's *Brutus* proposes to use a glorious myth of national foundation to exalt the poet himself. But it would be in his triumph "The Rape of the Lock" that Pope knit together his inclination toward epic grandeur and his lacerating satirical vision.

Pope's mock epic "Rape of the Lock" is a breezy portrait of a commodity-addled aristocracy and a statement lamenting the general loss of English martial vigor. Pope was writing his translation of Homer's *Iliad* as he worked on "The Rape of the Lock," and it is easy enough to see the poem as a teasing description of the English national character—cultures get the epic they deserve, after all. Between Brutus the plodder and Belinda the airhead, the English people are pretty short on epic heroes. But "The Rape of the Lock" is really a poem about longing and desire—the poet mourns his own distance from a glittering aristocratic world he desires but can never achieve, just as he mourns the heroic and classical past never to be recovered from the abyss of time. A seductive court culture is the milieu for this poem's satirical journey, but it is the poet himself who is most consumed and frustrated by desire.

Like so many of Pope's other poems, "The Rape of the Lock" is a balancing act between satirical mockery and authentic longing, between a desire to harm and the intoxications of delight. The opening lines of "The Rape of the Lock" establish a pattern of ironic revaluation, in which the poem's occasion, its subjects, its author, and his ambitions are all unsettled and recast as the work unfolds. The image of the poet himself (full of longing and self-laceration) is suited to the mock epic tone, of course, but it is also evidence of Pope's desire to maintain an ironic distance from the entanglements of epic, the genre of national ambitions.

The invocation of the poem introduces relational crossings of high and low, heroic and mock heroic, longing and detachment. Here are the opening verse paragraphs:

What dire offense from amorous causes springs,
What mighty contests rise from trivial things,
I sing—This verse to CARYLL, Muse! is due;
This, even Belinda may vouchsafe to view:
Slight is the subject, but not so the praise,
If she inspire, and he approve my lays.
    Say what strange motive, Goddess! could compel
A well-bred Lord to assault a gentle Belle?
O say what stranger cause, yet unexplored
Could make a gentle Belle reject a Lord?
In tasks so bold, can little men engage,
And in soft bosoms dwells such mighty rage?   (I, ll. 1–12)

True to form, Pope opens with a well-wrought couplet designed to announce and then complicate the thematic propositions of the poem. Effect precedes cause in each line—a suitably epic response has been incited by a cause of uncertain moral status.

Keeping our focus on the first two lines in the poem allows us to observe Pope at work. Notice the key terms in that opening couplet. "Amorous causes," "dire offense," and "mighty contests" are the matter of epic—these terms point explicitly to what we might call the high plot of the poem—its serious engagement with the effects of human desire and the consequences of human violence played out on a vast, world-historical scale. "Trivial things" is the anomaly here, although the poem turns its focus increasingly toward objects and commodities. The presence of trivial things at the end of this second line prevents the couplet from operating as a full-throated epic invocation; it crowds out the conventional "I sing." Epic must wait. Trivial things come first. The deferred invocation introduces the poem's pretenses toward epic, but it does so from a position of subordination.

The poet is equally elbowed out of the opening couplet's crucial exposition, much in the way Hervey crowds Pope out of his own self-portrait. The poet who tries to utter that epic "I sing" is a wallflower. He's either a pariah excluded from the glittering world of Am'rous Causes and Trivial Things or a disinterested skeptic voluntarily in exile from the hurly-burly of those two lines. As the poem unfolds, it becomes clear that the poet is both, pariah and satirical anthropologist. He longs for intimacy with the very courtiers he also despises. A vivid illustration of this stance unfolds in the last couplet of this section:

> In tasks so bold, can little men engage,
> And in soft bosoms dwells such mighty rage?   (I, ll. 11–12)

Relying on the couplet form to emphasize the crossing (in an X pattern) of key concepts and terms, Pope links "bold tasks" to "mighty rage" and "little men" to "soft bosoms." The first of these imputed bonds is the proper matter of epic, that genre of bold tasks, heroic actions, and mighty rage, while the second pairing describes only ridiculous desire. The "little men" in the first line is a reference to the diminutive Pope himself, and the pairing of "little men" and "soft bosoms" describes the poet's sexual (and frustrated) fascination with the beautiful if vacuous Belinda. "The Rape of the Lock" writ large describes the poet's desire both to be part of an alluring community and to inhabit a position of skeptical detachment from that same trivial and irretrievably corrupt *belle monde*.

But Pope had larger targets than just Belinda. In his "Essay on Man," for instance, he turns away from satire and unfolds some of the eighteenth century's most vivid and influential illustrations of a deist moral philosophy that for many modern readers looks like an unappetizing caricature of the "age of reason." But that poem is an expression of intellectual generosity, a program that offers up for public use a model of appealing philosophical consolation. Pope's cosmopolitanism is literally expansive;

the well-regulated self radiates outward in circles of charity:

> God loves from whole to parts: but human soul
> Must rise from individual to the whole.
> Self-love but serves the virtuous mind to wake,
> As the small pebble stirs the peaceful lake;
> The center moved, a circle straight succeeds,
> Another still, and still another spreads,
> Friend, parent, neighbor, first it will embrace,
> His country next; and next all human race;
> Wide and more wide, the o'erflowings of the mind
> Take every creature in, of every kind;
> Earth smiles around, with boundless bounty blest,
> And Heaven beholds its image in his breast.   (IV, ll. 361–72)

Pope describes the active transformation of the individual mind that must awake and arise in order to fulfill its native capabilities. The peaceful mind, supplied with the proper moral stimulus, transmits the soul outward from "individual to the whole" in concentric rings of sentimental identification: "Friend, parent, neighbor, first it will embrace, / His country next; and next all human race." These rings embrace increasingly wider communities of belonging without losing their original form or strength; the result is the harmonious integration of human and divine. The corrosive view of humanity we saw in "Epistle to Dr. Arbuthnot" or "The Rape of the Lock" has receded from view here; Pope instead offers us an invitation into a philosophical system that might offer real consolation.

As we have seen, Pope imagined himself as a cultural commissar and a private man, an arbiter of poetic style and a fragile soul, a star of contemporary media and a conduit to the classical past, a national poet and a cosmopolitan philosopher, a victim and an aggressor. These tensions spill out everywhere from his verse; his poetry contains energy, it juxtaposes without resolution, it pairs and complicates, and it lacerates and it elevates. Pope's poetry is endlessly inventive, a fractal rather than a reasoning machine, restless and searching within a strictly controlled idiom. That pairing of formal restraint and wild intellectual exuberance is at the core of poetry as an art form. It has no better illustration than in the poems contained in this volume.

—Elliott Visconsi

Selected Bibliography

Baines, Paul. *The Complete Critical Guide to Alexander Pope*. London and New York: Routledge, 2000.

Bloom, Harold, ed. *Alexander Pope*. Modern Critical Views. New York: Chelsea House, 1986.

Brower, Rueben Arthur. *Alexander Pope: The Poetry of Allusion*. Oxford: Clarendon Press, 1959.

Brown, Laura. *Alexander Pope*. Oxford: Basil Blackwell, 1985.

Deutsch, Helen. *Resemblance and Disgrace: Alexander Pope and the Deformation of Culture*. Cambridge, MA: Harvard University Press, 1997.

Edwards, Thomas R., Jr. *This Dark Estate: A Reading of Pope*. Berkeley and Los Angeles: University of California Press, 1963.

Erskine-Hill, Howard. *The Social Milieu of Alexander Pope*. New Haven, CT: Yale University Press, 1978.

————, and Anne Smith, eds. *The Art of Alexander Pope*. London: Vision Press, 1979.

Fairer, David. *Pope's Imagination*. Manchester: Manchester University Press, 1984.

————, ed. *Pope: New Contexts*. New York and London: Harvester, 1990.

Gee, Sophie. *The Scandal of the Season*. New York: Simon & Schuster, 2007.

Goldsmith, Netta Murphy. *Alexander Pope: The Evolution of a Poet*. Aldershot, England: Ashgate, 2002.

Griffin, Dustin H. *Alexander Pope: The Poet in the Poems*. Princeton, NJ: Princeton University Press, 1978.

Hammond, Brean, ed. *Pope*. New York and London: Longman, 1996.

Hunter, J. Paul. "Form as Meaning: Pope and the Ideology of the Couplet." *The Eighteenth Century: Theory and Interpretation* 37 (1996): 257–70.

Jackson, Wallace, and R. Paul Yoder, eds. *Critical Essays on Alexander Pope*. New York: G. K. Hall, 1993.

Johnson, Samuel. "The Life of Pope." In *The Lives of the English Poets*. London, 1779–81.

Knight, G. Wilson. *Laureate of Peace: On the Genius of Alexander Pope*. New York: Oxford University Press, 1955.

Mack, Maynard. *Alexander Pope: A Life*. New York: Norton, 1985.

————. *Collected in Himself: Essays Critical, Biographical, and Bibliographical on Pope and Some of His Contemporaries*. Newark: University of Delaware Press, 1982.

————. *Essential Articles for the Study of Pope*. Hamden, CT: Archon Books, 1964; 2nd ed., 1968.

————. *The Garden and the City: Retirement and Politics in the Later Poetry of Pope, 1731–1743*. Toronto: University of Toronto Press, 1969.

————, and James Winn, eds. *Pope: Recent Essays by Several Hands*. Hamden, CT: Archon Books, 1980.

McLaverty, James. *Pope, Print, and Meaning*. Oxford: Oxford University Press, 2001.

Morris, David B. *Alexander Pope: The Genius of Sense*. Cambridge, MA: Harvard University Press, 1984.

Parkin, Rebecca Price. *The Poetic Workmanship of Alexander Pope*. Minneapolis: University of Minnesota Press, 1955.

Rogers, Pat. *Essays on Pope*. Cambridge: Cambridge University Press, 1993.

Rosslyn, Felicity. *Alexander Pope: A Literary Life*. Macmillan Literary Lives. London: Macmillan, 1990.

Rousseau, G. S., and Pat Rogers, eds. *The Enduring Legacy: Alexander Pope Tercentenary Essays*. Cambridge: Cambridge University Press, 1988.

Rumbold, Valerie. *Women's Place in Pope's World*. Cambridge: Cambridge University Press, 1991.

Sherburn, George. *The Early Career of Alexander Pope*. Oxford: Clarendon Press, 1956.

Solomon, Harry M. *The Rape of the Text: Reading and Misreading Pope's* "Essay on Man." Tuscaloosa: University of Alabama Press, 1993.

Spence, Joseph. *Observations, Anecdotes, and Characters of Books and Men: Collected from Conversation*. James M. Osborn, ed. 2 vols. Oxford: Clarendon Press, 1966.

Tillotson, Geoffrey. *On the Poetry of Pope*. 2nd ed. Oxford: Clarendon Press, 1966.

———. *Pope and Human Nature*. Oxford: Clarendon Press, 1958.

Warren, Austin. *Alexander Pope as Critic and Humanist*. Princeton, NJ: Princeton University Press, 1929.

Williams, Aubrey L. *Pope's* "Dunciad": *A Study of Its Meaning*. London: Methuen and Co.; Baton Rouge: Louisiana State University Press, 1955.

Classic Poetry

THE WASTE LAND and Other Poems
T. S. Eliot
This edition contains many of T.S. Eliot's most important early poems, leading to perhaps his greatest masterpiece, "The Waste Land," which has long been regarded as one of the fundamental texts of modernism. By combining poetic elements from many diverse sources with bits of popular culture and common speech linked in a fragmented narrative, Eliot recreated the chaos and disillusionment of Europe in the aftermath of WWI.

EVANGELINE and Selected Tales and Poems
Henry Wadsworth Longfellow
Longfellow was the first American poet to employ the classic form and style of the Old World successfully to express the subjects and sentiments of the New. Distinguished poet Horace Gregory has chosen thirty-seven of Longfellow's most enduring poems for this edition, the only paperback of his poetry in print.

THE COMPLETE POETRY OF EDGAR ALLAN POE
From the exquisite lyric "To Helen," to the immortal masterpieces "Annabel Lee," "The Bells," and "The Raven," *The Complete Poetry of Edgar Allan Poe* demonstrates the author's gift for the form.

LEAVES OF GRASS (150th Anniversary Edition)
Walt Whitman
This collection remains the incomparable achievement of one of America's greatest poets—a passionate man who loved his country and wrote of it as no other has ever done.

Available wherever books are sold or at
signetclassics.com

READ THE TOP 20
SIGNET CLASSICS

ANIMAL FARM BY GEORGE ORWELL

1984 BY GEORGE ORWELL

THE INFERNO BY DANTE

FRANKENSTEIN BY MARY SHELLEY

BEOWULF (BURTON RAFFEL, TRANSLATOR)

THE ODYSSEY BY HOMER

THE FEDERALIST PAPERS BY ALEXANDER HAMILTON

THE HOUND OF THE BASKERVILLES
    BY SIR ARTHUR CONAN DOYLE

NARRATIVE OF THE LIFE OF FREDERICK DOUGLASS
    BY FREDERICK DOUGLASS

DR. JEKYLL AND MR. HYDE BY ROBERT LOUIS STEVENSON

HAMLET BY WILLIAM SHAKESPEARE

THE SCARLET LETTER BY NATHANIEL HAWTHORNE

LES MISÉRABLES BY VICTOR HUGO

HEART OF DARKNESS AND THE SECRET SHARER
    BY JOSEPH CONRAD

WUTHERING HEIGHTS BY EMILY BRONTË

A MIDSUMMER NIGHT'S DREAM BY WILLIAM SHAKESPEARE

NECTAR IN A SIEVE BY KAMALA MARKANDAYA

ETHAN FROME BY EDITH WHARTON

ADVENTURES OF HUCKLEBERRY FINN BY MARK TWAIN

A TALE OF TWO CITIES BY CHARLES DICKENS

S0154